The Flowering Plum a

The Flowering Plum and the Palace Lady

Interpretations of Chinese Poetry

Hans H. Frankel

中國詩選譯隨談

傅漢思著

張克和題

New Haven and London, Yale University Press

Library of Congress catalog card number: 75–8203
International standard book numbers:
0–300–01889–4 cloth 0–300–02242–5 paper

Designed by John O. C. McCrillis
and set in Baskerville type.
Printed in the United States of America by
The Alpine Press, Inc., South Braintree, Mass.

Published in Great Britain, Europe, Africa, and
Asia (except Japan) by Yale University Press,
Ltd., London. Distributed in Australia and
New Zealand by Book & Film Services, Artarmon,
N.S.W., Australia; and in Japan by Harper &
Row, Publishers, Tokyo Office.

Published with assistance from
the Mary Cady Tew Memorial Fund.

For Ch'ung-ho

Contents

Preface

This book offers new translations and interpretations of 106 Chinese poems, grouped under thematic and stylistic headings, and analyses of some common phenomena of Chinese poetic structure. It is not, however, a general introduction to Chinese poetry. Readers looking for such a work may turn to several good books available today, such as James J. Y. Liu, *The Art of Chinese Poetry*; A. C. Graham, *Poems of the Late T'ang*; and Burton Watson, *Chinese Lyricism*. The present work is intended for readers with an interest in Chinese poetry. It invites those who have not learned the Chinese language, as well as those who are in the process of studying it, or who are wondering whether such study is worth the effort. But those who have mastered the language, including specialists in Chinese poetry, will also (I hope) read beyond this point.

The viewpoint adopted for the interpretation of the poems is that of modern Western literary criticism, with due regard for the peculiarities of the Chinese literary tradition and the traditional Chinese approach to poetry.

The 106 poems selected for interpretation range in time from about the tenth century B.C. to the fourteenth century of our era. But the selection is not intended as a representative cross section of Chinese poetry during that time span. Rather, the poems chosen are personal favorites that seem to have yielded to my efforts to make them intelligible and enjoyable in translation. Some of them need hardly any comment, while others require a great deal of it. The explications offered vary from poem to poem in length and in kind, providing in each case what I feel to be necessary and helpful. The type of interpretation that I practice works only on poems which I like and admire, hence poems that strike me as inferior are excluded from this study.

My interpretations and judgments are obviously subjective. Reading poetry is after all a very personal affair, and no two individuals will understand a given poem in quite the same way. To counterbalance this subjectivity, I give close attention both to the formal and the nonformal structures of the poems, studying them as skillfully integrated organisms, as exquisitely coordinated creations of verbal art. Structure operates simultaneously and harmoniously on three levels: sound, syntax, and meaning. About phonetic features I say little, because the changing sound systems of the various historical periods are difficult to ascertain and hard to convey to nonspecialists. Hence our analyses will deal primarily with syntactic and semantic features.

This book is not oriented toward literary history and the lines of so-called development but toward an appreciation—rational, aesthetic, and emotional—of the material it deals with. To compare our intercourse with poetry to that with people, there are two ways of learning to know a person. You may make an effort to find out as much as possible about his childhood, background, parents, ancestors, relatives, teachers, friends, and associates, and about those who in turn have been influenced by him. Or you may accept him as he is, become familiar with him, study his appearance, listen sympathetically to whatever he has to say, and enjoy his company. I have chosen the latter way.

On the more technical side, however, since our ultimate concern is with understanding and appreciating each poem just as it was meant to be taken, we must learn as much as possible about its language, in the broadest sense of the word: the literary Chinese of the period and genre, the author's private language where it differs from other poets', the language of allusions and conventions such as were familiar to the author and his audience, and the language of the social and cultural milieu in which the poem was created.

The matter of the English versions deserves a few words. Much has been written on the problem of translating poetry from one language into another, and on the special difficulties of translating Chinese poetry into English.[1] Thus there is no need for going deeply into the matter here. Let me just clarify my stand on a few points.

I strike a compromise between a literal and a literary translation. I always keep intact the divisions of a poem into lines and stanzas. I change the word order as little as possible, and try to convey something of a pervasive poetic phenomenon that will occupy much of our attention throughout, namely, the word-for-word matching of lines, of half-lines, and sometimes of larger sections, which is known as parallelism and antithesis.* But I make no attempt to render other prosodic elements that are difficult or impossible to reproduce in English, namely, line length, rhyme, rhythm, and tonal balance.[2] In addition, I try (with uneven success) to keep intact that important but elusive phenomenon: imagery.

For the names of animals, plants, minerals, and the like, I make do with approximate translations. Precise equivalents could only be arrived at by experts in those scientific fields.[3] Besides, poets are usually not scientists, and even in cases where they are, they do not speak as such, and the medium of poetry is diametrically opposed to the scientist's precise and unequivocal statement, as has often been pointed out.[4]

On the few occasions where the translations are not my own, that fact will be acknowledged. I have profited from the use of earlier translations, commentaries, and studies, but I have not tried to find and peruse all existing secondary literature.

The poems selected are numbered from 1 to 106. (Fifty of them have not previously been translated into English, as far as I know.) They are cast in nine different poetic forms, which are explained in appendix 1. Legends, historical incidents, and other lore to which the poems allude appear in appendix 2, partly translated from the sources, and partly summarized.

I will say no more about the purpose and organization of the present volume. From my own experience as a reader I know that the way in which a book is used often has little in common with what the author had in mind. May the book speak for itself. Or better yet: may the poems speak for themselves.

*See especially chapter 11 below.

Acknowledgments

This book began to be written in 1965. In that year I had the good fortune to receive a Guggenheim Fellowship and a Yale Senior Faculty Fellowship. I spent six months at Academia Sinica in Nankang, Taiwan, in 1965–66, followed by three months in Kyoto. During my stay in Taiwan, I enjoyed the hospitable and congenial atmosphere of Academia Sinica, and benefited from the counsel and erudition of many Chinese scholars at Academia Sinica and National Taiwan University, especially Professors Chang Ping-ch'üan, Tai Chün-jen, T'ai Ching-nung, and Wang Shu-min. In Kyoto, I got helfpul advice on my work from several Japanese scholars, particularly Professors Ogawa Tamaki, Shimizu Shigeru, and Yoshikawa Kōjirō.

In my continuing work on the book, I was privileged to receive several grants from the Concilium on International and Area Studies of Yale University, which made possible some research trips to libraries outside of Yale, and the copying of needed materials. A final revision of the translations of the poems was supported by a grant from the A. Whitney Griswold Endowment Fund of Yale University, through the Council on the Humanities. On this revision I worked with Judith Wile. Thanks to her competence in Chinese and English, combined with a rare sensitivity for poetic diction in both languages, the translations were greatly improved. Two editors of the Yale University Press, Ellen Graham and Charles Grench, prepared the manuscript for publication with uncommon skill and loving care.

Permission to include previously published material is gratefully acknowledged as follows: Professor Bernhard Karlgren has given permission to quote from his translations of the *Shih ching* in *The Book of Odes* (Stockholm: Museum of Far Eastern Antiquities, 1950); Professor Angus C. Graham allows me to use, in appendix 2 under "Po Ya and Chung Tzu-ch'i," his translation in *The Book of Lieh-tzŭ* (London: John Murray, 1960); Professor Hugh M. Stimson, Secretary-Treasurer of the American Oriental Society, has given permission to use my translations and interpretations of Poems 24 and 31 from "Fifteen Poems by Ts'ao Chih," *Journal of the American Oriental Society* 84 (1964); Francke Verlag of Bern allows me to include Poem 1, previously translated and discussed in "The Plum Tree in Chinese Poetry," *Asiatische Studien* 6 (1952); and New York University Press has granted permission to include Poem 65, previously translated in "Classical Chinese," in *Versification: Major Language Types*, edited by W. K. Wimsatt, © 1972 by New York University.

The book owes much to many others, especially to my students and colleagues at Yale. Above all, I have received constant help and inspiration from my wife Chang Ch'ung-ho, who is herself a poet, a lifelong student of Chinese poetry, and a living embodiment of the finest in Chinese civilization.

1

Man and Nature

(Poems 1–11)

The relationship between man and nature is an aspect of Chinese poetry that has received much attention from Chinese literary critics over the centuries. They often point out the explicit and implicit relations between the human emotions (*ch'ing*) and the scenery (*ching*) described or created in a poem. Thus Hsieh Chen (1495–1575) said: "Scenery is the go-between of poetry, emotion is the embryo of poetry. By combining them a poem is made."[1] Those connections seem to me to be even more extensive and complex than has generally been realized.

We begin by looking at a poem in which a human figure and a semipersonified tree are made to interact, and in which the interaction renders an abstract notion. The poem is set in the imperial palace, and the author was himself an imperial prince who briefly reigned at the end of his life as a puppet emperor (Emperor Chien-wen of the Liang dynasty).

Poem 1, "The Flowering Plum"[2]
Hsiao Kang (503–51)
Form: *fu*

In the many-walled palace's
Sacred garden:
Wondrous trees, myriad kinds,
And countless plants in thousandfold profusion,   4
With light diffused and shadows mingled,
Twigs abound and trunks are everywhere.
When the cold sundial marks the change of season

蕭綱 「梅花賦」 層城之宮 靈苑之中 奇木萬品 (4)庶草千叢 光分影雜 條繁幹通 寒圭變節

And wintry ashes move in the calendar pipes,*   8
They all wither and fade,
Their beauty falls, destroyed by the wind.
The year turns, the ether is new,
Rousing the plants and stirring the earth.   12
The plum breaks into blossom before other trees,
She alone has the gift of recognizing spring.
Now, receiving *yang*,† she brings forth gold,
Now, mingling with snow, she wears a cloak of silver.   16
She exhales glamor and lights up the grove on all four sides,
She spreads splendor at the meeting of five roads.
As jades are joined and pearls strewn,
So ice is hung and hail spread.   20
Tender leaves sprout, not yet formed;
Branches pull out fresh shoots and stick them onto old twigs,
Petals from the treetop fall halfway and fly in the air,
Sweet scent goes with the wind to faraway places.   24
She suspends slow-drifting gossamer
And mingles with the heavy morning mist.
She vies with the cosmetic powder falling from upstairs
And surpasses the silk on the loom in sheer whiteness.   28
Now, opening into flower, she leans on a hillside;
Now, reflecting her own image, she overhangs a pool.
Stretching toward jade steps, she forms brilliant patterns;
Gently brushing a carved door, she lowers her branches.   32
Thereupon in the many-cloistered ladies' quarters an exquisite
    beauty,
Her appearance delicate and her mind refined,
Loves the early blossoms that spur in the season
And welcomes glorious spring's putting the cold to flight.   36

---

*A calendrical instrument of the imperial court: the ashes of reed membranes, placed in pipes, were supposed to indicate by their movements changes of season. See *Hou-Han shu,* "Chih," 1.23b–24a.

†The principle of light (contrasting with *yin* "darkness") as manifested in sunlight and spring.

(8)多灰徙筒　並皆枯悴　色落摧風　年歸氣新　(12)搖芸動塵　梅花特早　偏能識春
或承陽而發金　(16)乍雜雪而被銀　吐豔四照之林　舒榮五衢之路　旣玉綴而珠離　(20)
且冰懸而雹布　葉嫩出而未成　枝抽心而插故　標半落而飛空　(24)香隨風而遠度　挂靡
靡之遊絲　雜霏霏之晨霧　爭樓上之落粉　(28)奪機中之織素　乍開花而傍巘　或含影而
臨池　向玉階而結彩　(32)拂網戶而低枝　於是重閨佳麗　貌婉心嫻　憐早花之驚節
(36)訝春光之遣寒

Her lined gown is thinner now, unwadded,
Her silk sleeves are of single thickness.
She plucks the fragrant blossoms,
Raising her dainty sleeve.   40
She'll either stick some in her hair and ask how it looks,
Or break off some branches and give them away.
She hates too much bareness in front of her hair-knot
And is tired of the golden hairpin she has worn so long.   44
She looks back at her own shadow on the red lacquered
   steps
And posing, fondly eyes her graceful carriage.
She opens wide the spring windows,
She rolls up the silk curtains on all four sides.   48
"The spring wind blows plum petals—I'm afraid they will
   all fall,
So I knit my moth-eyebrows.*
Blossoms and beauties are all alike,
We always worry that time will pass us by."   52

We cannot be sure that this is the complete poem, since the text
has been reconstituted by modern editors from quotations in two early
encyclopedias.[3] But, complete or not, it is a well integrated work
whose dualistic approach to a single theme is reflected in its prosodic
structure.

Like other *fu* poems, it is divided into sections by three kinds of
devices: changes in meter, changes in rhyme, and a supernumerary
phrase (which has been set in italics here and throughout the book).
The meter is complex. There are six types of line, differing in length,
caesura, and the use of certain particles in fixed positions. Two types
of meter predominate, accounting for twenty-two lines each. The
changes in metric type divide the poem into twelve metric sections
(lines 1–2, 3–14, 15–16, 17–18, 19–32, 33–34, 35–36, 37–40, 41–44,
45–48, 49–50, and 51–52). The last four lines are set off from the
rest of the poem both metrically and stylistically to make the final
section (the technical term is *luan*) sound like a lyric poem or song.
Insertion of such lyric sections is not uncommon in the *fu* form.

---

*A beautiful woman's eyebrows were often likened to the antennae of a moth.

袷衣始薄　羅袖初單　折此芳花　(40)舉茲輕袖　或插鬢而問人　或殘枝而相授　恨鬢前
之太空　(44)嫌金鈿之轉舊　顧影丹墀　弄此嬌姿　洞開春牖　(48)四卷羅帷　春風吹梅
畏落盡　賤妾爲此斂娥眉　花色持相比　(52)恒愁恐失時

Changes of rhyme divide the poem into seven rhyme sections (lines 1–10, 11–16, 17–28, 29–32, 33–38, 39–44, and 45–52). Only half of these rhyme changes coincide with metric changes.

The third organizing device is the supernumerary phrase *yü shih* "thereupon." It occurs only once in this *fu*, at the beginning of line 33, which is one of the few places where meter and rhyme change simultaneously. With the three organizing devices coinciding, this point thus stands out as the one major dividing mark in this poem. Here the poet makes a fresh start, introducing the second of the two figures. He places the palace lady, like the plum tree, inside a multiple enclosure (lines 1, 33), and he enhances the similarities between them in other passages as well: both show off fine garments (lines 16, 37–38), both display their charms in all directions (lines 17, 48), both are dissatisfied with their old adornments and put on something new (lines 22, 41, and 44), and both assume coquettish poses (lines 29–32, 45–46).

The parallels are further brought out by the use of identical words (I have not always managed to reproduce this feature in my translation): *chin* "gold" (lines 15, 44); *ssu* "four" (lines 17, 18); *ch'a* "to stick" (lines 22, 41); *k'ai* "to open" (lines 29, 47); *hsin* "heart," "shoots," "mind" (lines 22, 34); *ying* "reflected image," "shadow" (lines 30, 45). Each figure becomes more significant through its association with the other. It is partly a poetic method of indirection. The poet chooses to say certain things about the flowering plum, not directly but by speaking about the palace lady, and he says certain things about the lady by speaking about the tree. What he says about one is also relevant to the other, and each can only be fully understood through its counterpart.

The poet's use of two separate figures does no harm to the unity of the poem because the two converge on a single theme: the transience of beauty. This is an abstract concept, and the reason why the Chinese poet does not deal with it directly, I suppose, is that he prefers concrete figures to abstract notions. And he creates a *pair* of figures rather than a single one because this makes possible a dramatic encounter. Throughout the poem, the method of presentation is dynamic rather than static. The two figures move toward each other; and in the opening passage, the exposition takes the form of a swift-moving narrative, which serves at the same time to give the flowering plum a central, superior, and unique position in the imperial garden:

a multitude of other plants are first displayed and then removed, leaving the plum to hold the stage alone.

These manipulations would be impossible if the plum did not play a dual role: as a tree and as a woman. It is in keeping with the conventions of the *fu* genre to devote an entire poem to a plant species or some other natural object or phenomenon. As far as personification is concerned, this is not quite as common in Chinese literature as in the West. But in Chinese folklore and popular religion (as in other countries) certain trees were early conceived as spirits or deities, some male, some female. The plum tree became established as a female figure. Hsiao Kang's *fu* is an early example of an important literary development which eventually made the flowering plum into a refined lady or a bewitching fairy, as in the following twelfth-century story.

> During the K'ai-huang era (581–601) of the Sui dynasty, Chao Shih-hsiung was sent to a post at Lo-fu.* Once, on a cold day, at the time of sunset, when he happened to be in a grove of plum trees, he saw a beautiful woman, made up sparingly and dressed simply but elegantly, coming toward him from a building next to a wine shop. It was already getting dark; the last remnants of snow had not yet melted, and the moon shone forth with a pale light. As Shih-hsiung spoke with her, her speech was most refined and beautiful, and her fragrance was enticing. So he took her to the wine shop and knocked at the door, and they drank together. After a while, a lad dressed in green merrily sang and danced for them. Shih-hsiung fell asleep, intoxicated. He only felt that the wind was cold, and the power of attraction was great. After a long time, when the east was already lighting up, he arose and, looking around, found himself under a large blossoming plum tree. Above there was a kingfisher, crying and gazing at him. The moon was setting, and Orion was on the horizon. Nothing was left but a feeling of disappointment.[4]

Here the equations are plain: the beautiful woman *is* the blossoming plum, the lad dressed in green *is* the kingfisher. Such stories of double identity and metamorphosis are as common in Chinese folklore as in the myths and tales of other civilizations. But in Chinese

---

*A mountainous region in modern Kwangtung, with an age-old reputation of being haunted by all sorts of spirits.

literature, they are found more often in prose fiction and drama than in poetry. There was no Ovid in China to make metamorphosis a focal point in poetry. That is why in Hsiao Kang's poem the relation between plum tree and woman is elusive and vague, in contrast to the twelfth-century story.

In the next poem we find again an association of two disparate figures, this time a girl and a deer.

Poem 2, *Shih ching*, no. 23
Anonymous (ca. tenth-sixth century B.C.)
Form: *Shih ching*

In the wilderness there is a dead roe,
Wrapped with white rushes.
There is a girl longing for spring,
A handsome man seduces her.

In the forest there are elms,
In the wilderness there is a dead deer,
Bound with white rushes.
There is a girl like jade.

Slow, easy, easy!
Don't touch my sash,
Don't make the dog bark.

In the first two stanzas, two themes are interwoven: the killing of a deer and the seduction of a girl. The last stanza is a dramatic flashback to the scene of seduction. Any interpretation of the poem must account for the remarkable combination of two themes in a single song. In the traditional Chinese explication, going back to the authoritative commentary by Cheng Hsüan (127–200), the poem is an appeal by a virtuous girl to her lover, asking him to give her a dead deer as a gift of betrothal. Modern readers will find this explanation hard to accept.[5] More convincing interpretations are offered by Arthur Waley and Bernhard Karlgren. Waley explains: "If people find a dead deer in the woods, they cover it piously with rushes. But there are men who 'kill' a girl, in the sense that they seduce her and then fail to 'cover up' the damage by marrying her."[6] According to

---

詩經23 「野有死麕」 野有死麕　白芽包之　有女懷春　吉士誘之　林有樸樕　野有死鹿
白茅純束　有女如玉　舒而脫脫兮　無感我帨兮　無使尨也吠

Karlgren, "A girl enticed into a love affair is likened to precious game carefully wrapped up and hidden by the lucky poacher."[7]

For a more satisfactory explanation, I suggest that we are dealing here with an archetypal pattern in which a hunter chasing (and sometimes killing) a deer is equated with a man pursuing (and sometimes raping) a woman. This pattern recurs frequently in the folklore and literature of various countries. In Goethe's *Faust*, for example, Euphorion likens the girls with whom he sports to "light-footed deer," and himself to "the hunter" (part 2, act 3). Two other instances are the British ballad "The Three Ravens" and the German ballad "Der Nachtjäger," or "The Night Hunter." It may be helpful to quote here all of the first poem and part of the second (in my translation, with the last fourteen lines omitted, as not pertinent to the present discussion).

The Three Ravens

There were three rauens sat on a tree,
   Downe a downe, hay down, hay downe
There were three rauens sat on a tree,
   With a downe
There were three rauens sat on a tree,
They were as blacke as they might be.
   With a downe derrie, derrie, derrie, downe, downe

The one of them said to his mate,
"Where shall we our breakefast take?"

"Downe in yonder greene field,
There lies a knight slain vnder his shield.

"His hounds they lie downe at his feete,
So well they can their master keepe.

"His haukes they flie so eagerly,
There's no fowle dare him come nie."

Downe there comes a fallow doe,
As great with yong as she might goe.

She lift vp his bloudy hed,
And kist his wounds that were so red.

She got him vp vpon her backe,
And carried him to earthen lake.

She buried him before the prime,
She was dead herselfe ere euen-song time.

God send euery gentleman,
Such haukes, such hounds, and such a leman.[8]

The Night Hunter

There is a town on yonder Rhine,
A noble hunter lives therein.

There is no hunter but carries a horn,
He hunts his prey, brings many to grief.

Out he rides with his greyhounds,
He came before some shrubs [?] so green.

There runs a doe by yonder woods,
A hunter chasing: she feels proud.

He came upon her track all right,
The doe, she ran ahead of the hounds.

"Run on, run on, you wild, wild beast:
A hunter is coming, he's got you, almost!"

She runs across mountains and valleys deep,
The hunter follows chasing behind.

The little doe, she took a jump,
The hunter lost her at that hour.

She ran through violets and green clover,
The hunter saw his prey no more.

He searches here, he searches there,
He found his prey, without evil intent,

He found her standing by a spring,
The hunter seized the game.

She had been running, she was warm,
She jumped into the hunter's arms.

He swung her into the clover green:
It hurts to part from your sweetheart.

The two together, they lay in great joy,
The hunter, he got his rendezvous.

What did he pull off from his hand?
He gave her a red gold finger ring.

"Look here, pretty love, this is for you,
With this you'll remember the hunter better."[9]

In the German ballad, the archetypal equation is quite plain, as far as it goes—death is not involved here. The British ballad is less explicit. With the vagueness characteristic of fine ballads, no explanation is given for the knight's death; but the fact that the doe—the knight's "leman"—also dies is an interesting analogue to the dead deer in the *Shih ching*. It is only in the German ballad that the man is clearly identified as a hunter. But in the British ballad, the combination of hounds, hawks, and deer also suggests hunting, and in the Chinese poem, too, there is a dog—possibly but not necessarily a hunting dog. Like "The Three Ravens," the *Shih ching* song refrains from telling the whole story, but through the juxtaposition of the two themes it equates the rape with a hunt, and the loss of virginity with death.[10]

We will now consider four poems in which man's relations with nature are rendered through events that are contiguous in time but diverse in substance. Chinese poetry has a special technique for contrasting successive events without narrating them one after another. This the poet accomplishes by occupying the exact point of transition, a vantage point from which he can view both the earlier and the later event or state simultaneously, without moving on in time. In the following poem there are several such contrasting states, with the poem always balanced between the two opposites.

Poem 3, "High Plateau"[11]
Wang Wei (701?–61?)
Form: *chüeh-chü*

The peaches' red holds the night's rain,
The willows' green is wrapped in spring mist.
Blossoms fall, the house boy has not swept them yet.
Orioles sing, the mountain guest is still asleep.

The pairs of opposites are: night and day; rain and clear weather;

王維 「高原」 桃紅復含宿雨 柳綠更帶春煙 花落家僮未掃 鶯啼山客猶眠

blossoms on the trees and falling; blossoms on the ground and swept away; the guest asleep and awake. The poetic moment maintains a delicate balance between past and future, clinging to the things that were but cannot last, and looking forward to what is inevitable but has not come yet. It is this balance that constitutes the charm of the situation and of the poem.

The balance of opposites also helps to save the poem from dullness. As it is, the fourfold repetition of similar patterns of thought and syntax comes dangerously close to monotony. The impression of wearisome uniformity is even stronger in the Chinese original than in translation because of the prosody. The poem is written in a rare meter which has six syllables to each line, and the six-syllable line is divided by two caesuras into three units of two syllables each, so that the poem from beginning to end runs in equal units of two syllables. This is never the case with the most popular meters of Chinese lyric poetry, whose lines have five or seven syllables. One reason, I suggest, why those two types of poem became favorites is precisely that they cannot be divided into equal parts and therefore are immune against such monotonous uniformity of prosodic and syntactic units as is exemplified in our present poem.

We now read another short poem by Wang Wei which also perches on points of transition.

Poem 4,
"Living in the Mountains, on an Autumn Evening"[12]
Wang Wei
Form: *lü-shih*

> On the empty mountain, just after rain,
> The air toward evening is autumnal.
> The bright moon shines among the pines,
> The clear fountain flows over the stones.
> The bamboo rattles: returning washerwomen;
> The lotus stirs: fishing boats going home.
> Spring fragrance ends at the season's command,
> But you, my prince, can stay as long as you like.

Though the poem does not move forward in time but seems to be

---

王維 「山居秋暝」 空山新雨後　天氣晚來秋　明月松間照　清泉石上流　竹喧歸浣女 蓮動下漁舟　隨意春芳歇　王孫自可留

standing still, it encompasses rain and clear sky, the transition from day to night, and the change of seasons (autumn and spring). The regular progression of time and the inevitable processes of change in the natural world are contrasted in the surprise ending with the voluntary lingering that is within the power of human beings.

A similar but earlier example of hovering is the following poem by Yang Kuang, better known as the last emperor of the Sui dynasty by the name of Sui Yang-ti (reigned 604–17).

Poem 5, "Feasting in the Eastern Hall"[13]
Yang Kuang (569–618)
Form: *ku-shih*

The rain has stopped, the splendor of spring is fresh,
The sun is setting, dusk's rosy clouds are radiant.
The coast pomegranates' bloom is about to end,
The mountain cherries' blossoms haven't yet flown.
Clear sounds issue from the singers' fans,
Floating scents waft from the dancers' clothes.
The blue-green canopy reaches all the way to the door,
The golden screen half hides the gate.
The gaiety of wind and flowers is infinite,
At dawn the birds return to the fragrant trees.

In describing the pleasures of a sumptuous feast, the poem does not focus on abundance and continuity but rather on changes and transfers: on transitions from rain to clear weather, from day to night, from night to day, from spring to summer, and also on transmissions from performers to audience and on contacts between indoors and outdoors. The notion is conveyed that the enjoyment of pleasures surpasses normal expectations. The feast lasts from dusk to dawn, and the spring mood continues indefinitely, despite the usual conception that spring blossoms are quickly blown away by the wind. Dwelling on changes has the advantage of suggesting variety rather than monotony, and of showing that the revelers benefit by each feature—and also by its opposite: clear weather is of course desirable, but the recent rain adds an appearance of moist freshness, and so forth.

楊廣　「宴東堂」　雨罷春光潤　日落暝霞暉　海榴舒欲盡　山櫻開未飛　清音出歌扇　浮
香飄舞衣　翠帳全臨戶　金屛半隱扉　風花意無極　芳樹曉禽歸

Let us now take a look at one more poem organized in a similar fashion. Its author is distinguished by a special brand of humor.

Poem 6, "On an Excursion
at Dawn, Looking at Clouds and Mountains"[14]
Yang Wan-li (1127–1206)
Form: *chüeh-chü*

The clearing sky is about to dawn but not yet bright.
Wherever you look there are wondrous peaks.
But one peak suddenly grows:
Now I know the ones that don't move are the real mountains.

The simultaneous presence of mountains, clouds, clearing sky, darkness, and growing daylight leads to a visual illusion, and then to a flash of recognition.

In the next few poems, nature appears to the beholder not as a single entity but as a combination of different worlds.

Poem 7,
"Ascending Solitary Islet in the Middle of
the River"[15]
Hsieh Ling-yün (385–433)
Form: *ku-shih*

South of the river I'm tired of seeing sight after sight,
North of the river I've long refrained from roaming.
I crave the new, but the roads wind too far;
I seek the unusual, but time is short.   4
The turbulent flow rushes against an upright bar:
Solitary Islet charms in midstream.
Clouds and sun reflect brilliance on each other,
Sky and water are equally pure and fresh.   8
No one appreciates such magic,
Who will transmit this truth?
In my fancy I picture the beauty of the Kunlun Moun-
    tains,*

---

*This mountain range between Tibet and Sinkiang was in Chinese Taoist tradition the abode of the Taoist goddess Hsi Wang Mu ("Queen Mother of the West").

楊萬里 「曉行望雲山」 霽天欲曉未明間 滿目奇峯總可觀 却有一峯忽然長 方知不動是眞山

謝靈運 「登江中孤嶼」 江南倦歷覽 江北曠周旋 懷新道轉迥 (4)尋異景不延 乱流趣正絕 孤嶼媚中川 雲日相暉映 (8)空水共澄鮮 表靈物莫賞 蘊眞誰爲傳 想像崑山姿

Letting the world's complications fade away.   12
Now at last I have faith in An-ch'i's* art
To make the most of the years by nourishing life.[16]

As we analyze the interplay of different worlds in this poem, we find that they belong to more than one set. In fact, we can distinguish three sets of interacting worlds: first, different elements of nature; second, different places; and third, different levels of consciousness. The boundaries between the sets are of course not rigid, and inter-action takes place across the boundaries as well as within the sets. I will take up the three sets in the order in which I have just enumer-ated them.

The various elements of nature that are mentioned in the poem are not viewed in isolation but in relation to each other. This is to be expected in any good poem of natural description, and amounts to saying that the poem is well unified. But the unity exhibited in this poem involves a special feature characteristic of Hsieh Ling-yün and other Chinese nature poets. Hsieh sees the different elements of the natural scene sharing and combining their qualities so as to form a harmonious whole:

> Clouds and sun reflect brilliance on each other,
> Sky and water are equally pure and fresh.

This visual harmony may be compared to the acoustic harmony in another poem by Hsieh Ling-yün (lines 7 and 8):

> Strange noises coming together make perfect listening,
> Different sounds combined are clear and superb.[17]

Turning now to the second set, which involves location, we find that this poem, like many others, evokes several different places. But the art of the poem is such that it is not immediately apparent how the places are related to each other, and in what respects they are alike or different. The opening couplet distinguishes two regions, "south of the river" and "north of the river." The antithetical phrasing suggests a contrast between the two regions, and such a contrast was indeed assumed by a seventeenth-century Chinese commentator, and accepted in modern annotated texts.[18] But as I read the poem, lines 1 and 2 (also lines 3 and 4) are cast in the rhetor-

---

*A Taoist sage, said to have lived as a recluse in Shantung, on a mountain named after him, to the age of a thousand years.

(12)緬貌區中緣　始信安期術　得盡養生年

ical pattern of *hu-wen* ("reciprocal phrasing") which will occupy our attention in chapter 12. This means, in short, that what is said about one region applies to the other as well. Thus it turns out that the contrast between the two banks is only apparent, not real. Both are equally distasteful to the speaker. He no longer roams on either shore because he has long since become satiated with both, and to go beyond the immediate banks would lead too far and take too much time. "North" and "south," then, are not in opposition but lumped together and jointly contrasted with another area which is neither north nor south of the river but in the middle. The central islet offers what the other two regions lack: its sights have not been seen previously by the speaker (lines 1, 2) but are "new" and "unusual"; the islet is not "too far" and can be reached without spending much "time."

The journey to the islet is remarkable in another respect. The shift of place is accompanied by a shift of consciousness. From the world that can be perceived by any traveler we pass to a world of which only the poet is aware, and hardly anybody else (lines 9, 10). In this case it is a Taoist world, devoted to communion with Nature and to the mysteries of nourishing and prolonging life. These two worlds—the ordinary and the spiritual—constitute the third of the three sets of worlds.

We can see now how closely the three sets are interrelated. A journey on the physical map drawn in the first part of the poem leads to the physical climbing of an island peak, which is at the same time a spiritual ascent, producing an unusual mental sensation. From the rarefied vantage point of the island world, the normally discrete natural elements fuse into a unified, harmonious whole of consummate beauty, while the ordinary world with its troubles recedes into the distance (line 12).

As the poet's mind rises to a higher level of consciousness, observation gradually gives way to "fancy" and to "faith." The island world frees him from the limitations of time and space that bothered him in the normal world (lines 3, 4). Thus the islet is linked to the distant, much bigger and higher Kunlun Range with its Taoist associations, and it induces thoughts of longevity and immortality (lines 13, 14).

The islet stands out from its environment in another way, too. Though it can be located on a map and reached in a short trip, it

is set apart from both shores, and it stands firm in the midst of a
turbulent river—according to line 5, which, if I read it correctly,
makes a point of contrasting "turbulent" with "upright." (This is
one of several standard patterns of parallelism and contrast within
a single line, see below, pp. 151–52, Pattern 1.) Evidently, the two
adjectives have moral and aesthetic overtones here. The newly
discovered spot is an island of uprightness, truth, and beauty in a
sea of turbulence and ugly mundane entanglements.

For a different association of worlds—in this case, the earth below
and the heavens above—we turn once more to Yang Kuang, the
last emperor of the Sui dynasty.

Poem 8,
"A Night of Spring River and Flower Moon"[19]
Yang Kuang
Form: *ku-shih*

> The evening river is smooth, it does not stir,
> The spring flowers are just in full bloom.
> The flowing waves go, carrying the moon;
> The tide water comes, bringing the stars.

This poem is unusual (though not unique) among Chinese lyric
poems in that it does not mention a single human being but concentrates exclusively on the natural scene. It also differs from the
other poems discussed in this chapter in being free from conflicts
and tensions, a freedom poetically conceptualized as the smooth
surface of the river, modified but not disturbed by the natural flow
of current and tide. The various elements of nature—spring, evening,
river, flowers, moon, stars—are all in complete harmony. We have
just seen a similar harmony in Hsieh Ling-yün (Poem 7), but in
that poem the concordant blending appeared side by side with op-
positions and contrasts. The last two lines of Poem 8 employ the *hu-
wen* pattern, which will be examined in chapter 12.

A special aspect of natural harmony in this poem is the coming
together of the celestial and the terrestrial world by means of an
optical projection. Reflection in water has always fascinated nature
poets in China as in other countries. Often, as in this poem, it is
tacitly linked to the philosophical notion of correspondences between

---

楊廣　「春江花月夜」　暮江平不動　春花滿正開　流波將月去　潮水帶星來

heavenly and earthly phenomena. It had long been a Chinese belief
that heaven and earth had been connected in the mythological past,
and that contact could be temporarily restored under special circumstances. It takes a poet to recognize the circumstances, and to recreate a paradise. Similar rapprochements of celestial and terrestrial
scenes occur in other cultures, with different philosophical and aesthetic backgrounds. Thus European baroque poets, basing themselves
on neoplatonic and Christian traditions, often represent a beautiful
landscape as a replica or reflection of Heaven. A Spanish play by
Antonio Mira de Mescua (born between 1574 and 1577, died 1644)
offers an example that may be translated as:

> This pleasant garden,
> Full of flowers, plants, and fruits,
> Gives us a picture of Heaven;
> That pond of silver
> Is crystalline Heaven;
> The wheels of that sluice, which is an artful
> Passage of water,
> Are *prima mobilia*;
> The roses are morning stars
> Of the beautiful firmament;
> The other fine flowers,
> The numerous host of stars.[20]

Another instance of the terrestrial and celestial worlds intermingling will be found in the hunting scene contained in Poem 106 below
(lines 278 and 279):

> Fires in darkness press to the sky,
> War chariots thunder and move. . . .

As the illumination for the nocturnal hunt turns night into day, the
man-made fires look like stars, and the hunting chariots rumble like
thunder.

A finely elaborate view of the blending of earthly and heavenly
beauty occurs in the following poem.

Poem 9,
"During the Night of the Mid-Autumn Festival,
in the Wu River Pavilion, Facing the Moon,

I Long for the Former Chief Minister Chang Hsien
and Send This Poem to Ts'ai Hsiang''[21]
Su Shun-ch'in (1008–48)
Form: *ku-shih*

Alone I sit, facing the moon, my heart is full of longing.
I cannot see my old friends, this makes me sad.
Tonight, men of past and present agree, is to be prized,
Especially here in the Pine River* Pavilion.   4
How lovely: Nature is in tune with human feelings,
After ten days of clouds and rain, clarity tonight.
This moon is honored not just by men,
Heaven, too, feels strongly about mid-autumn.   8
The endless sky is without blemish, revealing everything,
    inside and out.
In a gradual sweep, the rising moon's cold splendor glides
    along.
The river is smooth for thousands of acres, a true jade-green;
Above and below, clear and bright, a pair of jade disks float. 12
It seems as if my very heartbeat were visible;†
Fish and dragons worry about having no place to hide.
I don't feel that my body is on earth,
I'm only afraid if I go on a raft I'll meet the Dipper and
    the Herd Boy.‡   16
The scene is pure, the view superb, but something is lacking:
Alas! I have no companion to share all this.
My heart and soul grow cold and hot—at dawn I still can't
    sleep.
With an effort I write this to send to the capital.   20

As in Yang Kuang's poem, the rapprochement of the celestial

---

*Another name for the Wu River.

†On this night everything is so bright and transparent that even his pulse becomes
visible.

‡See appendix 2, "The Celestial Raft."

蘇舜欽 「中秋夜吳江亭上對月懷前宰張子野及寄君謨蔡大」 獨坐對月心悠悠 故人不見
使我愁 古今共傳惜今夕 (4)況在松江亭上頭 可憐節物會人意 十日陰雨此夜收 不
惟人間重此月 (8)天亦有意於中秋 長空無瑕露表裏 拂拂漸上寒光流 江平萬頃正碧色
(12)上下清澈雙璧浮 自視直欲見筋脈 無所逃遁魚龍憂 不疑身世在地上 (16)只恐槎
去觸斗牛 景清境勝反不足 歎息此際無交游 心魂冷烈曉不寢 (20)勉爲筆此傳中州

and the terrestrial world is brought about by an optical illusion: the moon's reflection in the water (line 12) makes it appear that the sky has come down to the earthly level. As the two worlds blend, the Wu River becomes the Milky Way ("The River of Heaven") through the allusion to the legend of the celestial raft.

A special feature of this special night is the unusual clarity of air and water, resulting in extraordinary visibility. What is normally hidden from sight can be seen at this time (lines 12–14). The special night is the Mid-Autumn Festival (the fifteenth day of the eighth month), when the moon is at its brightest (we call it the harvest moon). This festival is universally acclaimed by all men, and even by nature. The universality of the acclaim is rendered in the characteristic pattern of two complementary constituents: "men of past and present"; "not just by men, / Heaven, too." The same pattern serves to express the completeness of nature's beauty: "inside and out," "above and below." The beautiful scene is set off, on the one hand, by a contrasting period of bad weather immediately preceding the present, and on the other hand, by a feeling of loneliness and longing for friends. This sentiment plays a dominant role and is conspicuously placed at the beginning and the end.

In the next poem, the desired rapprochement between human affairs and natural processes takes the form of a magic spell.

Poem 10, *Shih ching*, no. 6
Anonymous
Form: *Shih ching*

The peach tree, young and tender,
Bright are its flowers.
This girl is being married,
Fit for her new home.

The peach tree, young and tender,
Plentiful is its fruit.
This girl is being married,
Fit for her new house.

The peach tree, young and tender,
Its leaves are lush.

詩經6 「桃夭」 桃之夭夭 灼灼其華 之子于歸 宜其室家 桃之夭夭 有蕡其實 之子于歸 宜其家室 桃之夭夭 其葉蓁蓁

This girl is being married,
Fit for her new family.

This is a wedding song, and thus speaks only of pleasant and auspicious matters. It celebrates the bride's resemblance to the tree—both are young and beautiful. It also serves as an incantation, seeking to transfer the tree's fertility to the woman. On such a festive occasion, everything is in harmony: the bride is just right for the groom and his family, and nature accords with the happy human event. The poem thus dwells on concords—actual and potential—between human affairs and nature.

To conclude this chapter, attention should be drawn to an aspect of nature poetry which plays an important role in Chinese poetry, though it can be found in other literatures as well. Chinese poets often feel the need for "placing" an emotion, that is to say, for attaching it to some concrete object, figure, scene, or natural phenomenon.[22] This kind of association is implied in many of the poems we have already discussed, and in others to come. It is also sometimes stated explicitly, usually in a negative way: the poet regrets the lack of a place to lodge his emotion, or he fears the loss of such a place, as in the following brief lyric.

Poem 11, "Autumn Night"[23]
Ch'en Yü-i (1090–1138)
Form: *chüeh-chü*

In the central courtyard a pale moon shines at midnight.
White dew washes the air, the Milky Way is bright.
Don't let the west wind blow all the leaves away,
Or there will be no place for autumn sounds.

之子于歸　宜其家人

陳與義　「秋夜」　中庭淡月照三更　白露洗空河漢明　莫遣西風吹葉盡　却愁無處著秋声

2

Personification

(POEMS 12–23)

Having already seen an instance of partial personification in Hsiao Kang's "Flowering Plum" (Poem 1), we will now consider other poems in which animals, plants, or natural phenomena are personified in a human setting. The following example is by a poet specializing in bold, unconventional imagery.

Poem 12, "South Garden"[1]
Li Ho (791–817)
Form: *chüeh-chü*

Flower branches and grass stems blossom before the eye,
Little white and long red: cheeks of a girl from Yüeh.
What a pity that at sundown the charming fragrance falls.
For her wedding with the spring wind, no matchmaker was
  employed.

The personifying image in line 2 is borrowed from a prose passage by Hsiao T'ung (501–31): "Lotus blossoms float in the water, attractive like the cheeks of a girl from Yüeh."[2] The region of Yüeh (southeastern China, approximately modern Chekiang and Fukien) was renowned for the beauty of its women. The most famous of these was the semilegendary Hsi Shih (see appendix 2).

In Li Ho's poem, the borrowed image is developed in a highly original manner. Unlike his prose model, Li Ho does not name any botanical species but focuses on certain qualities of the unnamed blossoms, their shape and color, their charm and fragrance. Also unlike his model, he sustains the personifying trope to the end of his composition, and matches the female figure with a male partner.

李賀 「南園」 花枝草蔓眼中開　小白長紅越女腮　可憐日暮嫣香落　嫁與春風不用媒

20

The personification of the spring wind as an impatient lover was not invented by Li Ho either, as an earlier poem to be quoted below will show (Poem 17). But here, too, he creates a novel configuration out of conventional materials. The services of a go-between have been required in Chinese weddings (down to modern times) to insure an arrangement fair to both families. By noting the absence of such a broker, the last line of our poem suggests that this is not a normal union but a violent, unilateral action. The falling of the blossoms is in the nature of a rape, a "defloration." On another plane, the final phrase, "no matchmaker was employed," undermines the fiction of personification in a sort of tragic irony.

Hsi Shih, the celebrated beauty from the land of Yüeh, appears again under the name of Hsi Tzu ("West Girl") in the following poem. Her presence there is appropriate because the poem was written (in 1073) at the scenic West Lake, near Hangchow (Chekiang Province), which is close to the region where the Hsi Shih of antiquity is reported to have lived.

Poem 13, "Drinking above the Lake
in Clear Weather Followed by Rain"[3]
Su Shih (1037-1101)
Form: *chüeh-chü*

The water's brightness, vast and rippling, looks
        best in clear weather;
The mountain's color, vague and misty, stands out
        even in the rain.
West Lake is like West Girl:
Whether the makeup's light or heavy, it always
        looks just right.

The comparison of West Lake and West Girl was often repeated by Su Shih himself and by later poets, as pointed out by the modern commentator Ch'ien Chung-shu. The principle of pairing, as it operates in this poem, brings together not only a lake and a woman but also clear weather and rain (compare Poem 4 above), plus two kinds of beauty—one subdued and refined, the other heavily but tastefully accented with adornments—and the two constituent

---

蘇軾 「飲湖上初晴後雨」 水光瀲灩晴方好 山色空濛雨亦奇 欲把西湖比西子 淡粧濃抹總相宜

elements of scenery, mountain and water (see below, p. 144). In the arrangement of these elements, polar opposites come together as the lake's water is coupled with dryness (clear weather), and land (mountain) with moisture (mist and rain). Or putting it differently, the juxtaposed entities—lake and mountain—exchange their essential attributes.

A natural phenomenon that is often singled out for personification is the moon. In Chinese lyric poetry it becomes not a deity but a semihuman companion of the lonely poet. A famous example is a humorous poem by Li Po in which he alternately builds up and destroys the illusion of personification.

Poem 14, "Drinking Alone
Beneath the Moon"[4]
Li Po (701?–63)
Form: *ku-shih*

Amidst blossoms, a pot of wine.
I drink alone, without a friend.
I raise the cup, inviting the bright moon.
With my shadow opposite, this makes three.   4
But Moon is not a drinker,
Shadow only follows me around.
With Moon and Shadow as makeshift companions
We make merry in keeping with the spring.   8
I sing, and Moon sways back and forth;
I dance, and Shadow runs helter-skelter.
As long as we're sober we share our happiness,
Once we're drunk we go our separate ways.   12
Joining forever in a passionless journey,
Let's meet far away at the Milky Way.

Li Po's genius manifests itself in the ability to create company out of loneliness, to make inanimate objects come alive, and to poke fun at himself and at the creatures of his imagination. His poem has been much admired over the centuries. Evidence of this is the following piece of verse.

李白 「月下獨酌」 花間一壺酒 獨酌無相親 舉杯邀明月 (4)對影成三人 月旣不解
飲 影徒隨我身 暫伴月將影 (8)行樂須及春 我歌月徘徊 我舞影零亂 醒時同交歡
(12)醉後各分散 永結無情遊 相期邈雲漢

Poem 15, "Going to Myriad Flower Valley
Two Days After the Double Ninth* with
Hsü K'o-chang and Passing the Cup in the Moonlight"[5]
Yang Wan-li
Form: *ku-shih*

This old man is thirsty, Moon is thirstier yet:
When wine flows into the cup, Moon goes in first.
He brings Blue Heaven along,
And Moon and Heaven both get soaked.   4
Heaven loves wine, old books report;
To say Moon is not a drinker is truly reckless talk.
I raise the cup and swallow Moon in one gulp;
I raise my head: Moon's still in Heaven.   8
This old man laughs loud and asks the guest:
"Is Moon one sphere or two?"
When wine enters the poet's guts, storm and fire arise;
When Moon enters the poet's guts, ice and snow are
      scattered.   12
Before one cup is downed the poem is done;
I chant the poem to Heaven, and Heaven is amazed:
Who'd have thought that once in a million years
      a hunk of bone
Would drink wine and swallow the full moon whole!   16

While Yang Wan-li undoubtedly had Li Po's poem in mind when
he wrote this piece (Yang's line 6 alludes to Li's line 5, Yang's line 7
to Li's line 3, and Yang's lines 5 and 8 to two other poems by Li),
yet this poem is no mere elaboration and mockery of a well-known
masterpiece. With some concepts taken from Li Po, Yang combines
fresh ideas to make up his own surprise package. Ignoring the shadow, he personifies both moon and heaven. Like Li Po and other poets,
he plays these personifications against the visible celestial features
that are part of the actual scene. He also exploits the duality of an

---

*The ninth day of the ninth month.

楊萬里 「重九後二日同徐克章登萬花川谷月下傳觴」 老夫渴急月更急　酒落杯中月先入
領取青天併入來　(4)和月和天都蘸溼　天旣愛酒自古傳　月不解飲真浪言　舉杯將月一
口吞　(8)舉頭見月猶在天　老夫大笑問客道　月是一團還兩團　酒入詩腸風火發　(12)
月入詩腸冰雪潑　一杯未盡詩已成　誦詩向天天亦驚　焉知萬古一骸骨　(16)酌酒更吞一
團月

object and its reflection. (We have discussed reflection of heavenly
phenomena with regard to Poems 8 and 9.) Finally, he uses the motif
of swallowing in a double sense, the literal and metaphorical one, in
accordance with traditional Chinese notions of psychology and poetic
creation, notions that may strike Western readers as strange and even
in poor taste. Thoughts and emotions were believed to originate in
the digestive system (lines 11, 12), and the absorption and production
of poetic material was often compared to eating and drinking. Verse,
like food and drink, is supposed to pass through the mouth, since
poetry is always chanted, no matter whether one is composing one's
own or reading the works of others. Besides, in China as elsewhere,
both moonlight and wine are known to inspire poetry.

   Another amusing personification of the moon occurs in the following poem, again by Yang Wan-li.

Poem 16, "Looking at the Moon
on a Frosty Night from 'Snow-Fisher Boat' "[6]
Yang Wan-li
Form: *ku-shih*

At the creek bank I stand for a time, doggedly waiting
   for Moon.
Moon, knowing my wish, perversely delays his rise.
I go home and shut the door; depressed, I decide not
   to look.
Suddenly he flies to the top of a thousand peaks.   4
Changing my mind, I climb aboard "Snow-Fisher" to
   watch awhile:
A wheel of ice hangs just at the tip of a pine branch.
The moon poets love best is the mid-autumn moon,
But if I am asked I shake my head.   8
Only in the twelfth month is Moon's yearlong splendor
Scrubbed with the essence of snow and washed with
   the water of frost;
In eight directions for ten thousand miles stretches
   one blue sky;
From an emerald pool floats a white jade dish;   12

楊萬里　「釣雪舟中霜夜望月」　溪邊小立苦待月　月知人意偏遲出　歸來閉戶悶不看　(4)
忽然飛上千峯端　却登釣雪聊一望　冰輪正掛松梢上　詩人愛月愛中秋　(8)有人問儂儂
掉頭　一年月色只朧裏　雪汁揩磨霜水洗　八荒萬里一青天　(12)碧潭浮出白玉盤

More yet: he invites Flowering Plum to be his partner;
How can the mid-autumn moon match this?

"Snow-Fisher Boat" is explained by Yang Wan-li in the preface
to another poem of his: "I had a small studio built for myself, shaped
like a boat, and named it 'Snow-Fisher Boat.' "[7] The name alludes,
I suppose, to the last line of a well-known poem by Liu Tsung-yüan:
"Alone fishing on the cold river in the snow."[8] In the present poem,
an imagery is developed to fit the studio's bizarre name: there is
water, ice, snow, and frost. As in the poems cited previously, the
Moon, personified, plays a prominent part. His partner this time is
neither Shadow nor Heaven but Flowering Plum, a figure familiar
to us in feminine garb from Hsiao Kang's *fu* (Poem 1). Toward the
speaker, Moon behaves at first in a refractory fashion: when wanted,
he refuses to appear; snubbed, he imposes his presence (lines 1–4).
It is a quarrel between proud lovers, of course, since Moon is evidently just as fond of his admirer as Yang is of Moon; thus, after two
couplets of hide-and-seek, the third couplet finds them contentedly
gazing at each other. There is a good deal of physical movement
going on in these six lines, with both partners taking up, in succession, three pairs of complementary positions—the typical pairing
pattern dominates throughout. In the second half of the poem (lines
7–14), narrative yields to a playful kind of objective judgment. It was
traditional for Chinese poets to set their personal opinions against
widely accepted views; and thus Yang begins by declaring his own
preference for the winter moon, and then proceeds to give his reasons.
In trying to prove his points, he lavishes laudatory metaphors on his
favorite; with no concern for consistency, he turns the previous
"wheel of ice" into a "white jade dish"; he has the moon first flying
up to the skyline, then hanging on a branch, and finally shining in
the midst of the open sky which suddenly becomes an emerald pool
with the moon floating on it. While in the first half of the poem the
Moon was a person with a mind of his own, he is now treated as an
impersonal object ("wheel," "dish") that can be scrubbed and
washed, to be personalized again toward the end (line 13). Each
image seems to be independent of the others, but they all collaborate
in eulogizing the same object and illuminating it with different
lights.

更約梅花作渠伴　中秋不是欠此段

Another form of personification is the universal literary phenomenon that John Ruskin (writing in 1856) named "the pathetic
fallacy." This feature, which we no longer consider a shortcoming
but a legitimate poetic device, consists in endowing elements of nature with human feelings. In Chinese poetry, as in other literatures,
the pathetic fallacy is usually reserved for moments of heightened
emotion, such as may be produced by grief or love. The following is
an excerpt from a threnody written in the year 217 by Ts'ao Chih
(192–232) on the death of his friend Wang Ts'an.

> The orphaned offspring fluttered helplessly,
> They cried and mourned his collapse and ruin.
> The hearse started from Wei in the North
> To go to Huai, far in the South.
> They passed successive mountains and rivers;
> They wept as if collapsing.
> Pitying winds rose with emotion,
> Passing clouds moved aimlessly back and forth.
> Traveling fish lost their waves,
> Retiring birds forgot their perch.[9]

All elements of the scene participate in the lament. Natural phenomena are rendered in terms of human actions, and conversely,
human behavior is phrased in language that normally refers to
nature. Thus *p'ien-p'ien* "fluttered helplessly" ordinarily applies to
birds, and *peng* "collapse," though a conventional euphemism for
the death of an exalted person, originally means "landslide" or
"collapse of a mountain."

In love songs, everything is centered on the speaker's overwhelming emotion, and the elements of nature are often assumed to share
that emotion to some degree. I will cite a few anonymous songs.

> Poem 17, "Spring Song"[10]
> Anonymous (fifth century A.D.)
> Form: *yüeh-fu*

> The spring grove's flowers are so charming,
> The spring birds' tone is so moving.
> The spring wind, too, is so emotional,
> He blows open my silken skirt.

「子夜四時歌 春歌」 春林花多媚 春鳥意多哀 春風復多情 吹我羅裳開

Flowers, birds, and the wind are all equally infected with the singer's spring fever, and the sense of similarity is enhanced by the unchanging repetition of two words—*ch'un* "spring" and *to* "so (much)"—in identical positions and syntax in each of the first three lines. This triple recurrence causes us to expect the same pattern in the concluding line, but we receive a surprise ending, brought about by the wind's unrestrained passion. The personification of the spring wind as an impetuous lover is already familiar from the (much later) poem by Li Ho (Poem 12).

The next two poems to be quoted belong to a loosely connected cycle of folk songs which begin, in turn, "One loom," "Two looms," and so on, to "Nine looms." "Nine Looms," the title of this and other cycles, became established as a tune pattern of the *tz'u* genre, and the songs bearing this title center on girls who make their living by spinning, weaving, and raising silkworms, which are fed mulberry leaves.

Poems 18–19[11]

Anonymous (twelfth century A.D.?)

Form: *tz'u*; tune pattern: "Nine Looms"

One loom—
Picking mulberry leaves on the field path, I wear my
    new spring dress.
The wind is clear, the sun is warm, I feel lazy and limp.
On the flowering peach branch
The singing oriole tells me
He won't hear of my going home.

———

Two looms—
The traveler stops his horse and hesitates.
What's deep in my heart I won't lightly reveal.
I turn my head and smile at him.
I go home through the blossoms,
Only afraid that the blossoms may know.

In these two songs, the speaker's amorous feelings are projected

---

〈九張機〉　一張機　採桑陌上試春衣　風晴日暖慵無力　桃花枝上　啼鶯言語　不肯放人歸

兩張機　行人立馬意遲遲　深心未忍輕分付　回頭一笑　花間歸去　只恐被花知

into the surrounding scene, as in the preceding example, but with different results. In the first of the present poems, the girl shifts to the personified oriole the responsibility for her own decision to linger—a clever conceit. At the same time, the oriole is made to act in conjunction with the wind, the sun, and the flowering peach in presenting the beauty of a spring day which one is loath to leave. All four of these images—oriole, wind, sun, and flowering peaches—are sex symbols.

In the second, a similar conceit involves the blossoms in a tacit conspiracy with the woman and the man, neither of whom is ready to put his feelings into words or action.

Poem 20, "Seven: Grief"[12]
Wang Ts'an (177–217)
Form: *ku-shih*

The barbarian land of Ching is not my home,
Why tarry any longer?
The double boat sails up the Great River,
The sunset saddens my heart.   4
On mountain ridges brightness lingers,
On steep slopes the darkness grows.
Foxes run to their caves,
Birds fly home to their forests.   8
Flowing waves make a clear sound,
Monkeys and apes cry on the banks.
A swift wind brushes the sleeves of my robe,
White dew moistens my collar.   12
Alone at night I cannot sleep,
Straightening my clothes, I rise to play the zither.
The silk strings and *t'ung* wood have human feelings,
For my sake they emit sad sounds.   16
Traveling without end,
Sad thoughts are heavy, hard to bear.

The poem displays a wide range of connections between the human situation and the natural scene, but before looking at these we have to clarify the nature of the river voyage. The poem, like most literary

---

王粲　「七哀詩」　荊蠻非我鄉　何爲久滯淫　方舟泝大江　(4)日暮愁我心　山岡有餘映　嚴阿增重陰　狐狸馳赴穴　(8)飛鳥翔故林　流波激清響　猴猿臨岸吟　迅風拂裳袂　(12)白露霑衣衿　獨夜不能寐　攝衣起撫琴　絲桐感人情　(16)爲我發悲音　羈旅無終極　憂思壯難任

works that are cast in autobiographical terms, is a combination of fact and fancy. As I read it, only the first two lines have a basis in fact, the rest is fancy. It is a historic fact that in A.D. 193 Wang Ts'an left Ch'ang-an, the capital, together with his family, to escape from the civil war ravaging North China, and went to Ching (modern Hsiang-yang, Hupei Province, Central China), whose governor, Liu Piao, had been a disciple of Wang Ts'an's grandfather. It is also known that Wang Ts'an was unhappy in Ching, not just because he was far from his home (Kao-p'ing in modern Shantung, Northeast China) but because he did not get along well with Governor Liu Piao. There is no record, however, of his leaving Ching until after Liu Piao's death in A.D. 208, when he joined the warlord Ts'ao Ts'ao. Hence the voyage up the Great River (from line 3 to the end of the poem) is likely to be purely imaginary, and those who have attempted to fit it into Wang Ts'an's biography seem to me to have failed.[13]

The voyage, then, is a poetic escape from the unpleasant reality of the sojourn at Ching. The poet's use of the epithet "barbarian" applied to the Ching region is an archaism, taken from poem number 178 in *The Classic of Songs*. Ching in Wang Ts'an's time was no longer on the periphery of Chinese civilization as it had been a millennium earlier when the ancient song was composed; the use of the derogatory archaic epithet reflects, I suggest, the poet's disgust. He makes his imaginary escape in grand style, traveling in a "double boat" —two boats lashed together, reserved for important travelers—and choosing the (or a) "Great River." But the voyage is an unhappy one: it goes upstream, that is, in the wrong direction, farther away from home, and it means "traveling without end."

Nature is in harmony with the traveler's mood: the sun sets, monkeys and apes cry, and the dew on his collar suggests tears. The screams of apes and monkeys sound sad to Chinese ears and are conventionally associated with melancholy in Chinese poetry, as in the following poem, said to be a song of the fishermen of Pa-tung (on the upper Yangtze, on the border of modern Szechuan and Hupei).

Poem 21, "Song(s) of the Three Gorges in Pa-tung"[14]
Anonymous (fifth century A.D.?)
Form: *yüeh-fu*

Of the three gorges in Pa-tung, Wu Gorge is the largest.

「巴東三峽歌」 巴東三峽巫峽長

When the apes cry three times, tears moisten our robes.
In the three gorges of Pa-tung, the apes' cries are sad.
When the apes cry three times tears moisten our clothes.

The cries of the apes, echoing from the steep banks, are combined here with the dangerous situation of passing through the rapids to produce an awesome effect.

Returning to Wang Ts'an's poem, we find that the juxtaposition of man and nature shows contrast as well as harmony. The animals' return to their habitats at nightfall is conventionally set against man's inability to go home (compare Poem 45 below). The simultaneous presence of brightness and gloom in the natural setting is beautifully expressed in lines 5 and 6 with the implication that complete darkness will soon prevail.

The harmonization of the human and the natural world reaches a climax near the end of the poem: the silk strings and the wooden body of the zither share the man's emotion and produce sad music for his sake. This is probably one of the earliest instances of pathetic fallacy in Chinese poetry.

In this and the preceding chapter we have seen elements of nature interacting with man, conversing with him or with each other, feeling and acting like him, with him, and for him. I will conclude this chapter with three instances of yet another kind of partnership, one where the poet communes with a mountain on a basis of equality and mutuality.

Poem 22, "Sitting Alone at Ching-t'ing Mountain"[15]
Li Po
Form: chüeh-chü

The flocks of birds up high have flown away,
One single cloud moves leisurely along.
For looking at each other without getting tired
There is only Ching-t'ing Mountain.

The silent companionship of man and mountain is not fully revealed until the very end of the poem. In the first half, Li Po prepares for the extraordinary conclusion by introducing two other natural phenomena, one representing togetherness and the other loneliness.

猿鳴三声淚沾裳　巴東三峽猿鳴悲　猿鳴三声淚沾衣

李白　「獨坐敬亭山」　衆鳥高飛盡　孤雲獨去閒　相看兩不厭　只有敬亭山

The wording of the first two lines recalls a poem by T'ao Ch'ien (365–427) which likewise contrasts a solitary cloud with a flock of birds.[16] In the first line of Li Po's poem, "up high" refers of course to the birds but is relevant also to the cloud and the mountain: it orients the whole poem by raising the gaze and keeping it high. Similarly, the words "single" and "leisurely" in the second line apply not only to the cloud but also to the human spectator (who, by the way, is never mentioned directly) and to the mood of the entire poem.

By first presenting and then removing the birds and the cloud, the poet intensifies the atmosphere of solitude and clears the stage for the two lone figures. (We may recall a comparable strategy in Poem 1.)

Li Po's poem inspired later poets to set up similar reciprocal relationships with favorite mountains. Thus Hsin Ch'i-chi (1140–1207) says in one of his *tz'u*:

> I think Green Mountain's really nice,
> I guess Green Mountain thinks the same of me.[17]

Also inspired by Li Po's poem is the following.

Poem 23, "Written on the Spot at Bell Mountain"[18]
Wang An-shih (1021–86)
Form: *chüeh-chü*

The creek water makes no sound as it flows around the bamboos.
West of the bamboos, flowers and grasses play soft in spring.
Under the thatched eaves, facing each other, sitting all day—
With not a single bird calling, the mountain is quieter still.

Bell Mountain is on the northeastern outskirts of Nanking. The last line is a conscious improvement over a couplet by Wang Chi (flourished early sixth century A.D.):

> With crickets chirping, the forest is yet more silent;
> With birds singing, the mountain is quieter still.[19]

As in Li Po's poem, there is no direct mention of the mountain's human partner. Furthermore, Wang's poem does not say outright who or what it is that the man faces, but in the light of Li Po's pre-

---

王安石　「鍾山卽事」　澗水無声遶竹流　竹西花草弄春柔　茅簷相對坐終日　一鳥不啼山更幽

cedent it is likely to be the mountain mentioned in the title and in the last line. The poem works its way toward the mountain gradually, almost step by step—"around the bamboos," "West of the bamboos." Three of the objects chosen for attention—bamboos, grasses, eaves— point upward and suggest mountain peaks. The silent birds are linked to the noiseless creek and enhance the mountain's sympathetic quiet. Everything contributes to the mood being created; one's eyes and thoughts are directed toward the mountain and its special re- lationship with man.

3

Man in His Relations with Other Men

(POEMS 24–28)

Since in China the writing of poetry was to a great extent a social activity, it is not surprising that a large proportion of Chinese poetry is concerned with social contacts among men, with chance encounters and planned reunions, with painful separations, and with longing for absent friends. From this vast corpus, five poems will be chosen for consideration in this chapter. The first is in the traditional ballad style known as *yüeh-fu*, by an early master of that genre, Ts'ao Chih, an imperial prince of the Wei dynasty.

Poem 24, "At The Gate There Is
a Traveler of Ten Thousand Miles"[1]
Ts'ao Chih
Form: *yüeh-fu*

At the gate there is a traveler of ten thousand miles.
I ask you, Sir, where is your home?
Gathering up my robe, I rise and follow him.
Thus I gain a heart-companion.
Clutching my robe, he weeps in front of me.
He sighs deeply and unburdens himself.
Once he was a lord in the northern region,
Now he is a commoner in the Southeast.
On and on, further on he must go,
Away and away, headed for the Northwest.

What are we to make of the two characters in this poem? Most critics down to modern times have identified the traveler with the

曹植 「門有萬里客行」 門有萬里客 問君何鄉人 褰裳起從之 果得心所親 挽裳對我泣 太息前自陳 本是朔方士 今爲吳越民 行行將復行 去去適西秦

poet (whose brother, the emperor, banished him from the capital, then transferred him from one enforced residence to another) or with one or more of his friends or relatives (who were similarly removed from the capital).[2] If the traveler is a close friend or relative of Ts'ao Chih then the speaker should be the poet himself—yet at the beginning of the poem the two men are complete strangers. If on the other hand the traveler is Ts'ao Chih himself, then the speaker is difficult to account for within the framework of an autobiographical reading.

Taking a different approach, contemporary scholars in Mainland China have said that the traveler represents the common people of North China who were forced to leave their farms and homes in the civil wars of the early third century. This reading equates the speaker with the poet, who is seen to identify and sympathize with the suffering masses.[3] This theory is patently incompatible with the text: the change of status from *shih* "gentleman," "lord" to *min* "commoner" indicates a dispossessed landlord rather than a peasant.

I see no profit in treating literary works of this nature as social, historical, or autobiographical documents.[4] As I read the poem the extrinsic identity of the persons is meant to remain vague because it is irrelevant to the intrinsic substance of the poem itself. There are two men—one of them is a householder, the other is a homeless wanderer. (The opening word, *men* "gate," conventionally implies the concepts of "home" and "household.") But their relationship is more than a confrontation of contrasting figures. Each of them becomes significant precisely through his contact with the other. It is this physical and spiritual contact that is verbalized in the poem. As the stranger comes to the gate, the speaker does not invite him in but asks him where his home is—a question to which, tragically, there can be no real answer. In fact, the wanderer does not answer immediately. During the delay, each man performs a simple act with a transcending significance. The speaker lifts up his garment, rises, and follows the stranger out into the road. "Gathering up the robe" is a conventional literary phrase, meaning "getting ready to walk." But in its context, I believe, the casual act acquires a symbolic value. As the speaker lifts up his robe, steps across the threshold, and goes out into the road with the stranger, he temporarily assumes the status of a traveler and thereby associates himself with the stranger. The wanderer, in turn, clutches the other man's garment (the same garment!) and thus makes physical contact with him. These two tacit gestures

bring about an essential rapport between the two men. They are no
longer strangers, and the traveler can now proceed to unburden
himself. Then he moves on. The encounter has been brief but
poignant. The two figures have potentiated each other.

The warm human encounter lasts only a moment, but this moment is presented as a segment of a continuing process. This is a
basic assumption underlying much of Chinese poetry: what is related in the poem is an excerpt from a larger (often limitless) sequence. In this case, the stop at the gate is a stage in a long journey.
We may note the reduplicated verb *hsing hsing* "on and on," more
literally "walk walk," in line 9 (adapted from the opening line of the
first of the "Nineteen Old Poems") matched in the final line by
ch'ü ch'ü "away and away," more literally "go go," producing a
cumulative effect of endless wandering. Grammatically, the theme of
incessant travel manifests itself in an uncommon abundance of prominently placed verbs. Not only do verbs abound, but in every single
line there is a verb in either first or second position, or in both. This
is a unique feature, not found in any other poem by Ts'ao Chih, and
rare, I presume, elsewhere in Chinese poetry. Combined with the
total lack of negatives throughout the poem, it marks positive, relentless, continuous movement punctuated by just one stop.

The following is a farewell poem.

Poem 25, "Seeing Off a Friend
on His Way to the Capital"[5]
Meng Hao-jan (691?–740)
Form: *chüeh-chü*

> You climb toward the blue clouds,
> I return to the blue mountain.
> At this point clouds and mountain separate,
> Tears soak my hempen robe.

The first two lines match closely, almost too closely. The subject
pronoun *yü* "I" at the beginning of line 2, normally unexpressed in
classical Chinese poetry, is used here for the sake of emphasis and
contrast.[6] Within the parallel structure, the juxtaposition of "clouds"
and "mountain" is brought to the reader's special attention by the
use of the same adjective for both. The juxtaposition is central to the

---

孟浩然　「送友入京」　君登青雲去　予望青山歸　雲山從此別　淚濕薜蘿衣

sense of the poem. "Clouds" and "mountain" perform multiple functions. They are parts of the landscape; they are, furthermore, symbols of the two friends' parting; and at the same time they represent their separate goals and their distinct ways of life: service at the imperial court and eremitism. The images are well chosen: one is constant, firm, and stationary, the other is mobile and unpredictable. The mobility of "clouds" makes possible the poetic representation of a temporary meeting, followed by the inevitable parting. The duality of place is thus linked to the conceptualization of two separate worlds.

In the following poem, the action moves from one place to another, and the two places signify two different sets of social relationships, and indeed two separate worlds.

Poem 26, "On the Following Day, Going Home Drunk"[7]
Yang Wan-li
Form: *ku-shih*

It's late, I rather feel like going home,
But my host insists that I stay.
I'm not against drinking,
But I'm always afraid of the drinking-game forfeits.   4
To oppose his desire is out of the question;
Though I'd like to leave I stay on.
As soon as I'm drunk he ends the party,
And my drunkenness leaves no room for sorrow.   8
On the way home my mind is confused,
The sun is setting on a corner of the mountain range.
Among the bamboos stands a farmhouse,
I'd like to stop and rest for a while.   12
An old man there is pleased to see me come;
He calls me "your lordship."
I tell him I'm not that.
He bows and, smiling, shakes his head.   16
His mind has long been made up.
It's still a case of gulls unwilling to alight.
The farmer deems me an outsider—
With whom can I enjoy myself?   20

楊萬里 「次日醉歸」 日晚頗欲歸 主人苦見留 我非不能飲 (4)老病怯觥籌 人意不可違 欲去且復休 我醉彼自止 (8)醉亦何足愁 歸路意昏昏 落日在嶺阪 竹裏有人家 (12)欲憩聊一投 有叟喜我至 呼我爲君侯 告以我非是 (16)俛笑仍掉頭 機心久已盡 猶有不下鷗 田父亦外我 (20)我老誰與遊

As indicated earlier, the poem evokes two worlds. One is the world of the elite, the poet's friends and peers. The other is the world of the farmers, the common people. The two worlds are presented in different settings, one at a drinking party and the other in front of a farmhouse. Corresponding to the shift from one location to the other, the poem is structurally divided into two parts: lines 1–8 are devoted to the first world, and lines 9–20 to the second. In the chronological sequence maintained in the poem, the poet travels from the first world to the second. The difference is one of life styles as well as social classes. As far as preference is concerned, the poet clearly favors the second, but to his chagrin he discovers that he has no choice: the farmer rejects him as an outsider, and he is compelled to remain in the milieu into which he has been born. As an upper-class gentleman he will never be accepted as an equal by the peasants, just as the sea gulls in the Taoist fable (line 18—see appendix 2) do not trust a man who lacks the Tao.[8]

In the next poem, the vicissitudes of separation are compared to the movements and phases of the moon.

Poem 27, "Feelings at Separation"[9]
Lü Pen-chung (1084–1145)
Form: *tz'u*; tune pattern: "The Mulberry Picker"

I wish you were like the moon on the river.
South, north, east, or west,
South, north, east, or west,
You'd always be near and never part.

I wish you weren't like the moon on the river.
Full for a time, it wanes again.
Full for a time, it wanes again.
How long the wait for full reunion?

The points of resemblance and distinction are deftly and neatly divided between the two stanzas, which are formally identical in this *tz'u* pattern. At the same time, likeness and unlikeness are mingled in both stanzas. The poet takes advantage of the formal structure, with its parallels, variations, and repetitions, to bring out the tensions between closeness and separation, between constancy and change. These features are also embodied in the length of lines: lines 1, 4,

---

呂本中 〈采桑子〉 「別情」 恨君不似江樓月 南北東西 南北東西 只有相隨無別離
恨君卻似江樓月 暫滿還虧 暫滿還虧 待得團圓是幾時

5, and 8 number seven syllables each; lines 2, 3, 6, and 7 have four
syllables apiece.

Correspondences and contrasts between the human and the
natural (or material) world are sometimes, as here, expressed as
similes, sometimes as coordinated states or events. We find both
forms of association in the following excerpt (lines 27–30) from
"Lady Pining at Home," a long poem by Hsü Kan (170–217).

> Since you went away
> The bright mirror has been dark, unpolished.*
> My missing you is like flowing water,
> There's never a time when it comes to an end.[10]

This four line excerpt set a pattern. "Since You Went Away"
became the opening line and title of many *yüeh-fu* ballads, twenty-one
of which are extant today, ranging from the fifth to the ninth century.[11] Three of them will be cited below (Poems 37–39).

The following is once more a farewell poem.

Poem 28,
"Seeing Off the Eighth Son
of the Hsüeh Clan at Kuang-ling"†[12]
Meng Hao-jan
Form: *lü-shih*

There is a man who hasn't reached his goal
And moves from perch to perch between Wu and Ch'u.
Our meeting at Kuang-ling is over,
The boat goes back to Lake P'eng-li.‡
The mast moves out from the trees by the river,
The waves join the mountains above the sea.
The wind-driven sail will be far off tomorrow,
Where will we catch up with each other again?

---

*Mirrors in Han times were made of bronze and other metals.

†Sons were numbered within the larger family (clan) in the order of their birth dates.
"Hsüeh the eighth [son]" was one way in which friends could refer to a man without
violating the taboo on his personal name. Nothing further is known about this friend of
Meng Hao-jan. Kuang-ling is the modern Chiang-tu, in Kiangsu Province.

‡An alternate name for Lake P'o-yang (in modern Kiangsi Province), about 400
English miles southwest of Kuang-ling by boat, going up the Yangtze River.

孟浩然 「廣陵別薛八」　士有不得志　棲棲吳楚間　廣陵相遇罷　彭蠡泛舟還　檣出江
中樹　波連海上山　風帆明日遠　何處更追攀

Figures, events, places, and elements of the scene are set against each other. Of the two figures, Hsüeh is more prominent than his friend the poet. The latter's presence is implied in the title and in lines 3 and 8. The first two lines clearly refer to Hsüeh. But in their wording they resemble passages in other poems where Meng Hao-jan casts himself in the role of the eternal wanderer who has been frustrated in his worldly ambitions. Some examples:

> As for me, what am I,
> Moving from perch to perch,* vainly asking about a
>   place to ford?[13]

> For thirty years I've hurried and scurried
> Without succeeding with pen or sword.[14]

> I too am one who has missed his chance.[15]

> Believing myself alone to have lost the way,
> I find you too out here in the wild.[16]

These four analogous passages, to which others could be added, incline me to believe that what is said about Hsüeh in the opening couplet of the poem is relevant also to the poet himself. The speaker projects himself into his friend, though their paths have crossed only briefly. As both are constantly on the move, their coming together is a rare and precious happening, and the prospect for a repetition of this event is uncertain. The final question which hopefully anticipates another meeting does not ask "when?" but "where?" The whole poem is oriented toward space rather than time, hence the unusually high proportion of place names and other words having to do with location and locomotion. The only word in the poem that clearly refers to time is *ming-jih* "tomorrow" (line 7), but it is immediately followed (in the Chinese original) by another space word, *yüan* "be far off."

The spatial orientation shows up also in the choice of verbs. Every line has a verb related to traveling or meeting: "reach," "move from perch to perch," "meet," "go back," "move out," "join," "be far off," "catch up."

---

*This phrase has a dignified, classical ring, since it was applied to Confucius in the *Analects*: "Wei-sheng Mou said to Confucius: 'Ch'iu, why do you thus move from perch to perch?' "

But every one of these verbs—except "join" and "move out"—has a negative or frustrated aspect: "reach" is preceded by "not"; "move from perch to perch" has the inherent negative connotation of being unsettled; "go back" and "be far off" in this context imply separation; "catch up" is tied to an indefinite place and may never be realized.

The description of the scene (lines 4–7) is an integrated combination of elements associated for the purposes of this poem. Mast and trees are joined together because they are seen together, resemble each other, and have a common origin. Waves and mountains, too, are linked because they are close together in this location, because they have similar shapes, and because together they make up the Chinese concept of landscape. (A common term for "landscape" is *shan-shui*, literally "mountains and water.") The subjects of lines 4–7—"boat," "mast," "waves," "wind-driven sail"—embody the lyric situation (the friend's departure) in a dynamic arrangement: concrete objects in motion. These moving elements are shown against a fixed background: "Lake P'eng-li," "trees," "river," "mountains," "sea." The impermanence of human affairs is set against the permanence of nature.

4

Recollections and Reflections

(Poems 29–34)

It is a common practice of poets everywhere to juxtapose the present with an earlier period of their lives. In the most ancient form of Arabic poetry, the *qaṣida*, it is obligatory to tell the story in retrospect: the poet represents himself as returning years later to the scene of the experience he is about to relate.[1] In English, there is Wordsworth's "Ode: Intimations of Immortality from Recollections of Early Childhood." Chinese poets have always been fond of recalling their own past while viewing the present. Here is one of many possible examples.

Poem 29, "Encountering Spring in the Eastern Capital"[2]
Han Yü (768–824)
Form: *ku-shih*

When I was young my spirit was truly wild,
Purposely competing with spring.
Every year in the second and third month
When all over the country the blossoms brighten each other, 4
When valleys and plains wear fresh clothes at dawn,
When peaches and plums in the morning make up their faces,
Then on reckless rides I knew no fatigue,
And getting dead drunk did not make me ill. 8
I ate and drank just as I pleased;
My writings were extravagant and overbearing.
Since then not much time has passed—

韓愈　「東都遇春」　少年氣真狂　有意与春競　行逢二三月　(4)九州花相映　川原曉
服鮮　桃李晨粧靚　荒乘不知疲　(8)醉死豈辭病　飲噉惟所便　文章倚豪橫　爾來曾
幾時

The mirror is suddenly full of white hair.   12
My old friends still insist on wildness,
My new companions are full of gaiety and criticism.
Now that my inner organs have changed,
I am ashamed to look at the season's splendor.   16
With time on my hands I do nothing;
What I want most is a rest from looking and listening.
In deep seclusion I live as though hiding from enemies;
I lie very still as if in darkness.   20
When the morning light enters my window
And birds call, I am drowsy and do not wake.
I can't be bothered to figure out my daily needs,
So I'm always running out of salt and rice.   24
When I sit I'm tired and forget to get up,
When my cap is awry I'm too lazy to straighten it.
Luckily I've been granted a post in the Eastern Capital,
Escaping from snares and pits.   28
My queer indolence and perverted pride
Have gradually corrupted my disposition.
What is past I cannot regain,
But in future I mustn't go on like this.   32
I have a boat on Lake Prince of Wei,
Often I drift in it alone.
The water's appearance and the sky's color—
Here everything is pure green.   36
The trees grow thick on the shore,
Toothed headlands weave lengthwise and across.
I longed to go home—alas! to no avail—
But now I have found this secluded spot.   40
What I seek is neither fame nor profit,
What I have is a match for both.
Removed from the world, I spend my days and nights;
Keeping to myself, I ignore distinctions of rank.   44
The ministers—how worthy!—

(12)白髮忽滿鏡　舊遊喜乖張　新輩足嘲評　心腸一變化　(16)羞見時節盛　得閑無所
作　貴欲辞視聽　深居疑避仇　(20)默臥如當瞑　朝曦入牖來　鳥喚昏不醒　爲生鄙計筭
(24)鹽米告屢罄　坐疲都忘起　冠側懶復正　幸蒙東都官　(28)獲離機与穽　乖慵遭傲
僻　漸染生弊性　旣去焉能追　(32)有來猶莫聘　有船魏王池　往往縱孤泳　水容与天
色　(36)此處皆綠淨　岸樹共紛披　渚牙相緯經　懷歸苦不果　(40)即事取幽迸　貪求匪
名利　所得亦以併　悠悠度朝昏　(44)落落損季孟　羣公一何賢

From on high they receive the Son of Heaven's wisdom.
Their planning follows the tracks of Yü the Great,
Everywhere stout heroes arise.   48
Supplies are distributed with diligent attention,
Absconders are hunted with military strictness.
At court, the hundred officials
Accept their duties, each with full respect.   52
I alone—what am I doing?
I sit and share these blessings with millions of subjects.
Like a bird in a cage
I raise my head to be fed.   56
I make this poem to tell my friends:
I bear my shame forever, to the end.

Change in the poet's own life is associated with the change of
seasons: youth is spring, old age (snow-white hair, line 12) is winter.
(Actually Han Yü was only forty-two years old when he wrote this
poem in the spring of 810.)[3] At the same time, the coming of spring
is also the occasion of the poem. Hence the former harmony between the persona's vital spirits and the recurring spring season is
set against the present discord between nature and self. The speaker
feels out of tune with his natural and human environment. He has
lost the vigor to enjoy the pastimes and activities of spring, and he no
longer participates with his peers in the political life of the imperial
court at the *Western* Capital. But he makes a manly effort to come to
terms with his environment (especially in lines 31–44) and to redress
the balance of past and present. Though the past was in many ways
preferable to the present, he also sees the negative sides of the past
and the advantages of the present. In the past, he was guilty of the
faults of youth: wild excesses in living, extravagance and pride in his
literary work. At present, the government is perfect (lines 45–52),
though he himself has no part in it. As a compensation, he makes the
best of his newly acquired tranquillity and detachment from political life by harmonizing with the natural world, as symbolized by the
lone boat drifting on the scenic, secluded lake. But he finds no real
remedy for his inability to keep step with the times. His final emotion
is shame.

上戴天子聖　謀謨收禹績　(48)四面出雄勁　轉輸非不勤　稽逋有軍令　在庭百執事
(52)奉職各祗敬　我獨胡爲哉　坐與億兆慶　譬如籠中鳥　(56)仰給活性命　爲詩告友生
負愧終究竟

In the following poem, past and present are confronted in a different way.

Poem 30[4]

Yen Chi-tao (1030?–1106?)

Form: *tz'u*; tune pattern: "The Immortal by the River"

> After the dream, locked in my tower;
> No longer drunk, shades rolled down;
> The grief of last year's spring just coming back:
> Falling petals, a man stands alone;
> Light rain, swallows fly in pairs.
>
> I remember first seeing little P'in,
> The word "heart" embroidered on both her gauze
>   garments.
> Strumming the guitar she sang a song of yearning.
> The same bright moon shines now
> That shone then while the brilliant cloud departed.

The formal structure is well coordinated with the unfolding of the poem's meaning. The first stanza deals with the present, the second recalls the past. But the past intrudes on the present as details of a remembered incident are gradually revealed. The opening couplet shows the persona's isolation and solitude, his desire to forget the present, and his temporary return to a happier past (as yet unspecified) in a dream. Line 3 narrows the incident as having occurred in spring, and from the combination of lines 3 and 4 it becomes clear that it is now late spring again: exactly one year has elapsed. Lines 4 and 5 are taken verbatim from a poem by Weng Hung (tenth century A.D.), but their borrowed origin in no way diminishes their effectiveness in this context. The powerful juxtaposition of "a man stands alone" and "swallows fly in pairs" further clarifies the past incident as involving love and separation.

The lover's identity is fully revealed in the second stanza. As it happens, we know from a postface which Yen Chi-tao wrote to his collection of *tz'u* that P'in was one of four singing-girls who once entertained Yen Chi-tao and two of his friends. The last line of the poem alludes to a couplet from a poem by Li Po:

晏幾道　〈臨江仙〉　夢後樓臺高鎖　酒醒簾幕低垂　去年春恨却來時　落花人獨立　微雨
燕雙飛　　記得小蘋初見　兩重心字羅衣　琵琶弦上說相思　當時明月在　曾照綵雲歸

I only regret that singers and dancers disperse;
Turning into brilliant clouds, they fly away.[5]

In Yen's poem, the "brilliant cloud" borrowed from Li Po refers perhaps to another of the four girls whose name was Yün, meaning "cloud." Her departure, then, conveniently left the two lovers alone.

The seventh line is difficult.* But no matter how it is interpreted, the double heart is an obvious image for P'in's love affair with the speaker.

While the whole poem hinges upon the tension between past and present, the tension is reduced in the last couplet through the image of the moon, which bridges the gulf between past and present just as in many other poems it bridges spatial separation. (See Poem 52 below.) In either case, the moon represents nature's constancy in contrast to the instability of the human condition.

The past which the Chinese poets confront with the present may belong not only to the speaker's personal life, as it did in the two poems just considered, but also to national history, as in the following poem.

Poem 31, "Seeing Off [the] Ying [Brothers?]"[6]
Ts'ao Chih
Form: *ku-shih*

On foot I climb the Pei-mang slope,
Afar I view the Lo-yang hills.
Lo-yang—how desolate!
The palaces completely burned;   4
The walls are all in ruins,
And brambles reach up to the sky.
I see no elders, friends of old,
But only youths, new and strange.   8
My steps are unsure, there are no paths;
The barren fields are tilled no more.
The wanderer has not been back for long,

Liang ch'ung hsin tzu lo i, literally "Two layers heart character gauze garment(s)." According to some commentators, "heart" is a kind of perfume; according to others, a collar or belt shaped like the character *hsin* "heart." I prefer to take it as a design embroidered on two transparent garments, worn on top of each other.

曹植 「送應氏」 步登北邙阪 遙望洛陽山 洛陽何寂寞 (4)宮室盡燒焚 垣牆皆頓擗 荊棘上參天 不見舊耆老 (8)但覩新少年 側足無行逕 荒疇不復田 遊子久不歸

He does not know the crisscross roads.   12
The countryside—how bleak!
A thousand miles without the smoke of men.
Remembering the home where long I lived,
I choke and cannot speak.   16

In the first six lines, the personal aspect does not appear. The speaker climbs a hillside and objectively views the ruins of Lo-yang, the eastern capital of the Han emperors. (Commentators plausibly account for the ruins as a consequence of the warlord Tung Cho's sack of Lo-yang, A.D. 190.) Ruins are conspicuous in poetic imagery, in the West as well as in China, precisely because they link the past to the present: they are visible, concrete remnants of past glory, painfully (or, to some eyes, beautifully) mutilated by the ravages of time and man.

In the second part of the poem (line 7 to the end), the objective detachment is replaced by personal involvement. The fate that has befallen the city is now seen as the speaker's private misfortune. The present is shockingly unlike the past: what had once been familiar is now strange. The old is no longer there or is changed beyond recognition. With a deft manipulation in lines 7 and 8, the semantic range of the contrasting notions "old—new" is expanded to include the related antonymous concepts "old—young" and "familiar—strange." In the entire second part, with its climax in the final couplet, the objective and the subjective view of the change from past to present blend into one as the national tragedy merges with individual grief.

The two parts are closely integrated (note for example the parallel structure of lines 3 and 13), but they are distinct in several respects, in addition to the subjective aspect of the second part that has already been noted. The first part emphasizes height, and the second, flatness. Part one has a verb of upward movement in its first line ("climb") and another in its last line ("reach up"), as well as many nouns expressive of height. (No adjectives are used here for this purpose.) In the flatness of part two, stretching a thousand miles, the only vertically rising phenomenon—smoke as a sign of human habitation—is conspicuous by its absence. Negatives, completely lacking in part

---

(12)不識陌与阡　中野何蕭條　千里無人煙　念我平常居　(16)氣結不能言

one, are found in part two in uncommonly high concentration: they occur in seven of the ten lines. They point up the negation of basic human endeavors and hopes.

The poem is filled with sights, but there is not a single sound. The only word suggesting sound is the last word of the poem, and even here the potential voice is muted. The silencing of the speaker's voice provides a convenient ending for a melancholy poem. This is a common poetic device which became conventional.

Poem 32, "Sentimental Thoughts
of Old Times in the Tower by the River"[7]
Chao Ku (flourished 844–47)
Form: *chüeh-chü*

Alone I climb the tower by the river, my thoughts far away.
The moon's splendor is like the water, the water is like the sky.
Where is the one who came with me to watch the moon?
The view is almost as it was last year.

In this confrontation of past and present, a maximum number of resemblances are marshaled to set off one crucial difference which is tacitly implied without being stated directly. Two figures are contrasted with one, and last year's event with the present. The setting as a whole remains unchanged in two successive years, and its component parts resemble each other. It is this tension between resemblances and differences, between constancy and change, that gives the poem its force.

In the following two poems, Han Yü relates the delicate personal relationships that he has developed with humanized flowering trees. As in Hsiao Kang's "Flowering Plum" (Poem 1), the plum trees are personified as attractive women. But in these two poems, as in Poem 48, we are dealing with a different species (*prunus salicina* or *prunus domestica*, Chinese *li*, as distinct from *prunus mume*, Chinese *mei*).

Poems 33–34, "Flowering Plums"[8]
Han Yü
Form: *ku-shih*

In the early morning I enter the western garden.

趙嘏 「江樓感舊」 獨上江樓思渺然　月光如水水如天　同來望月人何處　風景依稀似去年
韓愈 「李花」 平旦入西園

Some flowering pear trees look as if they were boasting.
Next to them is a single plum,
Her appearance sad as though stifling a sigh.   4
I ask, but she won't tell the reason.
Alone I walk around her a hundred times, till dusk.
Suddenly I recall having passed this tree before,
Just when the fragrance was first budding.   8
I was too drunk to notice,
Failed to see the jade branches holding frosty blossoms!
For your sake I shed a rain of tears,
Unable to turn back the sun's chariot.   12
When the east wind blows, she still looks unhappy;
Spreading far, the night air wraps her.

On an icy platter in summer they serve the purple fruit,
    full ripe.
Out of shame I send it back without eating, thinking of the
    blossoms.   16

In spring, heaven and earth compete in flowery
    splendor.
Especially in Lo-yang gardens there is a great melee.
Who has put on level ground a thousand piles of snow,
Cut out and carved these blossoms linked to heaven?   4
With the sun's red brilliance shining on them, they
    don't show off to advantage,
But when the bright moon is covered for a while they
    enhance each other's looks.

One night I took Chang Ch'e to see Lu T'ung.
Riding a cloud we both came to the Jade Emperor's
    house.   8
Tall girls, sweet-smelling, stood all around,

梨花數株若矜夸　旁有一株李　(4)顏色慘慘似含嗟　問之不肯道所以　獨繞百帀至日斜
忽憶前時經此樹　(8)正見芳意初萌牙　柰何趁酒不省錄　不見玉枝攢霜葩　汶然爲汝下雨
淚　(12)無由反旆羲和車　東風來吹不改顏　蒼茫夜氣生相遮　冰盤夏薦碧實脆　(16)斥
去不御虲其花

當春天地爭奢華　洛陽園苑尤紛挐　誰將平地萬堆雪　(4)剪刻作此連天花　日光赤色照
未好　明月暫入都交加　夜領張徹投盧仝　(8)乘雲共至玉皇家　長姬香御四羅列

All dressed alike in white silk skirts and kerchiefs.
Quiet purity and bright adornment were their offerings.
They saw I paid them no attention.   12
Their cold chastity cleaned my bones, sobered my heart.*
From now on, all my life I'll think no evil thoughts.

In the first of these two poems, we note: (1) it operates with three points in time; (2) it contrasts the several pear trees with the single plum tree; (3) starting with boastful pride, it ends with shame; (4) it treats the speaker, the pear trees, and the plum tree as equal members of a competitive, sensitive, interacting society.

The second poem needs more extensive comment. It opens with a familiar concept, namely, the juxtaposition of heaven and earth, which takes three forms here: competition (lines 1 and 2), connection (lines 3 and 4), and interaction (lines 5 and 6; note also the pairing of sun and moon). The idealization of the spring scene as a replica of heaven is appropriate as a compliment to Lu T'ung (died 835), in whose garden stood the plum trees celebrated in the poem. Lu T'ung and Chang Ch'e (died 821) were fellow poets and friends of Han Yü. Lu T'ung had given himself the byname Yü-ch'uan Tzu ("Master of Jade River"). That is why Han Yü makes him into "the Jade Emperor," a Taoist deity residing in heaven.[9]

The glorification of Lu T'ung's plum trees is enhanced by assigning them a unique position. Above all the vernal splendor of heaven and earth, the gardens of Lo-yang stand out, and from all the gardens of Lo-yang, Lu T'ung's is singled out. By a similar process of elimination, the day scene is rejected in favor of the night view (lines 5–6) and the visit takes place during a certain night. Both the spatial and the temporal concentration are completed at line 7 in the poem.

The celestial atmosphere built up in the first part of the poem envelops also the flowering plums. They are personified as attractive, virtuous, superhuman females. The poem ends on a note of Confucian morality. The concluding line alludes to a passage from the *Lun yü* (*Analects of Confucius*): "The Master said, 'The three hundred poems [of *The Classic of Songs*] can be summed up in one phrase: Think no evil thoughts.'"

---

*Literally, "liver and gall"—the seat of the emotions.

縞裙練帨無等差　靜濯明粧有所奉　(12)顧我未肯置齒牙　清寒瑩骨肝膽醒　一生思慮無由邪

5

Love Poems

(POEMS 35–41)

Love between the sexes is not as preponderant a poetic theme in China as in the West. This is because Confucian moralists discouraged the open expression of erotic sentiments in literature. Love, in their view, is essentially a private affair and therefore not a proper subject to be communicated by the man of letters to his public audience. Thus love poetry, by and large, is outside the mainstream of Chinese literature, and is to be found in certain types of popular and semipopular poetry, such as the anonymous *yüeh-fu* (see appendix 1) songs of the Southern Dynasties (fourth to sixth centuries) and the anonymous *tz'u* songs preserved in Tun-huang manuscripts (dating probably from the eighth century of our era). Men of letters, though restrained by the Confucian moral code from writing about love in their own high-class poetry, were often attracted to those folk genres and wrote love poetry in imitation of the *yüeh-fu, tz'u,* and other popular forms.

While the rules of decorum severely limited the use of amatory themes in poetry, they allowed much more freedom in the lower ranking genres of fiction and drama. Some of the most ardent and explicit erotic poetry is to be found in Chinese drama.

As a further result of the Confucian bias against eroticism, standard Chinese poetry tends to treat the subject of love in such a way as to de-emphasize sex. As will be seen in the next chapter, there is a rich body of poetry dealing with the negation and frustration of love.

An important corpus of love poetry is contained in the "Kuo feng" ("Airs of the States") section of the *Shih ching* (*Classic of Songs*). These songs of love, courtship, and wedding clearly originated as folk songs, though in their present form they seem to have been revised at the royal court. The frank eroticism of these charming songs was a matter of acute embarrassment to the Confucian scholars from Han times on. The *Shih ching* was, after all, a classic whose poems were believed to have been chosen by Confucius himself. They could not possibly deal with matters forbidden in polite literature. To get out of this dilemma, the Confucian scholars proceeded to provide the love poems in the *Shih ching* with allegorical and historical interpretations, so as to remove all erotic implications. Some of these moralistic interpretations, which completely distort the sense of the songs, are still widely accepted in our times by reputable Chinese, Japanese, and Western scholars. (See for example the traditional interpretation of the dead deer in Poem 2.) On the other hand, perspicacious minds such as the great neo-Confucian Chu Hsi (1130–1200) have debunked many of the false interpretations and restored the original sense of the songs.

We will now consider two love songs from the *Shih ching*.

Poem 35, *Shih ching*, no. 143

Anonymous

Form: *Shih ching*

The moon rises glistening—
The fair girl is sweet,
Slow-moving and graceful—
My troubled heart is sad.   4

The moon rises bright—
The fair girl is lovely,
Slow-moving and lithesome—
My troubled heart is grieved.   8

The moon rises shining—
The fair girl is illumined,
Slow-moving and lissome—
My troubled heart is upset.   12

Like many other poems in the *Classic of Songs* (cf. Poems 10, 36, 102, 103, and 104), this song reflects the alternation of similarities and differences in its formal structure: in successive stanzas, some lines and phrases are repeated verbatim, while others vary from stanza to

---

詩經143 「月出」 月出皎兮　佼人僚兮　舒窈糾兮　(4)勞心悄兮　月出皓兮　佼人懰兮
舒憂受兮　(8)勞心慅兮　月出照兮　佼人燎兮　舒夭紹兮　(12)勞心慘兮

stanza. The variations are sometimes very slight. For instance, *yao-shao* "lithesome" and *yao-shao* "lissome" are variants of the same two-syllable word, according to a modern commentary,[1] and neither one is very far from *yao-chiao* "graceful" in sound or meaning.

Through another acoustic device, this particular song emphasizes correspondences by an unusually high proportion of rhyming syllables. In most *Shih ching* songs (except the very short ones), the rhyme changes in the course of the poem, but here a single rhyme is maintained throughout, and the rhyming syllables outnumber the nonrhyming syllables, if we do not count the syllable *hsi* (this is its modern reading) which David Hawkes aptly calls a "carrier-sound."[2] Every stanza is built on the following scheme (+ represents a rhyming syllable, − a nonrhyming syllable):

$$- - + \textit{hsi}$$
$$+ - + \textit{hsi}$$
$$- + + \textit{hsi}$$
$$+ - + \textit{hsi}^3$$

The analogies between the bright, slow-moving moon and the girl are obvious, as is the tension between bliss and anxiety in the lover's mind. But the moon is more than an analogy: it is a part of the scene, as is made clear in line 10, where the moon lights up the girl's beauty. In ancient China as elsewhere, soft moonlight was ideally suited for trysts and amatory verse. Chinese lyric poetry derives much of its strength from such use of images which belong to the poem's physical setting, rather than being extrinsic to the world evoked in the poem ("her teeth are pearls," and the like). We may suspect that in a song discussed earlier (Poem 2) "the wilderness" where a deer had been killed might also be the scene of the human encounter of which the poem speaks. That suspicion is strengthened by the more obvious connection in the following song.

Poem 36, *Shih ching*, no. 94
Anonymous
Form: *Shih ching*

In the wilderness there are creepers,
The falling dew is heavy.
There is a beautiful woman,*

---

*Or: "a good-looking fellow."

詩經94 「野有蔓草」 野有蔓草　零露溥兮　有美一人

Clear, bright, and handsome.
Unexpectedly we meet,
Fitting my desire.

In the wilderness there are creepers,
The falling dew is thick.
There is a beautiful woman,*
Handsome, clear, and bright.
Unexpectedly we meet,
To be together with you is good.

Chu Hsi, a pioneer in freeing the *Classic of Songs* from traditional moralistic exegesis, recognized this poem as a love song and suggested that it speaks of a man and a woman meeting in an open field among plants covered with dew. This merging of scene and image gives this poem—and related poems—a marvelous cohesion. Creeping and clinging plants furnish good imagery for loving couples —a similar image is used in a widow's lament, no. 124 of the *Shih ching*—as does the dew.[4]

The next three poems are all cast in the same form, viz., the *yüeh-fu* pattern "Since You Went Away," whose prototype we encountered earlier (p. 38).

Poem 37, "Since You Went Away"[5]
Yen Shih-po (419–65)
Form: *yüeh-fu*

Since you went away
The scented curtains are never raised.
My missing you is like the whirling snow,
Wildly drifting, without continuing thread.

Poems 38–39, "Since You Went Away"[6]
Ch'en Shu-pao (553–604)
Form: *yüeh-fu*

Since you went away
The room is empty and the curtains light.

---

*Or: "a good-looking fellow."

(4)清揚婉兮　邂逅相遇　適我願兮　野有蔓草　(8)零露瀼瀼　有美一人　婉如清揚　邂逅相遇　(12)與子偕臧

顏師伯　「自君之出矣」　自君之出矣　芳帷低不舉　思君如回雪　流乱無端緒

陳叔寶　「自君之出矣」　自君之出矣　房空帷帳輕

My missing you is like the daylight candle:
The feeling heart does not seem bright.

I do not know why the curtains are said to be "light" (*ch'ing*).

Since you went away
Green grass has grown all over the steps.
My missing you is like the evening candle:
Tears drop till the cocks crow.

In Poem 37, the speaker's confused emotional state is well rendered by the mixed simile of snowflakes and threads ("being at loose ends," we would say): both indicate that there is no sense of direction, no guiding thread, only aimless drifting. In Poem 38, Ch'en plays on the double meaning of the word *hsin* "heart/wick," and in Poem 39 he employs the conceit of the candle weeping "tears." Both devices are used again in the following poem by Tu Mu, but Tu goes beyond Ch'en in making the candle act *for* the people to release the emotion they are unable to express.

Poem 40, "Presented at Parting"[7]
Tu Mu (803–52)
Form: *chüeh-chü*

Great passion seems like no passion at all,
We only feel, over the cups, that we cannot smile.
The candle has a heart, it pities our separation.
For our sake it sheds tears until the sky is light.

The personification of the candle in this poem is a powerful instance of the pathetic fallacy which we examined above (see chapter 2).

Poem 41, "To Be Sent Far Away"[8]
Li Po
Form: *ku-shih*

When the fair one was here, flowers filled the courtyard;
Since she left there is an extra empty bed.
On the bed the embroidered covers are rolled up and not
   slept under;

思君如晝燭　懷心不見明

自君之出矣　綠草遍堦生　思君如夜燭　垂淚著雞鳴

杜牧 「贈別」 多情卻似總無情　惟覺罇前笑不成　蠟燭有心還惜別　替人垂淚到天明

李白 「寄遠」 美人在時花滿堂　美人去後餘空牀　牀中繡被卷不寢

Even now, after three years, you can still smell the fragrance.
The fragrance, in the end, does not diminish;
The woman, in the end, does not return.
As I long for her, all the yellow leaves have fallen,
White dew moistens the green moss.

The flowers that bloom in harmony with the beautiful woman's presence and the four images of separation (the empty bed, the fallen leaves, the dew, the moss) are conventions. Particularly striking is the image of the unused bed covers. The poet emphasizes scent and color ("flowers," "embroidered," "fragrance," "yellow," "white," "green"). The key word "fragrance" links together the flowers, the bed covers, and the absent woman. Very effective poetically is the contrast between the persistence of lifeless things (bed, covers, fragrance) and human inconstancy. We also note nature's harmony with the speaker's changing mood: when the beautiful woman is present, flowers bloom; when her absence is felt, leaves fall.

至今三載聞餘香　香亦竟不減　人亦竟不來　相思黃葉盡　白露濕青苔

6

Lonely Women

(POEMS 42–46)

As we observed in the preceding chapter, erotic poetry occupies a less conspicuous place in Chinese than in Western literature. The reverse is true in regard to certain stock situations of frustrated women. Chinese poets, both male and female, early became obsessed with the figure of the lonely woman whose husband or lover has left her, either because duty has called him away or because he no longer cares for her. Many of these poems belong to the *tz'u* genre, which goes back to the eighth century and was fully developed in the ninth and tenth centuries in the milieu of singing-girls; hence the central figure is often a beautiful woman. I will give three examples by an early master of this form, taken from fourteen poems, all written to the same tune pattern, "Foreign Bodhisattva."*

Poems 42–44[1]
Wen T'ing-yün (812?–70?)
Form: *tz'u*

Within the crystal curtain, a glazed pillow.
Warm fragrance brings dreams—ducks embroidered on the cover.
The willows on the river are like mist,
Geese fly under a waning moon.

Lotus root fibers, the autumn color is light.
The man-shaped head ornament is cut zigzag.

---

*The fourteen poems do not form a cycle. Their title is unrelated to the text or meaning of the song-words; it merely identifies the original tune (which was lost early) and the prosodic pattern (which has remained constant, with minor variations, down to modern times).

溫庭筠 〈菩薩蠻〉 水晶簾裏頗黎枕 暖香惹夢鴛鴦錦 江上柳如煙 雁飛殘月天　藕絲秋色淺　人勝參差剪

56

The locks on her two temples are barred by fragrant red.
The jade hairpin on her head sways in the wind.

———

Yellow flower-powder boundless on her forehead,
Old makeup, a hidden smile, the gauze window was a barrier.
They met at the time of the peonies,
His visit was short, again were they apart.

The kingfisher hairpin has a stem of gold,
On the hairpin a pair of butterflies dance.
The heart's affairs—who really knows?
The moon is bright, blossoms fill the branches.

———

The peonies shed their blossoms, the orioles' song stops,
Green willows fill the walled garden, the moon is in the
    courtyard.
Remembering him, it's hard to dream.
She faces away from the window, the lamp is half bright.

Kingfisher hairpin, golden beauty marks on her face,
Lonely, she closes the scented bedroom door.
The man is distant, tears streak her face.
Swallows fly, spring again is waning.

When one dreamed of another person (as in Poem 44), it was believed
that either the dreamer's soul left the sleeping body to visit that
person, or the other person's soul came to visit the dreamer.

In each of the three poems, the scene is set in two places. The
single human figure is observed inside her apartment, but many of
the "events" are clearly situated outside: geese and swallows fly,
trees and flowers bloom and shed their blossoms, orioles sing and stop
singing. Unlike the persona in Hsieh Ling-yün's poem (Poem 7), the
lady in these poems does not move from place to place but stays in

---

雙鬢隔香紅　玉釵頭上風

藥黃無限當山額　宿妝隱笑紗窗隔　相見牡丹時　暫來還別離　翠釵金作股　釵上雙蝶
舞　心事竟誰知　月明花滿枝

牡丹花謝鶯声歇　綠楊滿院中庭月　相憶夢難成　背窗燈半明　翠鈿金壓臉　寂寞香閨
掩　人遠淚闌干　燕飛春又殘

her boudoir throughout, and whatever is said about the outside world can be seen and heard from inside.

Another difference between Hsieh's poem and the poems now under consideration is that Hsieh's natural world was the grand open wilderness, whereas here the natural elements are gentle and re-fined, in keeping with the femininity of these songs. One could almost say that Nature has become domesticated so as to be fit company for a lady. In fact, elements of the natural world that properly belong outdoors are somehow brought indoors. Mandarin ducks—symbolic of a happy couple—appear in an embroidery on the lady's quilt (42.2); red flowers are inserted in her hair as ornaments (42.7), while other flowers provide her with a yellow cosmetic powder (43.1); kingfisher feathers—noted for their blue green sheen—are used in her hairpins (43.5, 44.5), which in turn have the shape of butterflies (43.6).

Like other early *tz'u* poets, Wen often focuses on the places of con-tact between the lady's enclosed world and the external world, such as doors, windows, and railings. These barriers are poetically con-venient for viewing two separate worlds simultaneously.

Discrete worlds also come together in the phrase "lotus root fibers" (42.5). This phrase combines, it seems to me, three semantic ranges. First, it designates a color in the poetic language of the time (we do not know exactly which color). In connection with the three following lines it plausibly refers to the color of the lady's dress, as asserted by the commentators. Second, in the context of the line itself and the two lines preceding it, the lotus root fibers are a natural part of the autumn scene. Third, "lotus root" and "fibers" are conventional terms in Chinese amatory poetry, both singly and in combination, and each has a double meaning: *ou* "lotus root" is homophonous with *ou* "mate, companion, pair," and *ssu* "fiber" with *ssu* "thinking of, longing for (one's lover)." Such puns and exploitations of multiple meanings were as common and respectable in Chinese erotic poetry as in Elizabethan English verse.

A subtle contrast between the inside and the outside scene in the first poem, noted by Chinese specialists, is the glossy brilliance of the bead curtain and the hard pillow, made of glass or with a glassy surface in opposition to the misty, vague shape of the willows.[2] We may note similar contrasts and correspondences in the other two poems. In Poem 43, the "boundless" quantity of the makeup powder matches the abundance of the blossoms that "fill the branches," and tacitly contrasts with the emptiness of solitude. The woman's loneliness is enhanced by the "pair of butterflies." Similarly, in Poem 44, the fullness of willows and moonlight contrasts with the "half bright" lamp, the waning spring, and the distant man.

The following poem from *The Classic of Songs* establishes, like many other poems in that anthology, an analogy between the world of nature and the human situation. But while the juxtaposition is usually built on correspondences between the two worlds, this poem focuses instead on discords between them.

Poem 45, *Shih ching*, no. 66
Anonymous
Form: *Shih ching*

My husband is in the service,*
I don't know for how long.
When will he come home?
The chickens roost in a hole in the wall;
In the evening
The sheep and cows come down.
My husband is in the service,
How can I not long for him?

My husband is in the service,
Not just for days or months.
When will I see him again?
The chickens roost on the post;
In the evening
The sheep and cows come back down.
My husband is in the service,
I hope he's not hungry or thirsty.

The human and the natural world are in opposition. Any harmony between them is only a remote potentiality, an unfulfilled wish. While the domestic animals come home in the evening, the husband does not return. Nature moves in its regular, rhythmic pattern, but state

---

*Either military service or forced labor far from home.

詩經66 「君子于役」 君子于役　不知其期　曷至哉　(4)雞棲于塒　日之夕矣　羊牛下來　君子于役　(8)如之何勿思　君子于役　不日不月　曷其有佸　(12)雞棲于桀　日之夕矣　羊牛下括　君子于役　(16)苟無飢渴

service is without term. Also, the security of domestic life contrasts with the dangers of military campaigns (or corvée). Even the animals mentioned—chickens, sheep, and cows—are sources of food and thus stimulate the thought that the husband may be starving.

Through almost the entire history of Chinese poetry, especially from the sixth century A.D. on, we find a subgenre whose principal persona is the neglected palace lady. Most of the beautiful women of the imperial harem were inevitably, by their very numerousness, condemned to a life of boredom and frustration. One instance of the subgenre may be cited here.

Poem 46, "Palace Poem"[3]
Chang Hu (flourished first half of ninth century)
Form: *chüeh-chü*

Three thousand miles from her old country,
Deep in the palace these twenty years,
At the first sound of "Ho Man-tzu"
A pair of tears fall in front of her lord.

Or, more literally:

Old country three thousand miles
Deep palace twenty years
One sound "Ho Man-tzu"
Pair tears fall ruler's front.

"Ho Man-tzu" is the title of a dancing song current at the imperial court in the eighth and ninth centuries.[4] Different accounts agree that every performance had extraordinary effects on the dancer and the audience.[5] The performer in this poem may be an alien; even if she is a Chinese woman, she is far from home and suffers from long imperial neglect; this is always the given situation in the subgenre.

In the first two lines there are two juxtapositions of space and time, matching and interlocking with each other. Line 1 speaks of distance but begins with a temporal adjective ("old"). Line 2 measures time elapsed but opens with a spatial adjective ("deep").

The last two lines do not match word for word, but each of them begins with a numeral. Thus there is a number in every line, a large one in each of the first two lines and a small one in each of the last

---

張祜 「宮詞」 故国三千里 深宮二十年 一声何満子 雙涙落君前

two. This quantitative emphasis and the variation in the orders of magnitude go well with the import of the poem: the huge amount of accumulated grief produces a startling effect as soon as the first small dose of it is displayed.

7

Ballads

(Poems 47–49)

In this chapter we will take up three instances of narrative poetry. Two of them belong to the anonymous oral tradition while the third (Poem 48) is by a known man of letters. It is a striking fact that Chinese ballads have many features in common with ballads in other languages, without any possibility of mutual influence or cultural contact. This fact testifies to the universal typology of literary genres which transcend national boundaries.

Poem 47, "The Orphan"[1]
Anoymous (first or second century A.D.?)
Form: *yüeh-fu*

The orphan's life,
The orphan boy's encounter with life
Is fated to be nothing but bitter suffering.
When Father and Mother were alive   4
He rode in a strong carriage
Drawn by four horses.
Father and Mother are gone,
Big Brother and Sister-in-law make me travel as a peddler.*   8
South as far as Chiu-chiang,
East as far as Ch'i and Lu.[2]
In the twelfth month I come home,
Not daring to speak of my suffering.   12
His head is full of lice,

---

*Merchants ranked low in society; rich families carried on trade through slaves. This orphan is used by his elder brother as a slave.

「孤兒行」 孤兒生 孤子遇生 命獨當苦 (4)父母在時 乘堅車 駕駟馬 父母已去 (8)兄嫂令我行賈 南到九江 東到齊與魯 臘月來歸 (12)不敢自言苦 頭多蟣蝨

62

His face is full of dust.
Big Brother tells him to cook dinner,
Sister-in-law tells him to look after the horses.   16
He goes up to the great hall
And runs to the room below.
The orphan's tears fall like rain.

At dawn they send me to draw water,   20
At sunset, fetching water, I come home.
My hands are cracked,
No sandals on my feet.
It hurts, it hurts to tread the frost,   24
Where I walk there are many thorns.
I pull and break the thorns stuck in my legs,
It hurts so much I want to scream.
Tears come down, flowing, flowing,   28
Clear mucus, dripping, dripping.
No lined robe in winter,
No light clothes in summer.
Life in the world is misery.   32
It would be better to go soon,
To join them down below the earth at the Yellow Springs.

Spring air stirs,
Grasses sprout.   36
In the third month, silkworms and mulberry leaves;
In the sixth month, melons to pick.
Pushing that melon cart
On the way home,   40
The melon cart turns over.
Few are those who help me,
Many are the melon eaters.
I wish you'd give me back the stems,   44
Big Brother and Sister-in-law are strict.
I'd better hurry home—
They're bound to raise a fuss in reckoning.

面目多塵土　大兄言辦飯　(16)大嫂言視馬　上高堂　行取殿下堂　孤兒淚下如雨　　(20)
使我朝行汲　暮得水來歸　手爲錯　足下無菲　(24)愴愴履霜　中多蒺藜　拔斷蒺藜腸月
中　愴欲悲　(28)淚下渫渫　清涕纍纍　多無複襦　夏無單衣　(32)居生不樂　不如早去
下從地下黃泉　春氣動　(36)草萌芽　三月蠶桑　六月收瓜　將是瓜車　(40)來到還家
瓜車反覆　助我者少　啗瓜者多　(44)願還我蒂　兄與嫂嚴　獨且急歸　當與較計

Envoi

In the village—how much wrangling!   48
I want to send a letter
To Father and Mother below the earth:
Big Brother and Sister-in-law are hard to live with for long.

The poem abounds with actual or supposed facts, situations, and incidents. I proceed on the assumption that these events are all fictitious, if not in substance then at least in their poetic display, and that they are all full of meaning.[3]

Of the several principles which are at work in the choice, order, and phrasing of the occurrences, one is evidently the chronology. The poem has a chronological frame, indicated by three time markers: twelfth month (line 11), third month (line 37), sixth month (line 38). We can use these markers and a couple of other time indicators to make out a rough timetable of the narrative:

Unspecified time. The parents die; the eldest brother becomes head of the household; the orphan is sent out as a peddler (lines 7–10).

Twelfth month. He returns and is put to work at once[4] in the kitchen and stable (lines 11–19).

Still in winter ("frost," line 24). He draws and fetches water (from line 20 perhaps as far as line 34, but the end of the episode is not clearly marked).

Beginning of spring. Plants begin to grow (lines 35–36).

Third month. He feeds mulberry leaves to the silkworms (line 37).

Sixth month. He harvests melons (lines 38–51).

This chronological frame shows a constant forward movement. Significantly, each month mentioned is the last of its season: of winter, spring, and summer, respectively. (As the final incident takes place in summer, autumn is ignored.) The implication is perhaps, among other things, that the orphan is kept busy throughout the year.[5] But obviously this timetable covers only a small portion of what the poem reports. Coordinated with it is another scheme which jumps from one point in time to its polar opposite, linking and illuminating both like a flash of lightning: before the parents' death—after their death (lines 4, 7); dawn—sunset (lines 20, 21); winter—summer (lines 30, 31).

Here we see another principle at work, that of pairing. (This

---

(48)亂曰　里中一何譊譊　願欲寄尺書　將與地下父母　兄嫂難與久居

cardinal principle will be fully discussed in chapters 11 and 12.) In this poem, in addition to the three pairs just mentioned, other events are also arranged in pairs: hands hurt—feet and legs hurt (lines 22–27); silkworms to feed—melons to pick (lines 37–47); few help him—many help themselves (lines 42–47). Paired statements in Chinese poetry usually balance each other, but in the present poem they are remarkably uneven. The first member of the pair is mentioned only briefly in most cases, while the second is elaborated.

It remains for us to see how the events, as presented, relate to the poem's central concern; and here we will observe the movements of the principal figure in space as well as in time.

There is a dominant preoccupation with the boy's comings and goings. More specifically, we are told of three typical trips: to peddle goods, to draw water, and to harvest melons. In each case, his way out and way back are dealt with unequally (in accordance with a pattern already noted), in that the emphasis is placed on the troubles besetting his returns. This stress is pointed up by a triple recurrence, once for each trip, of the verb *kuei* "to return, come home," which is consistently and conspicuously placed at the end of the line (lines 11, 21, 46).

This particular preoccupation and this special emphasis both touch on the very core of the poem. The boy is pictured as being constantly on the run, without any rest. There are ceaseless pressures at work to expel him from his abode and to compel him to return there. His overriding concern is homecoming. But where is his home? A boy's home is where his parents are. This boy's parents are dead. His eldest brother and sister-in-law have taken over, and are exploiting him cruelly. Hence every homecoming involves some torture.

Where is the orphan's home? Is it where his parents used to live? Or is it where they are now? To the constant pull between coming and going is added a pull between two homes, one in this world and the other in the land of the dead—the Yellow Springs below the earth according to traditional Chinese eschatology. The prospect of death offers the orphan an alternative to his suffering in the world of the living. The theme of death is linked linguistically to the theme of going from place to place through the euphemism "to go" (*ch'ü*) for "to die," placed (in the original) like *kuei* "to return" in the prominent line end position: "Father and Mother are gone"; "It would be better to go soon / To join them down below the earth at the Yellow Springs."

The concept of descent to the Yellow Springs is also integrated into the imagery by various mental associations. To the hurrying and scurrying on the face of the earth, a third dimension has been added by repeated emphasis on *downward* movement (lines 18, 19, 28, 34, 50). We note also the persistent water imagery, suggesting perpetual motion, forever flowing downward: rain, tears, mucus, the place name Chiu-chiang ("Nine Rivers"), drawing water, the Yellow Springs. The tears, mentioned near the ends of the first and second stanzas (that is, following the returns from the first and second trips), seem to me to parallel the "letter" in the *envoi* which follows the third stanza (third trip): the tears flow down as a message to Father and Mother.

Other images, too, fit in with the general thematic and narrative structure. With the theme of being constantly on the move are connected widely different means of locomotion. First the boy rides in a fine carriage, then he is forced to travel long distances (mode of travel unspecified) and to run errands barefoot, and finally he pushes a cart. (The same Chinese word is used for "carriage" and "cart" in lines 5, 39, and 41.) The carriage of his good old days was called "strong," while the overturning of the cart can be taken as a drastic symbol of his unstable existence and as a dramatic condensation of the many upsets in his life. The horses, too, play contrasting roles: first they draw his carriage, then he has to take care of them.

These sets of images are all initiated in lines 5 and 6. In these two short lines, every word is pregnant with a significance that becomes apparent in the later context. Thus in the pattern of uneven pairs portentous matters can be concentrated in the briefer member of one pair and held there in abeyance for later use.

I would like to discuss one more feature of this ballad, namely, the change of person from "he" to "I." Though the subject need not always be specified in Chinese, the pronoun *wo* "I/me" is present in lines 8, 20, and 42 of the poem, while the third person is indicated in lines 1, 2, and 19. This change of person is a peculiarity of the ballad genre. It will be found again in the balled "Mu-lan" (Poem 49), where the first person is used in lines 49, 50, 51, 52, and 62, while the rest of the poem speaks of the heroine in the third person.

Such shifts are also found in English ballads, for example:

Down in London where I was raised,
    Down where I got my learning,
I fell in love with a pretty little girl;
    Her name was Barbara Ellen.

He courted her for seven long years,
    She said she would not have him.
Pretty William went home and took down sick
    And sent for Barbara Ellen.[6]

To understand such changes of person, one must take account of a
basic phenomenon in the art of balladry as practiced in China as
well as in other countries. The singer is free to switch, without warning, from objective relation of events to impersonating one or more
of the characters, and back again to his role as narrator.[7]

The following poem, though written by a man of letters, follows
in the tradition of the anonymous *yüeh-fu* ballad. It shows an interesting alternation of narration and dialogue.

Poem 48, "Tung Chiao-jao"[8]
Sung Tzu-hou (flourished early third century A.D.?)
Form: *yüeh-fu*

In Lo-yang, on the road East of the city wall,
Peach and plum* grow by the road.
Their blossoms shine on each other,
Their leaves face each other.   4
The spring wind rises in the Northeast,
Blossoms and leaves move up and down.
A girl from I don't know what family
Carries a basket to pick mulberry leaves.   8
Her delicate hands break their branches,†
Blossoms fall, tossed by the wind.
"Begging the lovely lady's pardon,
Why are you injuring us?"   12
"In the autumn months, when the sky is high,

---

*This plum is *li*, as in Poems 33 and 34, not *mei*, as in Poem 1.
†I take these to be branches of the peach and plum.

宋子侯 「董嬌饒」 洛陽城東路 桃李生路旁 花花自相對 (4)葉葉自相當 春風東北
起 花葉正低昂 不知誰家子 (8)提籠行采桑 纖手折其枝 花落何飄颺 請謝彼姝子
(12)何爲見損傷 高秋八九月

Bright dew will turn to frost.
At year's end you will whirl and drop,
You cannot keep your perfume long."   16
"In autumn we fall naturally,
In spring we are fragrant again.
We're not like people when they pass their prime
To be forgot forever by those who loved them."   20
I want to end this song,
This song grieves one's heart.
I'll go home and pour fine wine,
Grasp the zither and go up to the high hall.   24

The poem consists of three parts: ten lines of narration; ten lines of dialogue; and a conclusion in four lines. In the dialogue, the speakers are not expressly identified (a universal ballad feature), nor are the boundaries of the speeches marked; the Chinese original has, of course, no quotation marks, and also no personal pronouns (you, us, we, they) in the dialogue section. Everything has to be inferred from the situational context.[9] At the beginning of the conclusion, however, the personal pronoun (*wu* "I") is expressed; here the ballad singer speaks up, producing an ending made of conventional elements (the matter of this poem is so sad that it must be cut short and counter-acted with wine and music).

The fragility and transience of youth and beauty is a recurrent motif in Chinese poetry, as is the analogy of feminine charm and spring blossoms—(see Poems 1, 10, 33, and 34). In addition to the confrontation of the girl and the blossoming trees there are other, minor juxtapositions in this poem: peach and plum trees (line 2); blossoms and leaves (lines 3–6, note the emphasis on mutuality); the girl picks mulberry leaves for work and peach and plum blossoms for pleasure (lines 7–10); and finally, spring (throughout) and autumn (lines 13 and 17).

Poem 49, "Mu-lan"[10]
Anonymous (fifth or sixth century A.D.)
Form: *yüeh-fu*

Tsiek tsiek and again *tsiek tsiek*,
Mu-lan weaves, facing the door.

白露變爲霜　終年會飄墮　(16)安得久馨香　秋時自零落　春月復芬芳　何如盛年去　(20)
懽愛永相忘　吾欲竟此曲　此曲愁人腸　歸來酌美酒　(24)挾瑟上高堂

「木蘭詩」　唧唧復唧唧　木蘭當戶織

You don't hear the shuttle's sound,
You only hear Daughter's sighs.   4
They ask Daughter who's in her heart,
They ask Daughter who's on her mind.
"No one is in Daughter's heart,
No one is on Daughter's mind.   8
Last night I saw the draft posters,
The Khan is calling many troops,
The army list is in twelve scrolls,
On every scroll there's Father's name.   12
Father has no grown-up son,
Mu-lan has no elder brother.
I want to buy a saddle and horse,
And serve in the army in Father's place."   16

In the East Market she buys a spirited horse,
In the West Market she buys a saddle,
In the South Market she buys a bridle,
In the North Market she buys a long whip.   20
At dawn she takes leave of Father and Mother,
In the evening camps on the Yellow River's bank.
She doesn't hear the sound of Father and Mother calling,
She only hears the Yellow River's flowing water cry *tsien
     tsien.*   24

At dawn she takes leave of the Yellow River,
In the evening she arrives at Black Mountain.
She doesn't hear the sound of Father and Mother calling,
She only hears Mount Yen's nomad horses cry *tsiu tsiu.*   28
She goes ten thousand miles on the business of war,
She crosses passes and mountains like flying.
Northern gusts carry the rattle of army pots,
Chilly light shines on iron armor.   32
Generals die in a hundred battles,
Stout soldiers return after ten years.

On her return she sees the Son of Heaven,
The Son of Heaven sits in the Splendid Hall.   36

不聞機杼聲　(4)唯聞女嘆息　問女何所思　問女何所憶　女亦無所思　(8)女亦無所憶　昨
夜見軍帖　可汗大點兵　軍書十二卷　(12)卷卷有爺名　阿爺無大兒　木蘭無長兄　願爲
市鞍馬　(16)從此替爺征　東市買駿馬　西市買鞍韉　南市買轡頭　(20)北市買長鞭　且
辭爺娘去　暮宿黃河邊　不聞爺娘喚女聲　(24)但聞黃河流水鳴濺濺　且辭黃河去　暮至
黑山頭　不聞爺娘喚女聲　(28)但聞燕山胡騎鳴啾啾　萬里赴戎機　關山度若飛　朔氣傳
金柝　(32)寒光照鐵衣　將軍百戰死　壯士十年歸　歸來見天子　(36)天子坐明堂

He gives out promotions in twelve ranks
And prizes of a hundred thousand and more.
The Khan asks her what she desires.
"Mu-lan has no use for a minister's post.   40
I wish to ride a swift mount
To take me back to my home."

When Father and Mother hear Daughter is coming
They go outside the wall to meet her, leaning on each other. 44
When Elder Sister hears Younger Sister is coming
She fixes her rouge, facing the door.
When Little Brother hears Elder Sister is coming
He whets the knife, quick quick, for pig and sheep.   48
"I open the door to my east chamber,
I sit on my couch in the west room,
I take off my wartime gown
And put on my old-time clothes."   52
Facing the window she fixes her cloudlike hair,
Hanging up a mirror she dabs on yellow flower-powder.
She goes out the door and sees her comrades.
Her comrades are all amazed and perplexed.   56
Traveling together for twelve years
They didn't know Mu-lan was a girl.
"The he-hare's feet go hop and skip,
The she-hare's eyes are muddled and fuddled.   60
Two hares running side by side close to the ground,
How can they tell if I am he or she?"

The poem was composed when North China was ruled by the nomadic Toba. Hence the Toba Emperor, the "Son of Heaven," also bears the Altaic title "Khan." Characteristic of the oral ballad style is the sudden change from the third to the first person (lines 49–52)—a feature encountered already in Poem 47—and also several series based on repetition with variations of key elements. Another phenomenon typical of oral ballads is the repetitive "twelve (scrolls, ranks, years)," always in the same metric position, achieving a

策勛十二轉　賞賜百千彊　可汗問所欲　(40)木蘭不用尙書郎　願馳千里足　送兒還故鄉
爺娘聞女來　(44)出郭相扶將　阿姊聞妹來　當戶理紅妝　小弟聞姊來　(48)磨刀霍霍向
豬羊　開我東閣門　坐我西閒牀　脫我戰時袍　(52)著我舊時裳　當窗理霙鬢　挂鏡帖花
黃　出門看火伴　(56)火伴皆驚忙　同行十二年　不知木蘭是女郎　雄兔脚撲朔　(60)雌
兔眼迷離　雙兔傍地走　安能辨我是雄雌

musical effect at the expense of realism and consistency. ("Twelve years" in line 57 conflicts with "ten years" in line 34.)

One other detail may call for an explanation: the girls work and make up facing a door or window in order to get better light.

We note the special role played in this poem by sounds. Three different sounds are incorporated in the text through onomatopoeia: *tsiek tsiek*, *tsien tsien*, and *tsiu tsiu*. Each of these three sounds conveys a double meaning. The initial reduplicative *tsiek tsiek* is purposely ambiguous: it suggests the sound of the shuttle, and also of Mu-lan's sighs.[11] The noise of her regular activity—weaving—is confused with the sound of her sudden outburst of grief. As the latter supersedes the former, her normal life as a girl occupied with domestic duties is interrupted by the emergency which causes her to abandon her role as a woman in order to take up a man's job. The phrase "don't hear . . . only hear" (lines 3 and 4) marks the ambiguity and confusion of the two sounds. The recurrence of the same phrase in lines 23 and 24, and again in lines 27 and 28, indicates similar ambivalence in both cases. The surface meaning of the two passages is of course that Mu-lan cannot hear her parents because of the distance. But another meaning is simultaneously present: to the homesick girl, all the noises of her strange environment recall the sounds she would much rather hear.

Her dual role—as a woman and as a man—is represented in particular by the clothes she wears. The poem starts out with the making of clothes, which is a woman's normal function, and in the final scene she changes back into feminine dress.

The poem contains two instances of *hu-wen*, a phenomenon to be discussed more fully in chapter 12.

Lines 33 and 34:

> Generals die in a hundred battles,
> Stout soldiers return after ten years

cannot be taken at face value.[12] Surely the poet does not mean to say that only generals die in the war and only common soldiers survive. Rather, the two statements must be taken jointly: in this ten year war many battles are fought, many officers die, as do many soldiers; the survivors—officers and men—return at the end of the war. Among those who return is included, specifically, the heroine.

In lines 59 and 60 we have another instance of *hu-wen*:

> The he-hare's feet go hop and skip,
> The she-hare's eyes are muddled and fuddled.

What is said about the male hare also applies to the female, and vice versa: when both are running fast, neither of them can see clearly whether the other is a male or a female, and the same goes for soldiers busily fighting a war.[13]

8

Parting

(Poems 50–66)

This chapter will take up one of the most common themes found in Chinese lyric poetry: parting. Seeing off a friend or relative was originally a religious rite called *tsu-chien*, and it was designed to secure for the traveler divine protection against the hazards of the road. For this purpose, elaborate sacrifices of food and wine were offered to the God of the Road (Tao-shen), accompanied by music and dancing. After the feudal period, the religious aspect of this rite gradually receded into the background, and the ceremony became primarily a social affair. The offerings of food and wine were transformed into a banquet, the music and dances served to entertain the farewell party, and all those present—the departing traveler as well as those who came to see him off—would commemorate the occasion in poems. That is why such a large proportion of Chinese lyric poetry consists of poems of parting, some of which will be considered later in this chapter. But first we will examine a lengthy poem that was not written at the time of one particular leave-taking. Rather, it is a comprehensive work purporting to present all the various aspects of separation.

Poem 50, "Parting"[1]
Chiang Yen (444–505)
Form: *fu*

1

In darkness it dissolves the soul
Like nothing else: separation,
Especially between Ch'in and Wu—remote lands,

江淹 「別賦」 黯然銷魂者 唯別而已矣 況秦吳兮絕國

Or Yen and Sung—a thousand miles,   4
Now, when the spring moss begins to grow,
And then, when the autumn wind slowly rises.

2

Thus the traveler's heart is broken,
A hundred emotions make him sad.   8
The wind's sighing sounds unfamiliar,
The clouds' vast expanses look strange.
The boat stops at the water's edge,
The carriage lingers by the mountain side.   12
The oars lie idle, unmoving;
The horses whinny incessantly in the cold.
He covers up the golden cup—to whom can he drink?
He puts aside the jade-pegged zither and moistens the
        carriage-rail with tears.   16

3

The one left behind reclines in sorrow,
Deprived of her senses, like one bereaved.
Submerging its brilliance, the sun sets below the house wall;
Splendidly soaring, the moon rises above the balcony.   20
She observed dew on the red orchid;
She sees frost on the green catalpa.
She checks the lofty rooms and vainly closes them,
She strokes the embroidered curtains and finds them empty
        and cold.   24
She knows the departed one's dreams are unsteady,
She realizes the absent one's soul is soaring high.

4

Therefore, though parting is a single act,
Its manifestations are a thousand kinds,   28
Such as dragonlike horses and silver saddles,
Vermilion carriages and painted axles,
The farewell banquet at East Capital Gate,

---

(4)復燕宋兮千里　或春苔兮始生　乍秋風兮暫起　是以行子腸斷　(8)百感悽惻　風蕭蕭
而異響　雲漫漫而奇色　舟凝滯於水濱　(12)車逶遲於山側　櫂容與而詎前　馬寒鳴而不
息　掩金觴而誰御　(16)橫玉柱而霑軾　居人愁臥　怳若有亡　日下壁而沈彩　(20)月上
軒而飛光　見紅蘭之受露　望青楸之離霜　巡層楹而空掩　(24)撫錦幕而虛涼　知離夢之
躑躅　意別魂之飛揚　故別雖一緒　(28)事乃萬族　至若龍馬銀鞍　朱軒繡軸　帳飲東都

Seeing off the traveler at Gold Valley.*   32
The zither strikes the note *yü*, flutes and drums are arranged,
How touching, the songs of beauties from Yen and Chao!
Bedecked with pearls and jade, they entice in late autumn;
Dressed in gauze and silk, they charm in early spring.   36
Startled by the music, the feeding horses lift their heads,
And the red-scaled fish of the deep rise up.
When forced to let go of each other's hands they weep
With a feeling of desolation and spiritual injury.   40

5

Then there are knights-errant shamed by their lords' favors,
Young men bent on avenging their masters' grievances:
In the country of Han,† the privy of Chao,
The palace of Wu, the market of Yen.   44
They abandon their dear ones, suppressing their love,
Depart from their countries and leave their homes.
Shedding tears they separate forever,
Wiping off the blood they are weeping, they take a last
    look.   48
They spur their running horses without glancing back,
Occasionally seeing the travel dust rise.
Filled with a sense of mission, each concentrates his passion
    on the sword,
Without any thought of buying fame through death.   52
With the shaking music of metal and stone, they turn pale;‡
Their own flesh and blood suffer heartbreak and grief.

6

Or else the border provinces are not yet pacified,
So bearing arrows he marches with the army.   56
The Liao River goes on forever,

---

*For information on East Capital Gate and Gold Valley, see appendix 2 under "Shu Kuang" and "Shih Ch'ung."

†For information on Han, Chao, Wu, and Yen see appendix 2 under "Nieh Cheng," "Yü Jang," "Chuan Chu," and "Ching K'o," respectively.

‡See appendix 2, "Wu Yang."

(32)送客金谷　琴羽張兮蕭鼓陳　燕趙歌兮艷美人　珠與玉兮艷暮秋　(36)羅與綺兮嬌上春　驚駟馬之仰秣　聳淵魚之赤鱗　造分手而銜涕　(40)咸寂莫而傷神　乃有劍客慙恩　少年報士　韓國趙廁　(44)吳宮燕市　割慈忍愛　離邦去里　瀝泣共訣　(48)抆面相視　驅征馬而不顧　見行塵之時起　方銜感於一劍　(52)非買價於泉裏　金石震而色變　骨肉悲而心死　或乃邊郡未和　(56)負羽從軍　遼水無極

Mount Yen pierces the clouds.
At home, in the women's apartments, the wind is warm;
On the paths the grass is fragrant.   60
The sun rises in the sky with sparkling light,
The dew falls on the ground in glittering patterns.
Red dust is reflected in brilliance,
The life-force of spring bursts forth in profusion.   64
Plucking peach and plum sprigs, he cannot bear to leave;
At the beloved's farewell, tears soak her silk skirt.

7

Now consider: once he has gone to a remote land,
How can they ever meet again?   68
He looks at the tall trees in the old village,
At the northern bridge he takes leave forever.
The bystanders' souls are shaken,
The tears of relatives and guests pour down.   72
Perhaps they spread mats and exchange sad poems
Or they only pour wine and speak of their grief—
Right in the season when autumn geese fly,
Just at the time when white dew falls.   76
They hate, oh, they hate the winding route of distant
      mountains,
They go, oh, they go along the banks of endless rivers.

8

Again, suppose the husband lives in Tzu-yu,
The wife resides in Ho-yang.   80
They used to share the morning sunlight on their jade
      pendants
And the evening fragrance of the golden incense burner.
Now he ties official seals a thousand miles away,
Longing for the precious flower whose fragrance is wasted.   84
She feels guilty about the zither lying idle in her chamber,
Darkly on the high terrace the yellow silk curtains are
      drawn.

雁山參雲　閨中風暖　(60)陌上草薰　日出天而曜景　露下地而騰文　鏡朱塵之照爛　(64)
襲青氣之烟熅　攀桃李兮不忍別　送愛子兮霑羅裙　至如一赴絕國　(68)詎相見期　視喬
木兮故里　決北梁兮永辭　左右兮魂動　(72)親賓兮淚滋　可班荊兮贈恨　唯樽酒兮敘悲
值秋雁兮飛日　(76)當白露兮下時　怨復怨兮遠山曲　去復去兮長河湄　又若君居淄右
(80)妾家河陽　同瓊珮之晨照　共金鑪之夕香　君結綬兮千里　(84)惜瑤草之徒芳　慜幽
閨之琴瑟　晦高臺之流黃

The spring palace's gates are shut on the green moss,
The autumn curtains are filled with bright moon light; 88
The summer mats are cool, daylight does not fade,
In the winter lamps the oil thickens, how long the night!
As she weaves songs on silk, her tears are all shed;
As she composes revolving-verse poems,* alone with her
    shadow she grieves. 92

9

If there is a Taoist worthy in Hua-yin
He swallows drugs and returns to the mountains.
The art being subtle, he still continues his studies;
He has reached a stage of quietude but not yet full
    mastery. 96
He sticks to refining cinnabar without regard for others,
He smelts it in the metal tripod with firm determination.
Riding a crane, he rises to the Milky Way;
Mounting a *luan* bird, he soars to heaven. 100
A brief trip covers ten thousand miles,
A short absence lasts a thousand years.
But as in this world parting is a serious matter,
He takes leave of his hosts reluctantly. 104

10

In the world below there are the poem of the peonies,
The song of the beautiful lady,
The girl from Wei in Sang-chung,
The beauty from Ch'en in Shang-kung,† 108
The emerald color of the spring grass,
The clear waves of the spring river.
Seeing off the dear one at the southern bank,
How much grief! 112
As for the autumn dew like pearls,

---

*Artful compositions that contain many poems when read in different directions:
vertically and horizontally, forward and backward.
  †See Poem 104.

春宮閟此青苔色 (88)秋帳含妓明月光 夏簟清兮晝不暮 冬釭凝兮夜何長 織綿曲兮泣
已盡 (92)廻文詩兮影獨傷 儻有華陰上士 服食還山 術旣妙而猶學 (96)道已寂而未
傳 守丹竈而不顧 鍊金鼎而方堅 駕鶴上漢 (100)驂鸞騰天 蹔遊萬里 少別千年 惟
世間兮重別 (104)謝主人兮依然 下有芍藥之詩 佳人之歌 桑中衛女 (108)上宮陳娥
春草碧色 春水渌波 送君南浦 (112)傷如之何 至乃秋露如珠

The autumn moon like a jade disk,
Bright moon and white dew,
Light and shade come and go.   116
Parting from the dear one,
The loving heart is agitated.

11

Thus the ways of separation are unpredictable,
The causes of separation have a thousand names.   120
Those who are separated will grieve without fail,
Their grief will be abundant without fail.
As a result, men's feelings are violated, their minds are
   terrified,
Hearts are splintered, and bones dismayed.   124
Not even the superb ink of Wang Pao and Yang Hsiung,
The fine brushes of Yen An and Hsü Lo,
The dignitaries of the Golden Horse Gate,
The assembled flower of the Orchid Terrace,   128
Though their writing skill were said to pierce the clouds
And their eloquence were likened to carving dragons,
None could depict the aspects of temporary separation
Or describe the feelings of irrevocable parting.   132

The poem is divided into eleven sections. Each new section begins
with a supernumerary phrase, a metric shift from a longer line to a
four-syllable line, and a change of rhyme. There are only two exceptions: line 17 has no supernumerary phrase, and at line 119 the four-
syllable meter does not constitute a change from the meter of the
preceding portion. The supernumerary phrases normally consist
of two syllables (the only exception in this poem is *ku* "therefore" in
line 27), and each of them is used only once in the course of the poem,
with the exception of *shih i* "thus" (lines 7 and 119).

The manner of presentation is determined to a large extent by the
conventions of the *fu* genre: a single subject is treated in exhaustive
detail, not from the vantage point of one person (as would be the
case in a lyric poem) but in a series of shifting scenes. Concentration

秋月如圭　明月白露　(116)光陰往來　與子之別　思心徘徊　是以別方不定　(120)別理
千名　有別必怨　有怨必盈　使人意奪神駭　(124)心折骨驚　雖淵雲之墨妙　嚴樂之筆
精　金閨之諸彥　(128)蘭臺之羣英　賦有凌雲之稱　辯有雕龍之声　誰能摹暫離之狀
(132)寫永訣之情者乎

on a single subject leads to hyperbolical treatment and explicit exclusion of other topics: the pain of parting is unique (line 2), it cannot be described even by the most talented writers (lines 125–32), it causes men to weep blood (line 48), it breaks not only hearts but even bones (line 124, an instance of *hu-wen*). The emotion produced by separation is so powerful that it affects even animals and inanimate objects, in a sort of pathetic fallacy (lines 11–14).

In addition to the universality of parting, the poet emphasizes its unity in diversity: "Though parting is a single act, / Its manifestations are a thousand kinds" (lines 27–28); "The ways of separation are unpredictable, / The causes of separation have a thousand names" (lines 119–20). Despite the diversity, the result in every case is infinite grief (lines 121–22, and passim).

Throughout the poem, the distinction between the specific and the general is deliberately blurred. Six historical persons who had memorable experiences of parting are referred to without mentioning their names. Rather, each person is evoked by means of a place name that suggests to the erudite reader the incident in question: "The farewell banquet at East Capital Gate, / Seeing off the traveler at Gold Valley" (lines 31–32); "In the country of Han, the privy of Chao, / The palace of Wu, the market of Yen" (lines 43–44). As a result of this use of place names and omission of personal names, the historical and fixed episodes assume the same external appearance as those fictitious and floating situations where the poet arbitrarily sets up a pair of separate locations without having in mind a specific historical occurrence: "separation . . . between Ch'in and Wu—remote lands, / Or Yen and Sung—a thousand miles" (lines 2–4); "The Liao River goes on forever, / Mount Yen pierces the clouds" (lines 57–58); ". . . the husband lives in Tzu-yu, / The wife resides in Ho-yang" (lines 79–80); ". . . a Taoist worthy in Hua-yin" (line 93).

Conversely, in the passages just quoted, the fictitious nature of these scenes is concealed by the concrete details with which they are depicted—details of location in these cases. Elsewhere, the same purpose is achieved by details of time and season: "Now, when the spring moss begins to grow, / And then, when the autumn wind slowly rises" (lines 5–6); "Submerging its brilliance, the sun sets below the house wall; / Splendidly soaring, the moon rises above the balcony" (lines 19–20); "The life-force of spring bursts forth in

profusion" (line 64); "Right in the season when autumn geese fly, /
Just at the time when white dew falls" (lines 75–76). Another effective use of concrete detail within an invented scene is the last look
at familiar landmarks: "He looks at the tall trees in the old village, /
At the northern bridge he takes leave forever" (lines 69–70).

The particular bits of detail as they arise and disappear to create
one scene after another bring about an illusion of timeless actuality.
It no longer matters that some of the events did occur once in history,
that others allude to earlier literary treatments of parting (lines 105–
08, 111), and that the remaining ones were invented specifically for
this poem—all of them are typical scenes that might take place at
any time, illustrating different aspects of the topic. On the other
hand, there are many details that seem to have no bearing on the
theme of parting. But they serve a purpose nevertheless. Lines 81–
82 bring out the poignancy of separation by setting forth the pleasures
of togetherness before the parting. Other passages dwell on the beauty
of the home environment which is (or will be) missed by the traveler
(lines 19–20, 59–64, 84, 87–88, 109–10, 113–14). In one scene, a
fabulous display of wealth and luxury forms a stark contrast with the
impending separation (lines 29–38). In the same vein, phrases like
"the golden cup," "the jade-pegged zither," "their jade pendants,"
"the golden incense burner," "the precious flower," "the autumn
dew like pearls, / The autumn moon like a jade disk," and even
place names like "Gold Valley," "Golden Horse Gate," and "Orchid Terrace" contribute to the atmosphere of luxury pervading the
background against which the painful aspects of parting stand out
sharply. This is a strategy that we observed earlier (see discussion of
Poem 1, above): a large amount of wealth is accumulated at one
stage in order to achieve a dramatic effect from its removal at a later
stage.

The juxtaposition of pleasant and unpleasant features connected
with separation may also be seen as a manifestation of the general
principle of pairing that is so pervasive in Chinese poetry. Joy is
coupled with grief, companionship with isolation, abundance with
desolation, and the state of mind of the traveler is contrasted with
that of the person who stays behind.

While a large variety of different situations are produced so as to
bring out the universality of parting, a selection is made in favor of
those times, places, and circumstances that are most likely to be

connected with separation. A partial exception is the departure of the Taoist adept from this world (section 9). He has freed himself from emotional entanglements and is able to disregard the normal restrictions of space and time. Yet even he is subject to the established tradition which makes parting a reason for regret. In this exceptional scene, the power of the emotion is demonstrated by showing how it prevails even under the most unlikely circumstances.

We will now proceed to sort out various notions associated with parting in this poem and in others. The images occurring most frequently in "Parting" are dew, spring, and autumn; each of these is used five times ("dew" in lines 21, 62, 76, 113, 115; "spring" in lines 5, 36, 59–66, 87, 109–10; "autumn" in lines 6, 35, 75, 88, 113–14). Dew has several different associations in Chinese poetry. We have already encountered its use as a sexual symbol (above, Poem 36). Another common signification of dew is imperial favor (which comes from above like dew from the sky). In this sense it is often coupled with rain, for example in the following opening line of a poem by Tu Fu, titled "Presented to the Imperial Reception Officer and Diarist, Secretary T'ien":

The Reception Office is close to the rain and dew.[2]

(That is to say, the office where the recipient of the poem is employed is close to the Emperor's palace, and he is showered with imperial favors.) Neither of these two uses of dew fits our present poem. But dew has another poetic association that was already well established at the time when "Parting" was written. We find it in the following bearers' song:

Poem 51, "Dew on the Wild Onion"[3]
Anonymous (third century B.C.?)
Form: *yüeh-fu*

Dew on the wild onion,
How easily it dries!
When dew has dried it falls again the next morning—
Once a man is dead and gone, when will he come back?

The same image occurs in this section from the thirteenth of the anonymous "Nineteen Old Poems" (first or second century A.D.?):

「薤露」　薤上露　何易晞　露晞明朝更復落　人死一去何時歸

> In endless alternation, *yin* and *yang* take turns,
> Our fated years are like the morning dew.
> Human life is sudden, like a temporary lodging.
> Long life is not as solid as metal or stone.[4]

Dew, then, symbolizes instability and evanescence. It is therefore an appropriate image for a situation that compels a person to make do with "a temporary lodging" and separates him from his normal environment. Dew, as well as other images of instability that we shall meet later, occurs often in Chinese poems dealing with separation and other states of transience. A special use of the dew image is found in Li Ho, for example in the opening section of his poem entitled "Autumn Chill: A Poem sent to My Elder Paternal Cousin, the Twelfth in His Generation, the Collator":

> Closing the gate I feel the autumn wind,
> Long have I been separated from your noble person.
> Over the vast expanse grows a white sky,
> The breadth of heaven and earth is filled with forbidding air.
> Bright dew weeps on withering orchids,
> Insect sounds continue through the night.[5]

The identification of dewdrops with tears is one of Li Ho's favorite images, though not exclusively his. (It is used, for example, by Po Chü-i; see Poem 61 below.) It also occurs in Western poetry. Ovid once explains the morning dew as the tears shed by Aurora (Dawn) in mourning for her dead son Memnon:

> luctibus est Aurora suis intenta, piasque
> nunc quoque dat lacrimas et toto rorat in orbe.[6]
> [Aurora is bent on her mourning, and the pious
> Tears she still sheds now bedew the whole earth.]

The Spanish poet Francisco de Quevedo (1580–1645), in a *silva* (addressed to a fountain) lamenting his separation from his beloved, has the following lines:

> Aquí la vez postrera
> vi, fuente clara y pura, a mi señora,
>
> . . . .
> Aquí me aparté de ella
>
> . . . .

Ya me viste gozarla,
y en medio del amor, con mil temores,
llorar más que la aurora en estas flores.[7]

[Here for the last time
I saw, clear and pure fountain, my lady,

. . . .
Here I parted from her

. . . .
You saw me enjoy her,
And amid love, with a thousand fears,
Weep more than does dawn on these flowers.]

The French poet Charles de Montausier (1610–90) employs the same conceit when he has the Rose say: "Quand l'Aurore au matin m'arrose de ses pleurs. . . ."[8] In the following line, the Chinese poet Ts'ao Chih also uses the dew image for human tears: "Tears come down like falling dew."[9]

We turn now to spring and autumn. They are the seasons of change and shift, of growth and decline, in contrast to summer and winter, which are periods of stability and rest. Hence spring and autumn go together with separation, which is a state of mobility and instability. (Summer and winter are each mentioned only once in "Parting": lines 89 and 90. Like spring and autumn, they are paired.)

Corresponding to the seasons of spring and autumn, the times of day most frequently associated with parting are morning and evening, the times of transition and change. Both occur twice in "Parting" (morning in lines 61 and 81, evening in lines 19–20 and 82).

In addition to marking the time and hinting at instability, the periods of the day and the year also serve two other poetic functions in "Parting." The first of these is accomplished by the use of multiple rather than single time-markers. The juxtaposition of spring and autumn in lines 5 and 6 indicates the passage of time, emphasizing the *length* of separation, just as in the preceding couplet the mention of two pairs of place names brings out the vast *distances* involved in separation. Similarly in lines 87–90, the successive mentioning of the four seasons in four consecutive lines is a way of saying that the separation continues from season to season, without relief. The same painful continuity is rendered by the repeated juxtaposition of spring and autumn in lines 109–16. The remaining poetic function of the concepts "spring," "autumn," "morning," and "evening" consists in their evocation of beautiful scenery, which sharpens the pain felt by those who travel and those who stay behind.

Other images from nature that are used in "Parting" and other poems on the same theme are wind, clouds, dust, sky, sun, and moon. (Wind occurs in "Parting," lines 6, 9, 59; clouds in lines 10, 58, 129; dust in lines 50, 63; sky in lines 61, 99–100; sun in lines 19, 61; moon in lines 20, 88, 114, 115.) All of these are natural elements to which the traveler is exposed, and all of them (except the sky) are themselves in motion. Wind, clouds, and dust are particularly apt as images of sudden, unpredictable movement and of instability. Furthermore, wind, dust, and sun are features that contribute to the discomforts of traveling, thus adding physical pain to the mental anguish of separation. Clouds are used quite commonly to represent the traveler. Take for example the final line of a poem by Meng Hao-jan, entitled "Seeing Off Personnel Officer Wang the Seventh in His Generation to Sung-tzu and Reaching the Clouds at Yang Terrace": "Following the traveling clouds, you go and do not return."[10] And a poem by Tu Fu (712–70) titled "Dreaming of Li Po" begins:

> The floating cloud travels all day,
> The wanderer has not come for so long.[11]

The moon, with its waxing and waning, is a favorite emblem of change and inconstancy. We saw it so used in the second stanza of Lü Pen-chung's "Feelings at Separation" (Poem 27), though in the first stanza of that poem it was held up as a symbol of permanence, in contrast with the separation of the two human beings. This aspect of the moon, too, is commonly used in Chinese poetry. To console those who are far apart, the moon serves as a link that brings them together. "Those who are separated by a thousand miles share the same moon," says Hsieh Chuang (421–66) in his *fu* "The Moon."[12]

Conventional Chinese views of the moon in connection with parting and meeting are well brought out in a poem by Su Shih, written at the time of the mid-autumn festival. This festival, falling on the fifteenth day of the eighth Chinese month when the full moon is at its brightest (it is the harvest moon of the autumnal equinox), is traditionally the occasion for a family reunion—a full moon signifies a complete family. Su Shih in this poem laments the absence of his younger brother Su Ch'e (1039–1112, courtesy name Tzu-yu).

Poem 52, "During the Mid-Autumn Festival in the Year *ping-ch'en* [1076], Making Merry and Drinking till Dawn, I Got Very Drunk and Wrote This Poem, Longing for Tzu-yu"[13]
Su Shih

Form: *tz'u*; tune pattern: "Water Melody Overture"

The bright moon—how long has it existed?
Holding a cup, I ask the blue sky.
I do not know what year it is up there
Tonight in the palaces of Heaven.   4
I want to go there riding the wind,
I only fear among the jasper towers and jade roofs
Up there the cold must be unbearable.
I start to dance and play with the bright moonlight—   8
Is there anything like this in the world of men?

It turns among the crimson pavilions,
It comes down to the latticed window,
It shines on my sleeplessness.   12
There should be no resentment—
Why is it always full at parting time?
People have sorrow and joy, separation and reunion;
The moon is dark and bright, full and incomplete;   16
These things from of old have been hard to match.
I only hope that our lives will last,
That we may share this beauty across a thousand miles.

There is always a difference, the poet notes, between the celestial and the human timetable (lines 1–4, 14–17). If human life were ideal, the alternation of human affairs would coincide with the natural cycle that manifests itself in the phases of the moon, the seasons of the year, and the like. But the rhythm of nature is fixed and regular, while man's vicissitudes are erratic and unpredictable. The two worlds are different and separate. The moon that seems so close and yet cannot be reached also represents the distant brother, or at least the hoped-for family reunion. What man should do—the poet

---

蘇軾 〈水調歌頭〉「丙辰中秋歡飲達旦大醉作此篇兼懷子由」 明月幾時有 把酒問青天 不知天上宮闕 (4)今夕是何年 我欲乘風歸去 惟恐瓊樓玉宇 高處不勝寒 (8)起舞弄 清影 何似在人間 轉朱閣 低綺戶 (12)照無眠 不應有恨 何事長向別時圓 人有悲 歡離合 (16)月有陰晴圓缺 此事古難全 但願人長久 千里共嬋娟

concludes—is to accept the separateness of the two worlds and the separation of family members, and to enjoy the few links that are available.

Besides waxing and waning, and being visible simultaneously to persons in different places, the moon has other aspects that can be associated with parting. It shines on lovers' trysts and nocturnal farewells; it may be a symbol of feminine grace and charm (see Poem 35 above); and it often serves to enhance the beauty of a scene that contrasts with the pain of parting, thus performing the same function as images noted earlier in this chapter.

The sun, too, is sometimes merely a part of the beautiful scene. But it is especially the *setting* sun that we find in poems of parting (see "Parting," line 19)—an obvious image of gloom, disappearance, and loss, akin to the images "evening" and "autumn" that have already been discussed.

In view of this preference for images with negative, uncomfortable implications, such as "setting sun," "autumn," and "dust," it is not surprising that three lines in "Parting" speak of cold (lines 14, 22, 24) but only one of warmth (line 59). In this connection we may also mention frost ("Parting," line 22), which is naturally often coupled with autumn and which is another form of dew. We may add to our previous remarks on dew that it sometimes has the unpleasant connotations of cold and dampness in poems that speak of spending the night with a departing friend, or spending a lonely night outdoors.

As noted earlier, images frequently have more than one function. The juxtaposition of dew on the orchid and frost on the catalpa ("Parting," lines 21–22) indicates the progress of time (the change of tense in the translation is of course absent in the original), besides contributing to the beauty of the changing natural scene (again the tension between natural beauty and personal grief).

Other natural features that figure importantly in poems of parting are rivers and mountains (rivers in "Parting," lines 11, 57, 78, 110; mountains in lines 12, 58, 77, 94). The two are often paired (as they are in three of their four occurrences in "Parting"). For the traveler they are both obstacles and scenery. For the one who stays behind they are barriers preventing the dear one from returning; but they are also visible links to the distance. Both are symbols of nature's constancy and endurance. (Their use in this sense is of course not limited to poems of parting.) Thus they are related to time. Rivers, in particular, often represent the ineluctable flow of time, the impossibility of bringing back the past, and the endless continuity of grief. We may recall Hsü Kan's lines,

> My missing you is like flowing water,
> There's never a time when it comes to an end.

(See above, p. 38.) A river may also be associated with the flow of tears, as in Poem 65 below. (Cf. the water imagery in Poem 47.)

Mountains and rivers are used together as images of separation and travel in the opening of a poem by Ts'ao P'ei (187–226):

> The day of parting—how easy! The day of meeting—
>   how hard!
> The mountains and rivers are distant and far, the road
>   goes on and on.[14]

This recalls a poem in the *Classic of Songs* (no. 232), which begins:

> Steep, steep, those rocks,
> How high!
> The mountains and rivers are distant and far,
> How fatiguing!
> The soldiers march east,
> They have no days off.
>
> Steep, steep, those rocks,
> How lofty!
> The mountains and rivers are distant and far,
> When will they ever end?
> The soldiers march east,
> They have no relief.

The river that forever flows east (as most rivers do in China), symbolizing an endless series of partings and other forms of suffering, is a powerful image in two poems by Li Yü, the last ruler of a small, weak state known as Southern T'ang.

Poem 53[15]

Li Yü (937–78)

Form: *tz'u*; tune pattern: "Crows Cawing at Night"

李煜　〈烏夜啼〉

The flowering trees of the grove have dropped their spring
    red
All too quickly.
Unbearable, the cold rain coming in the morning and the
    wind at night.

Tears smear the rouge,
Drunk at the farewell—
When again?
Inevitably human life is always grief, the river always
    flows east.

The image of the flowering trees will be taken up shortly. The wind, already familiar to us in connection with parting, has an additional function here as a destroyer of spring beauty, in conjunction with the cold rain—another favorite image of parting and loneliness. Note also the parallel of the red blossoms washed away by rain and the rouge diluted by tears. The first stanza maintains an objective stance, while the second stanza is subjective. But the phrase *wu nai* "unbearable" is deliberately ambiguous, being equally relevant to the blossoms and the persona.

Poem 54[16]

Li Yü

Form: *tz'u*; tune pattern: "The Beautiful Lady Yü"

Spring blossoms and autumn moon—when will they end?
How much has happened in the past!
On the balcony last night, again an east wind,
The moon was so bright, I couldn't bear to look toward
    the old land.

The carved galleries and jade steps must still be there,
Only the rosy cheeks have changed.
I ask you, how much sorrow can there be?
It's just like a whole river full of eastward flow in spring.

This poem must have been written after 976 A.D., when Li Yü, having lost his small state of Southern T'ang with its capital at Chin-ling (modern Nanking), was taken as a prisoner to the Sung

---

林花謝了春紅 太匆匆 無奈朝來寒雨晚來風 胭脂淚 相留醉 幾時重 自是人生長恨水長東

李煜 〈虞美人〉 春花秋月何時了 往事知多少　小樓昨夜又東風　故国不堪回首月明中
雕闌玉砌應猶在　只是朱顏改　問君能有幾多愁　恰似一江春水向東流

capital of K'ai-feng. This should be kept in mind to understand the
multiple meanings of the last line of each stanza. In the fourth line,
ku kuo "the old land" means both "homeland" and "lost realm."
The final line answers not only the question of the preceding line
("How much sorrow can there be?") but also another, unspoken
question ("What is sorrow like?"). As most of his poems (except some
early ones) are melancholy, the river's eastward flow signifies for
him not just the flux of time but specifically the continuity of sorrow
and the irretrievable loss of past happiness and position.

When poems of parting speak of rivers, they sometimes localize
the scene more specifically by mentioning a bridge or a river bank.
There are three instances in "Parting" (lines 70, 78, 111). Two of
these have literary antecedents. Line 70, "At the northern bridge he
takes leave forever," is lifted verbatim from the eighth of the "Nine
Regrets" by Wang Pao (first century B.C.), which is part of the *Ch'u
tz'u* anthology.[17] From the same anthology derives line 111, "Seeing
off the dear one at the southern bank": it is based on a line from the
eighth of the "Nine Songs," which literally says: "Seeing off the
beautiful lady at the southern bank."[18] These localizations of parting
in the *Ch'u tz'u* pieces and in Chiang Yen's "Parting" became established by convention, and were often used in later poetry. Hsieh
T'iao (464–99), for example, matches them with each other in the
opening of his poem, "Song of Seeing Off One Who Is Going Far
Away":

> At the northern bridge we have a farewell banquet,
> At the southern bank I see her off.[19]

Here are two more instances of "southern bank," and one of "northern bridge."

> The southern bank was the place of parting;
> In the east wind, magnolias are plentiful.[20]

> Since we parted at the southern bank
> I've been grieved to see the lilacs bud.[21]

> I truly lament the day set for the westward journey,
> I am moved even more by the song of the northern bridge.[22]

The last example is remarkable in that "song of the northern bridge"
functions almost like on Old Germanic *kenning,* that is, a conventional

circumlocution for an unnamed thing (such as "dragon's lair" for "gold"). The educated Chinese reader is aware of the literary antecedents and knows that a "song of the northern bridge" must be a farewell poem; he is alerted to this special meaning by the matching phrase "day [set] for the westward journey" in the preceding line.

Turning now to plant imagery, we may recall that spring blossoms were associated with parting in the two poems by Li Yü just quoted (Poems 53 and 54). In earlier chapters we repeatedly encountered flowering trees as images of feminine beauty, with emphasis on the transience of loveliness (see Poems 1, 10, and 48). We can see now that when poets use the flower image in connection with separation, they view this special condition as a manifestation of the general instability to which man is subject. In this sense, flowers function in a similar way as dew, spring, autumn, wind, clouds, and moon. But the flowers that are shed will grow again the following year. In this respect, they represent the constancy of nature, in tragic contrast with the limitations of man's fate. Furthermore, blossoms also contribute to the beauty of the scene where the parting takes place, or where the absent person is missed (see "Parting," lines 21, 22, 65, 105).

Other plants that figure prominently in poems of parting are grass ("Parting," lines 60, 109) and moss ("Parting," lines 5, 87). Grass is an effective image of parting because it combines several qualities. Its fragrance leaves a strong sensuous impression at the time of parting and recalls that moment in later years. Every year, grass disappears and returns like a traveler; but unlike the movements of human beings, its periodic comings and goings take place at regular, fixed intervals. This imagistic function resembles that of the spring blossoms. At the same time, the grass of meadows stretches far into the distance. Thus it brings out the vast space separating the two persons and simultaneously forms a link between them. In this sense, it works in the same way as mountains, rivers, and roads. An early example of this use of the grass image is found in the first half of an anonymous *yüeh-fu* ballad, probably composed between the second century B.C. and the second century A.D., entitled "Watering the Horses at the Water Hole by the Great Wall":

> Green, green, the grass on the river bank;
> Stretching away, the far road I think of;

> The far road, beyond the reach of thought.
> Last night I saw him in a dream,
> I saw him in a dream, at my side;
> Suddenly I woke in another village,
> In another village, each of us in a different district;
> I tossed and turned, he could no longer be seen.[23]

We note the association of grass with the river bank and the road, all stretching into the distance. There is a desperate attempt to establish a link with the beloved man, but he can never quite be reached, not even with thoughts or in dreams. The notion of spring grass transmitting a love message is found also in a couplet from a poem by Lo Pin-wang (ca. 640–84):

> In the mountains there is spring grass,
> It grows as if sending thoughts of longing to my love.[24]

In the animal world, the creatures named most often in conjunction with separation are birds. The correspondences are manifold. Birds are always on the move, like travelers; they are seen singly, in pairs, or in a flock, thus harmonizing or contrasting with human situations of separation and togetherness. Unlike human beings, they move about swiftly and freely, crossing boundaries, rivers, and mountain ranges at will.

One of the favorite birds in poems of parting is the wild goose ("Parting," line 75). Its migrations differ from human travel by occurring at regular, predictable intervals, in harmony with the seasons of the year. Also, according to Chinese folklore, the goose helps separated lovers and friends by carrying messages from one to the other. By 815 the use of wild geese and ducks in poems of separation had become common enough to be mentioned by Po Chü-i in his letter to Yüan Chen on the principles of poetry: "In poems of parting, pairs of wild ducks and single wild geese are used as images."[25]

Another frequently mentioned animal is the horse ("Parting," lines 14, 29, 37, 49). Its connection with travel is obvious, as is the role played by carriages (lines 12, 16, 30) and boats (lines 11, 13) in such poems. Noteworthy is a passage of pathetic fallacy in "Parting" (lines 11–14), where the boat and its oars, the carriage, and the horses join in the man's reluctance to part.

While carriages and boats are obvious images of travel, the state of mind of being left behind is often symbolized by the house that remains cold and empty after the dear one's departure ("Parting," lines 19–20, 23–24). Sometimes the poet focuses on a particular, crucial object within the house, such as an empty bed, the departed person's clothes, curtains ("Parting," lines 24, 86, 88; Poems 37 and 38), an incense burner ("Parting," line 82), a lamp ("Parting," line 90), a candle, or a gate. The candle often appears in scenes of parting as well as in situations of loneliness, and as we saw earlier, it may express its sympathy by shedding "tears" (Poems 39 and 40).

Finally, communication between those who are separated is often said to be achieved in a dream ("Parting," line 25), in accordance with the belief that the soul of a sleeping person may leave the body and travel abroad.

Having concluded our survey of the principal images found in Chiang Yen's "Parting," we will now look at some other poems of separation, with particular attention to their imagery.

Poem 55, "Seeing Off a Friend"[26]

Wang Wei

Form: *chüeh-chü*

In the mountains, after seeing you off,
At sunset I close the brushwood gate.
The spring grass will be green again next year,
Will you, my prince, return or not?

Like many poems in the *chüeh-chü* form, this one divides into two halves. The first couplet relates past and present events, the second one looks into the future. The opening of the first line ("in the mountains") states in a general way the location of the scene, and the corresponding phrase of the second line ("at sunset") fixes the time. Another function of the initial phrase "in the mountains," in conjunction with "the brushwood gate" which concludes the first half, is to indicate that the speaker has voluntarily chosen eremitism as his mode of life.

The last two lines have a literary antecedent: "You, my prince, went wandering and have not returned, / The grass of spring grows, oh! so lush," reads a couplet in "Summons for a Gentleman Who Became a Recluse," a poem of the second century B.C., preserved in

---

王維　「送別」　山中相送罷　日暮掩柴扉　春草明年綠　王孫歸不歸

the *Ch'u tz'u* anthology.[27] The same *Ch'u tz'u* couplet also inspired a poem by Hsieh T'iao which will be cited below (Poem 91). In Wang Wei's poem, the spring grass works as a multiple image of separation, expanding distance, affectionate linkage, and possible reunion.[28] The seasonal regularity of plant growth is juxtaposed with the uncertainty of human activity. The last line is that type of interrogative sentence (more common in spoken than in literary Chinese) which places two alternatives side by side (it literally says, "return not return"), thus implying an exhortation and a wish that the departing friend will choose the alternative that accords with the natural cycle and with the speaker's desire.

Besides the grass, other images of parting in this poem are the mountain, the sunset, and the gate. The prevailing mode of the first half is finality: the farewell is over, the sun is setting, the gate is closed. The gate, standing at the center of the poem, where past and present give way to the future, faces in both directions. The same gate that closed after the friends' departure may open again on his return. Thus the gate is not only an image of gloom but also one of hope. It is probably no accident that *fei* "gate" is made to rhyme with *kuei* "return."

Poem 56[29]
Li Yü

Form: *tz'u*; tune pattern: "Music in the Modes *ch'ing* and *p'ing*"

Since we parted, spring's been halved.
It strikes my eye, and my sad heart breaks:
Beneath the steps, the falling plum blossoms are
    like a flurry of snow;
I brush them off but still they cover me.

Wild geese come but messages don't get through.
The road is far; it's hard to meet in dreams.
The grief of separation is just like grass in spring:
No matter how far you go, it's growing still.

In the first line, the use of *pan* "half" as a verb (half of spring has passed already) is ingeniously fitted to the theme of parting (cutting in half). In the third and fourth lines, the poet achieves a magnif-

---

李煜 〈清平樂〉 別來春半 觸目愁腸斷 砌下落梅如雪亂 拂了一身還滿 雁來音信無憑 路遙歸夢難成 離恨恰如春草 更行更遠還生

icent combination of images: petals and snowflakes signify separation, decay, and confusion; they are the continuous grief that cannot
be brushed off. In the second stanza, wild geese and dreams fail in
their normal function of affording communication. The irrepres-
sible growth of the spring grass has both a spatial and a temporal
dimension, and the two final words—*huan sheng* "it's growing still"—
admirably convey this double aspect. They echo and surpass the
ending of the first stanza, *huan man* "still fill/cover." We recall the
endings of two other poems by Li Yü (Poems 53 and 54), which
similarly expand into infinite time and space, employing the image of
the river.[30]

Poem 57, "Feelings at Parting"[31]

Chou Pang-yen (1052–1121)

Form: *tz'u*; tune pattern: "A Magpie Flying at Night"

At the river bridge, where I saw him off,
What was it like, that lovely night?
The setting moon dropped its extra splendor far and wide.
In the copper dish, the candle's tears no longer flowed.   4
Dripping, dripping, cold dew soaked our clothes.
At the farewell meeting,
In the wind we heard drums at the ford.
The treetops touched the Flag of Shen.*   8
The piebald understood;
Though the whip was raised, it deliberately walked slow.

In the distance the road winds through the clear expanse of land.
Human voices gradually fade;   12
In vain, carrying my grief, I return.
Why do red leaves cover the ground again?†
The hairpin, left behind, has disappeared;
The steep paths all lead nowhere.   16
Mallows and wild oats.
Toward sunset,

---

*A constellation, including some stars of Orion.
†A variant reads: "Why do I pass again the former place?"

周邦彥　〈夜飛鵲〉　「別情」　河橋送人處　良夜何其　斜月遠墮餘輝　(4)銅盤燭淚已流
盡　霏霏涼露霑衣　相將散離會　探風前津鼓　(8)樹杪參旗　花驄會意　縱揚鞭亦自行
遲　迢遞路回清野　(12)人語漸無聞　空帶愁歸　何意重紅滿地　遺鈿不見　(16)斜徑都
迷　兔葵燕麥　向殘陽

Alone with my shadow,
I just walk to and fro and have straw spread to sit.   20
Sighing, I pour wine
And gaze at the far western horizon.

Line 7, in conjunction with line 3, derives from a line in a poem by
Wang An-shih: "As the moon sets I hear drum sounds at the ford."[32]

The poem contains several standard images of parting: the river
bridge, the moon, the candle with its "tears," the cold dew, the wind,
the sympathetic horse, the road leading far away, the sunset. Since
the action of the two stanzas takes place at different times, the
poet manages to include both a setting moon and a setting sun.
Throughout, he uses language denoting decline, decay, and forlorn-
ness: "setting," "dropped," "far and wide," "no longer flowed,"
"in the distance," "clear expanse of land," "fade," "in vain," "left
behind," "has disappeared," "lead nowhere," "sunset," "alone,"
"walk to and fro," "sighing," "far western horizon."

In place of the typical farewell banquet (as in "Parting," lines 31
and 74) we have here a solitary drinker. This substitution of a single
person for the usual social gathering emphasizes the speaker's loneliness, as does line 19, where his only companion is his own shadow
(cf. "Parting," line 92). By this time, all other human figures have
been eliminated (line 12). Nothing could bring out more effectively
the stark solitude of the scene.

There is one important image of parting that we have not encountered in the poems discussed so far: the willow.[33] The earliest
literary association of this tree with traveling occurs in the last stanza
of a poem in *The Classic of Songs* (no. 167), speaking of soldiers on the
march:

> When we left
> The willows were lush;
> As we come back
> Snow is falling.
> We walk on the road slowly,
> We are thirsty, we are hungry.
> Our hearts are pained,
> No one knows our suffering.

影与人齊　(20)但徘徊班草　欷歔酹酒　極望天西

In the symbolism of this ancient poem, the luxuriant verdure of spring obviously represents the comforts of home, while the snow of winter goes with the toils of the military campaign. The juxtaposition of green willows and falling snow also indicates the passage of time, and later Chinese readers came to associate the willows in this poem with long trips, absence from home, and the hardships of campaigning soldiers.

Beginning with the Han dynasty (206 B.C.–A.D. 220), it became customary to present a willow branch to a departing friend as a farewell gift, as attested in the following passage from a description of Ch'ang-an, the imperial capital: "The Pa Bridge is east of Ch'ang-an, it is a bridge spanning the [Pa] River. In Han times, people accompanied their guests as far as this bridge, and broke off a willow branch as a farewell present."[34] One reason for using willow branches on this occasion is probably the fact that the word *liŭ* "willow" is homonymous with *liŭ* "to keep, detain" (also read *liú*, the standard reading in modern Mandarin). The Pa Bridge, incidentally, became a standard fixture in poems of parting. The plucked willow branch was believed not only to have the power to delay the friend's departure but also to lure him back if sent to him while he was traveling.

The next poem is unusual in that it is the traveler himself who breaks off the willow branch.

Poem 58, "Plucking the Willow Branch"[35]
Anonymous (North China, fifth or sixth century A.D.)
Form: *yüeh-fu*

He mounts his horse but does not grasp the whip.
He turns back, breaks off a willow branch,
Gets off his horse, and blows the long flute.
Sad to death is the traveling lad.

The young man is reluctant to leave. He therefore performs the symbolic act of plucking a willow branch, which is to counteract his planned departure, and substitutes the branch for the similarly shaped horsewhip, which represents traveling. It is perhaps no accident that the flute, which he uses to vent his melancholy, resembles the whip and the branch in appearance. Flute-playing, at any rate, is often associated with the willow in poems of parting.

「折揚柳枝歌」 上馬不捉鞭 反拗楊柳枝 下馬吹長笛 愁殺行客兒

The following is another early instance of the willow as an image of separation.

Poem 59, "Plucking Willows"[36]

Hsiao I (505–55)

Form: *yüeh-fu*

The mountain is high, the Wu Gorge is long,
The drooping willow, the weeping willow,
It joins hearts together and breaks them together,
The old friend longs for his old home.
The mountain is as charming as lotus blossoms,
The flowing water glitters like the bright moon.
In the cold night, the gibbons' cries pierce his heart;
The wanderer's tears soak his clothes.

The reference to lotus blossoms involves a pun which often occurs in amatory *yüeh-fu* poems of this period: *lien* "lotus" is a homonym of *lien* "to sympathize, love." The sight of the willow reminds the traveler of his home and his beloved, and particularly of the moment of parting, when he was given a willow branch to "join hearts together." The broken branch is linked here—and in many other poems—to broken hearts.

Similar conceits are found in the next poem. The slender, pliant willow twigs growing in spring are often likened to silk-floss, and the threads are said to tie together the hearts of lovers. This again involves a pun that was first used in Southern *yüeh-fu* poems of the fourth century A.D.: *ssu* "silk threads" has the same sound as *ssu* "to think of, long for (an absent lover)." In poems where I believe this pun to be intended, I translate *ssu* as "love-threads."

Poem 60, "Willow Branches"[37]

Liu Yü-hsi (772–842)

Form: *yüeh-fu*

On the palace dike by the Green Gate, sweeping the ground
    they hang,
A hundred strands of gold thread, a thousand strands of
    love-threads.

蕭繹 「折楊柳」 山高巫峽長　垂柳復垂楊　同心且同折　故人懷故鄉　山似蓮花艷　流
如明月光　寒夜猿声徹　遊子淚霑裳

劉禹錫 「楊柳枝」 御陌青門拂地垂　千條金縷萬條絲

Now they're tied to make a love knot,
Later they'll be sent to the traveler—does he know?

We shall look at two more poems of the *yüeh-fu* genre before taking
up some willow poems in the *tz'u* form.

Poems 61–62, "Willow Branches"[38]
Po Chü-i (772–846)
Form: *yüeh-fu*

The leaves hold heavy dew like crying eyes,
The branches bend in the light wind like dancing waists.
The young tree can't bear the pain of being plucked,
I beg you, leave two or three twigs.

———

People say willow leaves are like sad eyebrows,
Even more a sad heart is like willow love-threads.
When willow love-threads are broken, when hearts are
      broken,
Neither can ever be restored.

In these two poems—and in many others—the willow is personified
as an attractive woman. Its slender branches, gracefully swaying in
the wind, suggest the slim waist of a dancing girl, and its leaves are
likened to eyes and to eyebrows. Whenever the willow is thus
personified, it is likely to be endowed with human feelings. The
dewdrops in the first line of Poem 61 are turned into tears, shed presumably in sympathy with the persons who are parting from each
other.

Poem 63[39]
Ou-yang Hsiu (1007–72)
Form: *tz'u*; tune pattern: "Walking on Sedge"

The plum trees at the lookout tower have lost their flowers,
The willows by the stream bridge are delicate.
The grass was fragrant, the wind was warm, it shook the
      horse's reins.

如今綰作同心結　將贈行人知不知

白居易 「楊柳枝」 葉含濃露如啼眼　枝裊輕風似舞腰　小樹不禁攀折苦　乞君留取兩三條
人言柳葉似愁眉　更有愁腸似柳絲　柳絲挽斷腸牽斷　彼此應无續得期

歐陽修 〈踏莎行〉 候館梅殘　溪橋柳細　草薰風暖搖征轡

The grief of separation grows infinite as the distance grows.
Far, far—endless, like the spring river.

Inch by inch her tender heart is torn,
The flow of tears ruins her makeup.
The building is tall—don't lean over the high railing.
Where the grass of the plain ends there are spring mountains;
The traveler is even farther, beyond the spring mountains.

The viewpoint is that of the woman left behind by the traveler, and the scene is the very spot where they parted, as indicated by the combination of "willow" and "bridge." Line 3 expressly recalls the time of parting. (This line derives from Chiang Yen's "Parting," lines 59–60). But whether lines 1 and 2 refer to the present moment of recollection, or to the past moment of separation, or to both, remains unspecified, perhaps deliberately so. The last two lines describe the view from the lady's balcony, where she may have ascended despite the warning voiced in line 8.[40] Or one may take the last three lines to mean: it would be useless to ascend because the traveler is too far away to be seen.

The willow in this poem is simply one of several images that blend together to convey the mood of separation. These other images are familiar to us from poems discussed earlier: the fading plum trees, the bridge, the fragrant grass, the wind, the spring river, the vegetation spreading across the plain, and the distant mountains. They are combined in such a way as to relate to space and time simultaneously, expanding both into infinity. This configuration of images accords with the progress that takes place in the course of the poem, gradually enlarging the scope from the persona's location into the distance, and from the present into the past and future. This process of spatial and temporal expansion is characteristic of the *tz'u* genre.

Poem 64,
"Matching Chang Chieh's 'Willow Catkins' "[41]
Su Shih

Form: *tz'u*; tune pattern: "In the Water Sings the Dragon"

They are like blossoms, yet not like blossoms,
And no one pities them as they fall.

離愁漸遠漸無窮　迢迢不斷如春水　寸寸柔腸　盈盈粉淚　樓高莫近危闌倚　平蕪盡處是春山　行人更在春山外

蘇軾　〈水龍吟〉「次韻章質夫楊花詞」　似花還似非花　也無人惜從教墜

They leave home and drop by the roadside.
Examine them and you find
They lack feeling but have longing.*
Their tender hearts are knotted and hurt,
Their lovely eyes are tired and drunk,
Wanting to open but staying closed.
In dreams they follow the wind a thousand miles,
Seeking the place their lover went,
Only to be wakened by the oriole's cry.

I don't regret that these blossoms have all flown away,
I regret that in the West garden the fallen red petals
      are hard to gather.
In the morning, after the rain,
Where are their remains?
All over the pond, a scattering of duckweed.
Of all the colors of spring,
Two thirds become dust,
One third flowing water.
When you look closely
They are not willow catkins, dot after dot,
But tears of separated people.

The personification of the willow that we noticed earlier is carried much farther here. Again the willow leaves are "lovely eyes." The catkins travel, like human wanderers, and pursue their lover. Regarding their transformation into duckweed, we have a note on this poem by Su Shih himself: "When willow blossoms fall into water they become floating duckweed. Upon investigation this turns out to be truly so."[42] This note records a popular belief, playfully adopted by Shu Shih. Throughout the poem, one can see a persistent preoccupation with the multifaceted identity of the willow: it is a flowering tree, and yet it is not; though a plant, it behaves like a human being; it lacks feeling, yet displays emotional behavior; it is metamorphosed into duckweed, and this in turn becomes human tears.

---

*Love-threads.

拋家傍路 (4)思量卻是 無情有思 縈損柔腸 困酣嬌眼 (8)欲開還閉 夢隨風萬里 尋
郎去處 又還被鶯呼起 (12)不恨此花飛盡 恨西園落紅難綴 曉來雨過 遺蹤何在 (16)
一池萍碎 春色三分 二分塵土 一分流水 (20)細看來 不是楊花點點 是離人淚

The floating duckweed, by the way, is another poetic image of aimless wandering and separation. An early example is found in the *Ch'u tz'u* anthology:

> I lament the floating duckweed
> That drifts without roots.[43]

Ts'ao Chih has a poem titled "Floating Duckweed" that deals with a deserted wife.[44]

Poem 65[45]

Ch'in Kuan (1049–1100)

Form: *tz'u*; tune pattern: "The City by the River"

The willow in the West City shows off her springtime softness
And stirs up the sadness of parting,
Tears are hard to restrain.
I still remember her great sympathy—
For our sake she tied up the departing boat—
The green plain, the vermilion bridge, that day's events.
The woman is gone,
The river flows in vain.

Spring's flowering does not linger for the young,
Long, long is my grief,
When will it end?
At the time of flying catkins and falling blossoms, when I
  ascend the tower—
Even if the spring river were all tears
Its current could not bear away
This much sorrow.

The willow, personified in the first line as a graceful woman, is associated again with the river, the bridge, the boat, the green plain, and the falling blossoms. In an earlier poem (Poem 60), the willow's "love-threads" were said to tie two hearts together in a love knot. Here—and in many other poems—another conceit is used: in order to delay the parting, the sympathetic willow "tied up" the boat with its threads (twigs), though these are not expressly mentioned.

秦觀 〈江城子〉 西城楊柳弄春柔　動離憂　淚難收　(4)猶記多情　曾爲繫歸舟　碧野
朱橋當日事　人不見　(8)水空流　韶華不爲少年留　恨悠悠　幾時休　(12)飛絮落花時
候一登樓　便做春江都是淚　流不盡　許多愁

On a more earthly level, the poem suggests that the speaker tied his
hawser to a willow near the bridge where he had his tryst.

A new poetic aspect is given to the river. In addition to being an
image of the pitiless flux of time, the river also represents the flow of
human tears. The same conceit can be found in European baroque
poetry, for instance in Quevedo's *silva* addressed to a fountain, from
which we quoted earlier:

> ¡Qué pobre de agua tu corriente baña
> la tierra que dió flores y da abrojos!
> ¡Cómo se echa de ver en tus cristales
> la falta del tributo de mis ojos,
> que los hizo crecer en ríos caudales!
> . . . .
> Ya no te queda, fuente, otra esperanza,
> tras prolija tardanza,
> de cobrar tu corriente y su grandeza,
> sino la que te doy con mi tristeza,
> de aumentarte llorando,
> por no saber de Aminta, mi enemiga.

> [With how little water does your current bathe
> The earth which once produced flowers and now
>   produces thistles!
> How visible in your crystal mirror
> Is the lack of my eyes' tribute,
> Which made them grow into abundant rivers!
> . . . .
> Now there remains for you, fountain, no other hope,
> After prolonged delay,
> Of recovering your current and its greatness
> Than that which I give you with my sadness,
> To augment you, weeping,
> For knowing nothing of Aminta, my enemy.]

Poem 66[46]

Chou Tzu-chih (flourished mid-twelfth century)
Form: *tz'u*; tune pattern: "Walking on Sedge"

Feelings are like drifting love-threads,

周紫芝 〈踏莎行〉 情似遊絲

People are like flying catkins.
With tear pearls fixed in our eyes, we stare at each
    other in vain.
All along the stream, from the misty willows a
    thousand love-threads hang,
But they have no way to tie up the magnolia boat.*

Wild geese pass the setting sun,
The misty isle is hidden in the grass.
Right now our grief is infinite,
Don't think what it will be like tomorrow morning.
How will we ever get through this night?

Once again, the flying catkins become an image of the human traveler, and the willow twigs are "love-threads." This time they do not perform their potential function of delaying departure by tying up the man's boat.

The poem contains a heavy dose of words suggesting vagueness, distance, infiniteness, and melancholy: "drifting," "flying," "tears," "stare," "in vain," "misty," "thousand," "wild geese," "setting sun," "misty," "hidden," "grass," "grief," "infinite." The willows play an essential part in the poem's imagistic structure. They are linked to the magnitude of the emotional upheaval ("a thousand love-threads hang"), to the specific situation of parting and travel, to the vagueness pervading the atmosphere ("misty willows"), to the infinity of space ("all along the stream"), and, by implication, to the prospect of endless suffering which dominates the last three lines (now—tomorrow—tonight).

---

*"Magnolia boat," i.e., a boat made of magnolia wood, is common poetic usage for a precious boat.

人如飛絮　淚珠閣定空相覷　一溪烟柳萬絲垂　無因繫得蘭舟住　雁過斜陽　草迷煙渚　如今已是愁無數　明朝且作莫思量　如何過得今宵去

9

Contemplation of the Past

(POEMS 67–80)

The keen interest of the Chinese literati in their country's history has been a salient feature of Chinese civilization from early times. The man of letters was normally a highly educated scholar, and a large part of his education was concerned with history. One of the uses of history was to take it as a guide for moral behavior. In the words of *The Record of Etiquette*, one of the Confucian Classics, "the Confucian lives among men of the present and studies the men of old. What he has learned he practices in the present age, and later generations will take him as their model."[1] The writing of history was done by the same class of men who wrote literary prose and poetry. It is therefore not surprising that Chinese poetry abounds with evocations of historical events, situations, and personalities. Such evocations of the past tend to fall into definite patterns, which evolved over a long period and became fixed by poetic convention. It is these conventional patterns of association that will be studied in the present chapter.[2]

One important category of poems was called *yung shih*, which may be freely rendered as "poems on historical themes." The first author to write such poems was Pan Ku (32–92). As he is known primarily as a historian—he compiled the official *History of the Former Han Dynasty*—his interest in history is a natural matter. But his one surviving *yung shih* poem[3] is not particularly illuminating in our present context. More interesting to us is Tso Ssu, who composed the earliest extant "poems on historical themes" after Pan Ku. Of his series of eight poems bearing this title, we will examine three.

Poems 67–69, "On Historical Themes"[4]
Tso Ssu (250?–305?)
Form: *ku-shih*

I admire Tuan-kan Mu,
Without effort he protected the ruler of Wei.
I revere Lu Chung-lien,*
With joking words he made the Ch'in army withdraw.
Throughout their lives they prized being unrestrained;
Faced with difficulties, they knew how to deal with
　them;
Their tasks accomplished, a sense of shame made them
　reject rewards;
Their great integrity stood out above the herd.
Lu refused to tie the sash of office around his waist,
He would not accept the jade of enfeoffment.
Signets twice brought glory to his house,
He shrugged them off as "floating clouds."†

————————

Chu-fu sought office but failed,
His own flesh and blood despised him.
Mai-ch'en wore himself out collecting fuel,
His wife did not stay in his house.
Ch'en P'ing owned no real estate,
At day's end he huddled against the city wall.
When Ch'ang-ch'ing returned to Ch'eng-tu,
How empty were the bare walls of his home!
These four worthies‡ were surely great,
Their recorded deeds shine in the history books.
But until their time came
It was their sad lot to be fill for ditches and gullies.
Heroes do encounter trouble,

---

　*See appendix 2 for Tuan-kan Mu and Lu Chung-lien.
　†"The Master said: '. . . Wealth and status without righteousness are to me as floating clouds' " (*The Analects of Confucius*, sec. 7, "Shu erh").
　‡See appendix 2: "Chu-fu Yen"; "Chu Mai-ch'en"; "Ch'en P'ing"; Ch'ang-ch'ing under "Ssu-ma Hsiang-ju."

左思 「詠史」 吾希段干木 偃息藩魏君　吾慕魯仲連　談笑却秦軍　當世貴不羈　遭難能
解紛　功成恥受賞　高節卓不羣　臨組不肯紲　對珪寧肯分　連璽耀前庭　比之如浮雲
主父宦不達　骨肉還相薄　買臣困采樵　优儷不安宅　陳平無產業　歸來翳負郭　長
卿還成都　壁立何寥廓　四賢豈不偉　遺烈光篇籍　當其未遇時　憂在塡溝壑　英雄有屯邅

From ancient times it's always been like that.
In every age there are outstanding talents
Abandoned to live in pastures and marshes.

———

Fluttering, fluttering, the bird in the cage,
Raising his wings, bumps against the four corners.
Lonely, lonely, the scholar in the poor alley,
With his shadow as company, keeps to his empty hut.   4
When he steps out of his door there is no open road,
Thorns and brambles block his path.
His plans and proposals are rejected, never accepted,
He is left all to himself, like a fish in a dried-up pond.   8
Outside his home, no hope of the slightest emolument;
Inside, not one peck of grain.
His relatives despise him,
His friends stay away from him day and night.   12
Su Ch'in traveled north to persuade,
Li Ssu* presented a memorial in the West.
Glance down and up: they are covered with glory,
Say alas: they wither away.   16
When the mole drinks in the river it only wants to fill
    its belly;
It craves sufficiency, no more.
The tailorbird builds its nest on a single twig;
These can serve as models for the wise scholar.   20

Tso Ssu, as these examples show, makes a highly selective and
subjective use of his historical themes. Rather than devoting a single
poem to each historical personality, he deals with two men in Poem
67, with four in Poem 68, and again with two in Poem 69. The historical figures in these poems are grouped in pairs—in accordance
with the basic principle of which we have seen many instances. (Such
pairing is not obligatory in this type of poetry but it is very common.)
One detail: the names are sometimes trimmed in order to produce a

---

*See appendix 2 for Su Ch'in and Li Ssu.

由來自古昔　何世無奇才　遺之在草澤

習習籠中鳥　舉翮觸四隅　落落窮巷士　(4)抱影守空廬　出門無通路　枳棘塞中塗　計策
棄不收　(8)塊若枯池魚　外望無寸禄　內顧無斗儲　親戚還相蔑　(12)朋友日夜疏　蘇
秦北游說　李斯西上書　俛仰生榮華　(16)咄嗟復彫枯　飲河期滿腹　貴足不願餘　巢林
棲一枝　(20)可爲達士模

perfect match, thus in Poem 68, Chu-fu Yen is shortened to Chu-fu (using the surname only), while the matching Chu Mai-ch'en is abbreviated to Mai-ch'en (using the given name only); in the same poem, Ssu-ma Hsiang-ju is called by his courtesy name, Ch'ang-ch'ing, matching Ch'en P'ing, whose full name has just two syllables and therefore remains intact.

Another detail: the matching lines 15 and 16 in Poem 69 have multiple imagery. "Glance down and up" and "Say alas" indicate speed: In no more time than it takes to glance down and up, the two men rose, and just as quickly (before you can say alas) they fell. At the same time, the image of the shifting glance fits the sudden lift from humbleness to prominence, and the sigh is a proper accompaniment of their calamity.

Our poet makes no attempt to create well-rounded portraits of these personalities. Instead, he focuses on those qualities and achievements which in his view are worthy of attention and emulation. He is quite plain about his personal interest in these matters: "I admire . . . ," "I revere . . . ." He also brings out the universal applicability of the lessons taught by history: "From ancient times it's always been like that./In every age . . ." Writing poetry on historical themes means to him making history relevant to one's own time and one's personal situation. (Coming from a rather humble family and living in an age when the better government posts were reserved almost exclusively for members of the aristocracy, Tso Ssu, like his father, never rose above the rank of a petty official.)

It is a curious fact that historical matters, with their universal applications, are not the only concern of these poems "on historical themes." In Poem 69, only four of the twenty lines (lines 13–16) deal with historical figures, the rest of the poem takes its themes from the animal world. Similarly, the second poem of the series (not translated here)[5] opens with a plant simile: the tip of a tall pine tree at the bottom of a valley does not reach as high as a tiny grass on the mountain above the valley—men of noble birth have better careers than able commoners; the poem continues with historical examples.

Allusion to historical precedent, then, is one of two strategies that the poet uses side by side. The other is reference to nonhuman nature in its well-known constancy. By contemplating the present through the mirror of the past, or by viewing human affairs in terms of the world of nature, he creates an aesthetic distance that gives greater depth to his poem and puts it in the perspective of universal truth.

A different kind of past-oriented poetry developed from the seventh century on. There we find historical reminiscences stimulated by visits to historic sites. Several such poems were written by Ch'en Tzu-ang. We will consider two of them.

Poem 70,
"At White Emperor City, Cherishing the Past"[6]
Ch'en Tzu-ang (661–702)
Form: *p'ai-lü*

The sun is setting, it's evening on the Big River.
Stopping the oars, I inquire about the local atmosphere.
The city looks down on the Viscount of Pa's land,
The King of Han's palace has vanished from the terrace.   4
This land, though distant and wild, belonged to the royal
    domain of Chou;
The mountains, forbidding and deep, can still be approached
    through the merit of Yü.
Precipices hang, green walls break off;
The terrain is difficult but the jade-green river comes
    through.   8
Ancient trees grow to the edge of the clouds,
The home-bound sail pokes through the mist.
The river route goes on without limit,
The traveler's thoughts linger on without end.   12

To understand this poem, one must be aware of a few facts of geography, history, and mythology. White Emperor City is modern K'uei-chou (Feng-chieh) in eastern Szechuan Province, and Ch'en Tzu-ang was himself a native of Szechuan. The city was founded by Kung-sun Shu (died A.D. 36), who styled himself "The White Emperor." It is situated on the Yangtze, "the Big River," which narrows at this point. This part of Szechuan was anciently called Pa, and in antiquity, during the feudal Chou period, it was the domain of the Viscount of Pa. The King of Han mentioned in line 4 is Liu Pei, who founded the state of Han in 221 and had a palace built at White Emperor City before he died in 223. Yü, the mythical founder of the Hsia dynasty, is a culture hero, credited with regulating the

---

陳子昂 「白帝城懷古」　日落滄江晚　停橈問土風　城臨巴子國　(4)台沒漢王宮　荒服仍
周甸　深山尙禹功　巖懸靑壁斷　(8)地險碧流通　古木生雲際　歸帆出霧中　川途去無
限　(12)客思坐何窮

course of rivers throughout China. It was thus due to him that this remote and forbidding area became accessible (lines 5–8). The term "local atmosphere," literally "the wind of the land," includes the physical and spiritual atmosphere of the place, as shaped by topography, climate, history, and local customs and manners.

The bulk of the poem (lines 3–10) may be taken as an answer to the speaker's inquiry in line 2. In this core section, the known facts of history combine with the presently visible sights. Much of the past has disappeared: Yü, the Chou dynasty, the Viscount of Pa, and Liu Pei's palace. But though Yü himself is gone, his great work endures, linking the remote past to the present, and making possible the later historical developments as well as the present journey. The ancient trees, too, belong to both past and present, and their bridging of temporal distances is matched on the spatial plane: they reach from earth to heaven. The continuity in time is expressed also by the adverb *shang* "still" (line 6).

The tension between transience and continuity, between destruction and survival, between disappearance and visibility, runs through the whole poem and can be observed in the choice of words. On the negative side, we have "setting," "evening," "stopping," "vanished," "distant," "break off," "difficult," "edge," "mist," "limit," and "end." On the positive side, the words are "looks down on," "approached," "comes through," "grow," "pokes through," and "goes on." But it should be noted that the negative words "limit" (line 11) and "end" (line 12) are both negated, which makes them positive. The river, appearing at the beginning and again near the end, is an image of continuity in space and time. It represents the speaker's continuing journey, temporarily interrupted at this point to view the past intermingling with the present. But it also represents the passage of time (thus constituting another link between past and present) and, through the conventional implications contained in the phrase "the traveler's thoughts," the continuity of human sorrow.

Poem 71,
"At Mount Hsien, Cherishing the Past"[7]
Ch'en Tzu-ang
Form: *p'ai-lü*

Feeding my horse I look down on the wild land,
Climbing high I gaze at the old capital.

陳子昂　「峴山懷古」　秣馬臨荒甸　登高覽舊都

I lament at the Pillar of Dropping Tears
And think of the Sleeping Dragon's design.
From cities and towns in the distance I make out Ch'u,
Mountains and rivers half enter Wu.
Hills and peaks stand out by themselves,
How many worthies and sages have perished!
Dark mist cuts across the plateau,
The tower at the ford stands solitary in the evening air.
Who knows the traveler of ten thousand miles,
Cherishing the past as he paces to and fro?

Again we must begin our discussion of the poem by mentioning a few facts from geography and history. Mount Hsien is in modern Hupei Province, just south of the city of Hsiang-yang, the former capital of the Ching Region ("the old capital"). The Pillar of Dropping Tears was erected to commemorate Yang Hu (221–78), who as Protector of Ching became a popular administrator of this area. His official biography reports: "On Mount Hsien, at the place where Hu used to go for recreation, the people of Hsiang-yang erected a pillar and built a shrine. At the time of the seasonal festivals they offered sacrifices there. No one could look at the pillar without weeping. Tu Yü therefore named it the Pillar of Dropping Tears."[8] (Tu Yü* was a friend of Yang Hu's.) "The Sleeping Dragon" is an epithet of Chu-ko Liang (181–234), the famous statesman and general of the state of Han (Shu) in the period of the Three States,† and his "design" is a stone maze which he is said to have constructed to work out a superior strategy. (It is actually a prehistoric relic.) As Chu-ko Liang never succeeded with his plans to defeat the hostile states of Wei and Wu, the evocation of his design strikes a tragic note, matching the Pillar of Dropping Tears.

While at White Emperor City (Poem 70) the poet was seen to find both glory and sorrow in his contemplation of the past and its remnants, here at Mount Hsien his mood is predominantly melancholy. An apparent exception occurs in lines 5 and 6, since they speak neither of the past nor of sadness and seem to describe the

---

*Not to be confused with the mythological Tu Yü of appendix 2.
†He is also the subject of Poem 79 below.

猶悲墮淚碣　(4)尙想臥龍圖　城邑遙分楚　山川半入吳　丘陵徒自出　(8)賢聖幾凋枯　野樹蒼煙斷　津樓晩氣孤　誰知萬里客　(12)懷古正踟躕

visible scene without any reference to the past. But in their context these two lines set the enduringness of mountains and cities against the ephemerality of individual human endeavor. This contrast is made quite explicit in the following couplet (lines 7–8), which cannot be fully appreciated unless we are aware of its literary antecedent. Line 7 comes almost verbatim from a ditty in the *Biography of Mu, the Son of Heaven*, sung by the Queen Mother of the West to her visitor, King Mu:

> White clouds are in the sky,
> Hills stand out by themselves.
> The road is far,
> Mountains and rivers block the way.
> If you don't die
> You can come again.[9]

The hills, then, represent Nature's permanence in contrast with man's mortality.

Another quality emphasized in this poem is loneliness. It informs the entire scene, the hills, the man-made structures, and also by implication the solitary traveler. Just as in the preceding poem, the melancholy engendered by the contemplation of the past leads to general reflections on the brevity of human life and blends with the personal sadness of the homesick traveler. The time of day in this poem, as in the preceding one, is evening, fitting the theme of decline and solitude.

Before dealing further with the implications of Ch'en Tzu-ang's poems, we will consider a poem by a younger contemporary of his which speaks of a visit to the same Mount Hsien.

Poem 72,
"Ascending Mount Hsien with Several Gentlemen"[10]
Meng Hao-jan
Form: *lü-shih*

Human lives succeed each other and decay,
They come and go, becoming past and present.
Rivers and mountains keep their scenic beauty;
We, too, climb up to have a look.

孟浩然 「與諸子登峴山」 人事有代謝 往來成古今 江山留勝跡 我輩復登臨

The water level sinks, the fishing sluice is shallow;
The weather is cold, Lake Meng-tse is deep.
Lord Yang's pillar is still here,
After we read it, tears soak our robes.

The complexity of this poem is caused in part by its moving on two different time scales. On the one hand, it records a momentary experience: the poet and his companions ascend Mount Hsien, take in the view from the top, and are moved by the reading of the stele commemorating Yang Hu. On the other hand, Yang Hu, the poet, and his friends are seen as links in a long chain of history, subject to its eternal laws of succession and disintegration. The transition from the larger to the smaller time scale is achieved near the middle of the poem, in line 4, which is ambiguously worded so as to fit both scales. "We, too" means, on the wider scale, that the poet and his contemporaries have their turn in the succession of generations. On the lesser scale, it means that they come on this day to visit the scenic spot, as others have done before them.

We cannot fully appreciate the wording of the evocation of Yang Hu in this poem unless we have before us another passage from his official biography:

> Hu loved natural scenery. Whenever the weather was fine, he would visit Mount Hsien, where he had wine served and poetry recited, without tiring all day long. Once he heaved a deep sigh, looked at his followers (Tsou Chan and others), and said to them: "From the beginning of the world, this mountain has always been here. All along, worthy and outstanding men have climbed up here to enjoy the distant view. There have been many like you and me, who have perished without leaving a reputation behind. This makes one sad. If a hundred years from now there are conscious souls they are still bound to climb up here." Chan said: "Your virtue caps all within the four seas, in your conduct you are the heir of former sages. Your noble reputation, your noble fame will surely be preserved together with this mountain. As for the rest of us, it will be as you have said."[11]

Clearly the first half of the poem takes its motifs from the biography, but the wording is nevertheless quite original and striking,

---

水落魚梁淺　天寒夢澤深　羊公碑尚在　讀罷淚沾襟

with its artful combination of two time scales, of past and present, of natural phenomena and human affairs. The second half of the poem speaks of what is seen from the mountaintop, beginning with objective descriptions and ending with a personal, sentimental reaction, an effusion of grief which is all the more forceful because up to this concluding line the poet refrains from injecting any lament into his observations. Tears at this point are quite appropriate because in this respect, too, the poet follows in the tradition set by preceding visitors to this mountain and this pillar, which goes back ultimately to the lament voiced by Yang Hu himself.

Why is it that in so many of these poems the contemplation of the past is coupled with the ascent of a mountain? We saw in Tso Ssu's poems (Poems 67–69) that reflections on history often go hand in hand with contemplation of the physical scenery. Mountains have a particular role to play for several reasons. For one thing, they represent, as we have seen, the permanence of nature in contrast with human transience; they are relics of the hoary past, surviving into the present. For another, they transcend the normal limits of space and time, they take the viewer above the ordinary here-and-now, offering a grand vista of the natural and the human world, of the past and the present. A third reason is that a mountain is often the site of some specific historic remnant or monument, such as the Pillar of Dropping Tears. A fourth element is the ancient tradition associating ascent with the writing of poetry. This practice was supposed to have been prescribed by Confucius himself. A passage in the *Han-shih wai-chuan* (second century B.C.) embodies this tradition in words which, whatever their original import, could be taken to mean: "Confucius went on an excursion to the top of Mount Ching. . . . Confucius said: 'When a gentleman climbs to a high place, he must compose poetry.' "[12]

In addition, the poetic association of climbing a mountain with the process of decay in the natural and the human world, and with loneliness and homesickness, can be traced back to a long poem by P'an Yüeh (247–300), titled "The Mood of Autumn," from which I will cite a passage. The excerpt begins with a quotation from the opening of the "Nine Arguments" ("Chiu pien"), attributed to the legendary Sung Yü.[13]

> Sung Yü said it well:
> "How sad is the breath of autumn!

> Rustling it shakes shrubs and trees so they drop
>   their leaves and wither.
> Autumn is grievous, like traveling far,
> Climbing a mountain, looking down on a river, or
>   seeing off a friend on his way home."
> Now seeing off a man on his way home involves
>   affection for a companion;
> Traveling far brings the trouble of lodging abroad;
> Looking down on a river, one is stirred by the flow
>   of water and laments its going;
> Climbing a mountain, one cherishes what is far and
>   resents what is near.
> These four sad experiences make the heart sick,
> Meeting them all on the same road is hard to bear.[14]

The words "one cherishes what is far and resents what is near" are likely to refer to time as well as space. The idea of the past being superior to the present was firmly established in Chinese ideology from early times. The ancient philosopher Chuang Tzu testifies to this: "To exalt antiquity and belittle the present—that is the fashion of scholars."[15] And a melancholy brooding as the prevailing mood of the poet on the mountaintop is noted by a poet of the early tenth century in this couplet:

> From ancient times climbing high has always been sad,
> But never so much as today—tears fill my kerchief.[16]

Reaching an elevated position does not necessarily require a mountain. The view from a tall building will inspire the Chinese with the same kind of reflections, as can be seen in the following poem.

Poem 73, "The Myriad-Year Tower"[17]
Wang Ch'ang-ling (698–765?)
Form: *lü-shih*

Lofty above the river, the Myriad-Year Tower,*
How many thousand autumns has it braved?

---

*Located at Jun-chou (modern Chen-chiang, Kiangsu Province) on the Yangtze River.

王昌齡 「萬歲樓」 江上巍巍萬歲樓　不知經歷幾千秋

Year after year there's joy in seeing the mountains
    endure,
Day after day there's grief in watching the water just flow.
Why did the monkeys leave the evening mountains?
The cormorants aimlessly drift around the cold island.
Who can bear to climb and look into the clouds and mist?
Toward evening the vastness stirs the traveler's grief.

Most of the imagery in this poem is already familiar from other poems discussed in this and the preceding chapter. The lookout tower provides not only the same kind of elevated vantage point which in other poems was afforded by a mountaintop; the tower also functions, together with the mountains that form part of the visible scene, as a symbol of endurance contrasting with nature's complementary law of destruction and disappearance, represented by the river and also by the supplementary images of autumn, evening, coldness, clouds and mist, and aimless drifting far from home (lines 5, 6, 8). While the mountains are juxtaposed with the river within the antithetical framework of the *lü-shih* pattern (see chapter 11), the enduring tower is physically situated next to—and above—the flowing river.

A related but somewhat different view of the past is displayed in the following poem.

Poem 74, "Old-Time Poem"[18]
Ch'ang Chien (*chin-shih** 727)
Form: *ku-shih*

Grazing horses by the ancient road,
By the road are many ancient tombs.
The desolation is deathly sad,
Crickets sing in the aspen trees.
I turn my head and look toward the capital—
A piled up growth of dust and mist.
Wealth and rank—how can they last?
When I return I'll stick to simplicity and truth.

---

*Highest degree in the civil service examinations.

年年喜見山長在　日日悲看水獨流　猿犹何曾離暮嶺　鸕鶿空自泛寒洲　誰堪登望雲烟裏
向晚茫茫發旅愁

常建　「古意」　牧馬古道傍　道傍多古墓　蕭條愁殺人　蟬鳴白楊樹　廻頭望京邑　合沓
生塵霧　富貴安可常　歸來保眞素

The poem consists of two equal halves, with the persona making its appearance at the beginning of the second half. The view of the past here is general, vague, and one-sided. No particular events, personalities, or epochs are evoked. Nothing is said of the positive aspects of history. The only products of the past are desolation, destruction, and death. Its visible remains are tombs and a lonely landscape—an autumnal landscape, as line 4 indicates. Even the road and the grazing horses in the context are images of instability, of painful wandering and separation from home. The negative aspects of the flow of time are combined with a moral condemnation of an educated man's conventional activities and aspirations. The harried life of a bureaucrat in the capital is seen as "dust and mist." The values most highly prized by the man of the world—wealth and rank—are subject to the universal law of destruction (line 7). Hence in the final line, the speaker resolves to stop seeking the unstable goals of the wandering life and to go back to the eternal, imperishable values of truth and simplicity.

A word should be said about the title of the poem, "*Ku i*," which I have loosely rendered as "Old-Time Poem." It is used repeatedly by poets of the T'ang period, and implies that the poem partakes of the past both in subject matter and in style. Our present poem has much in common, in its theme and language, with the anonymous "Nineteen Old Poems." In its diction it recalls many anonymous *yüeh-fu* poems of the Han period. It also shares with some of them the device known in Chinese rhetoric as *ting-chen t'i* ("thimble design"), which means that the last words of a line are repeated to form the beginning of the next line. (In this poem, the phrase *tao p'ang*, literally "the side of the road," occurs at the end of line 1 and at the beginning of line 2.)

We go on to consider a cycle of five poems by Tu Fu.

Poems 75–79, "Poetic Thoughts on Ancient Sites"[19]
Tu Fu
Form: *lü-shih*

Forlorn in the Northeast in wind and dust,
Drifting in the Southwest between heaven and earth,
In towers and terraces at the Three Gorges, lingering
    for days and months,

杜甫 「詠懷古跡」 支離東北風塵際 漂泊西南天地閒 三峽樓台淹日月

With the costumes of the Five Streams sharing clouds
    and mountains;
The barbarian, serving the ruler, in the end could not
    be trusted,
The wandering poet, lamenting the times, had no
    chance to return.
Throughout his life, Yü Hsin was most wretched,
In his waning years his poetry stirred the rivers and
    passes.

————

"Decay and decline": deep knowledge have I of Sung
    Yü's grief.
Romantic and refined, he too is my teacher.
Sadly looking across a thousand autumns, one shower of
    tears,
Melancholy in different ages, not of the same time.
Among rivers and mountains his old abode—nothing
    left but his writings;
Deserted terrace of cloud and rain—surely not just
    imagined in a dream?
The palaces of Ch'u have suffered the most destruction,
The fishermen pointing them out today are doubtful.

————

Groups of mountains and thousands of streams run to
    Ching-men.
It's still there, the village where Ming-fei was born
    and bred.
As soon as she left home the crimson terraces linked her
    to the northern desert.
All that remains is the green tomb facing the yellow
    dusk.
The painting showed imperfectly her spring-wind face,
With tinkling pendants, in the moonlit night, her soul
    comes back in vain.

五溪衣服共雲山	羯胡事主終無賴	詞客哀時且未還	庾信平生最蕭瑟	暮年詩賦動江關
搖落深知宋玉悲	風流儒雅亦吾師	悵望千秋一灑淚	蕭條異代不同時	江山故宅空文藻
雲雨荒台豈夢思	最是楚宮俱泯滅	舟人指點到今疑		
羣山萬壑赴荆門	生長明妃尚有村	一去紫台連朔漠	獨留青塚向黃昏	畫圖省識春風面
環珮空歸月夜魂				

For a thousand years the lute, speaking its barbarian
    language,
Has clearly expressed her sorrow in songs.

―――――――

The ruler of Shu had his eyes on Wu and reached
    the Three Gorges.
In the year of his demise he was in the Palace of
    Eternal Peace.*
The blue green banners can be imagined on the empty
    mountain,
And the jade palace in the void, deserted temple.
Cranes nest in the pines of the ancient shrine;
At summer and winter festivals the only ones to come
    are village elders.
The Martial Count's memorial shrine is ever nearby;
Together, sovereign and minister share the sacrifices.

―――――――

Chu-ko's great name hangs across the world,
His portrait is majestic and pure.
Triple division and separate states twisted his plans,
A single feather in a sky of a thousand ages.
Not better nor worse was he than Yi and Lü;
Had his strategy succeeded, he would have bested
    Hsiao and Ts'ao.
As revolving fate shifted the fortunes of Han, they
    could not be restored;
His purpose was cut off and his body destroyed as he
    toiled with the army.

    The "ancient sites" to which these five poems are devoted are less
easy to establish than the historical personalities that are invoked.
We will therefore begin with the latter. The first poem deals with Yü

―――――――

*In modern Feng-chieh District, Szechuan Province. This is where he established
his headquarters in the campaign against the state of Wu; it is also the place where he
died, and the site of his memorial temple.

千載琵琶作胡語　　分明怨恨曲中論

蜀主窺吳幸三峽　　崩年亦在永安宮　　翠華想像空山裏　　玉殿虛無野寺中　　古廟杉松巢水鶴
歲時伏臘走村翁　　武侯祠屋常隣近　　一體君臣祭祀同

諸葛大名垂宇宙　　宗臣遺像肅清高　　三分割據紆籌策　　萬古雲霄一羽毛　　伯仲之間見伊吕
指揮若定失蕭曹　　運移漢祚終難復　　志決身殲軍務勞

Hsin (513–81), a great poet who got caught in the conflicts that plagued China during the Period of Disunion. He served the Southern Chinese court of the Liang dynasty at its capital Chien-k'ang (modern Nanking) until 549, when the "barbarian" general Hou Ching staged a coup d'etat and captured Chien-k'ang. Yü Hsin then went to Chiang-ling (in modern Hupei), where Emperor Yüan of Liang established his new capital. From there Yü Hsin was sent as ambassador to Ch'ang-an, where the Western Wei, a Northern dynasty, had its capital. He was compelled to remain at Ch'ang-an the rest of his life, frustrated in his desire to return South. He unwillingly served the Western Wei and, from 557 on, its successor, the Northern Chou. His longest poetic work, "Ai Chiang-nan fu" ("Lament for the Southland"), written toward the end of his life, laments the decline and fall of the Liang dynasty.

The hero of Poem 76 is Sung Yü, a nebulous figure supposed to have lived in the state of Ch'u in the third century B.C. He is said to have been a romantic person, and a follower of the great Ch'u poet Ch'ü Yüan. The extant poems attributed to him are of doubtful authenticity, but in Tu Fu's time they were accepted as genuine.

Poem 77 is devoted to Wang Ch'iang (see appendix 2). Her sad fate was much celebrated in prose and poetry. One extant poem is attributed to Wang Ch'iang herself.[20] This attribution was taken seriously in Tu Fu's time, though discounted by modern scholarship.[21] The chief repository of *yüeh-fu* poetry also contains fifty poems about her by various authors,[22] most of them earlier than Tu Fu, and the topic continued to be a favorite with later poets as well.

Poem 78 deals with Liu Pei (161–223), the first ruler of the Shu-Han dynasty (reigned 221–23), and Poem 79 with his loyal minister and general Chu-ko Liang (181–234; the "Sleeping Dragon" of Poem 71), who failed in his campaigns to end the division of China into three states. His posthumous title was "Martial Count."

As far as the localities are concerned, it is usually assumed that the poems were "each inspired by Tu Fu's visit as a sightseer to some place of interest associated with a famous historical personage."[23] This is indeed what the title of the cycle indicates, but actually it cannot be true for all five poems, and may not even apply to any of them. Professor William Hung, an expert on the biographical background of Tu Fu's poems, states in respect to Poem 75 that "the subject of the poem was the site of Yü Hsin's home in Chiang-ling" and then goes on to point out that "Tu Fu, when he wrote the poem, had not yet been to Chiang-ling, and therefore, had not seen the site of Yü Hsin's early home." In regard to Poem 77, too, Professor Hung doubts that Tu Fu actually visited Wang Ch'iang's native village.[24] It seems to me slightly more likely that the poet had gone to this village than that he had been to Yü Hsin's dwelling in Chiang-ling, since the former is mentioned in the text while the latter is not. But it is not necessary to assume that Tu Fu at the time of writing the cycle had visited *any* of the sites. His visits to the past are spiritual journeys rather than travel records. In this respect the cycle differs from other poems discussed in this chapter, such as Poems 70–73.

We are now ready for a closer examination of the five poems. In Poem 75 it is remarkable that Yü Hsin's name is not mentioned until the penultimate line, and that the wording of the first six lines is ambivalent, so that it may be taken to refer either to that poet or to Tu Fu himself. Thus line 1 on first reading brings to mind the outbreak of An Lu-shan's rebellion in Northeast China in 755, and line 2 suggests Tu Fu's travels in the Southwest in the 760s. But when one comes upon Yü Hsin's name in line 7, one realizes that the first two lines also refer to the disorders of the sixth century, and to Yü Hsin's travels. In this reading, the juxtaposition of "Northeast" and "Southwest" is not to be taken literally (as it was in the first reading) but as an instance of *hu-wen*. The couplet would then amount to saying that there was strife all over China—north, east, south, and west—and a man was wandering from one part of the country to another. Correspondingly, "the barbarian" of line 5 can be identified with Hou Ching of Yü Hsin's time as well as with An Lu-shan of Tu Fu's, and "the wandering poet" is both Yü Hsin and Tu Fu. The phrases "had no chance to return" and "most wretched" recall a couplet in Yü Hsin's Preface to his "Lament for the Southland": "The stout knight does not return, / The cold wind makes a wretched sound."[25] This couplet is based in turn on the song that forms part of the story of Ching K'o (see appendix 2):

> The wind soughs wretchedly, the I River is cold.
> Once the stout knights are gone they do not return again.[26]

In the final line of poem 75, the phrase "river(s) and pass(es)" also alludes, I believe, to Yü Hsin's "Lament for the Southland." As mentioned above, that poem was written late in the poet's life—hence

Tu Fu says "in his waning years," and its title literally means "*Fu* of Lamenting [the Land] South of the River." While writing it, Yü Hsin was living at Ch'ang-an, in the region known as Within the Passes. The phrase "river(s) and pass(es)" would then point to the two regions, [South of the] River and [Within the] Passes, or by extension, South and North China.[27] The paired nouns "river(s) and pass(es)" exemplify the pattern of complementary pairs that will be discussed in chapter 11. In this poem there are five such pairs, representing various aspects of nature, all placed at or near the end of a line (lines 1, 2, 3, 4, and 8).

In the first half of Poem 76, Tu Fu adopts as his own certain sentiments voiced in the poetry of Sung Yü, to whom this poem is devoted. Three words in the first line—"decay [and] decline," "grief"—are taken verbatim from the opening couplet of Sung Yü's "Nine Arguments." The phrase "cloud and rain" alludes to a couplet in the description of the goddess in the "Kao-t'ang fu," attributed to Sung Yü: "In the morning I am the dawn cloud, / In the evening I am the driving rain."[28] The goddess in that poem appears to the King of Ch'u in a dream; that is why our poem says, "surely not just imagined in a dream."

The destruction of palaces is a motif that we have already encountered in other poems contemplating the past. But here the familiar *topos* receives a special significance through the wording: "the *most* destruction . . . ," implying a comparison with other objects that have not been destroyed as thoroughly as the Ch'u palaces, whose very location is uncertain (line 8). Thus the poem sets up a series of objects with varying degrees of destruction and survival: (1) the royal palaces of Ch'u, completely destroyed; (2) Sung Yü's house, largely destroyed; (3) Sung Yü's literary works, remaining intact[29] (like Clara Robinson's in Robert Frost's "A Fountain, a Bottle, a Donkey's Ears and Some Books").

There is a tradition that Sung Yü's house in Chiang-ling was inhabited by Yü Hsin after the latter fled from Chien-k'ang to Chiang-ling at the time of Hou Ching's rebellion.[30] The house thus forms a link between Poems 75 and 76. Another link is the phrase "romantic and refined" (76.2), which had been used by Yü Hsin in regard to another man.[31] Yet another link is the word "too" (line 2), which I take to mean that Sung Yü, like Yü Hsin, is one of Tu Fu's literary models.[32] A further bond between Tu Fu and his admired model

Sung Yü is implied in line 4: though they lived at different times, their melancholy fate was similar.

In Poem 77, the verb "run" imparts a dynamic quality to the description of the landscape. Also possible is another reading, as given in David Hawkes's translation: "By many a mountain and many a thousand valley *I come* to the Gate of Ch'u." Perhaps the line is intentionally ambivalent, as is often the case in Tu Fu's late poetry. "The crimson terraces" refers to the imperial palace. The same phrase had been used in two earlier poems about Wang Ch'iang.[33] The legendary "green tomb" is juxtaposed with the "yellow dusk" in the same line ("yellow" is a conventional attribute for "dusk") and also with the "crimson terraces" in the preceding line. This simultaneous use of parallelism within the line and in the couplet is very effective.

The last two lines of Poem 77 show the influence of a poem by Yü Hsin (the subject of Poem 75) which ends as follows:

> The barbarian wind is cold as it penetrates the bones,
> The evening moon is bright as it shines on the heart.
> As soon as I play a tune on the zither
> It changes to barbarian flute music.[34]

In the context of Tu Fu's poem, the "barbarian language" of the lute song has a double relevance, each involving a paradox. On the one hand, the lute (*p'i-pa*) was a barbarian instrument, brought to China by Central Asian nomads together with other musical instruments and many Central Asian tunes and dances. The lute became very popular in China, both as a solo instrument and to accompany *yüeh-fu* songs. Hence its mention is very fitting in connection with Wang Ch'iang's *yüeh-fu* song (and its later imitations over a period of nearly "a thousand years") about her journey to her new home among the nomads. Yet line 7 is paradoxical because the "language" of music is international, its use and understanding are not restricted by national boundaries. On the other hand, the barbarian song represents Wang Ch'iang's unusual situation: though Chinese, she is forced to live among barbarians as their queen. The alien, unwelcome environment imposes itself on her and becomes a foreign song. What makes this facet of the image paradoxical is the fact that the poem attributed to Wang Ch'iang is in Chinese, not in a "barbarian language." Thus the final couplet admirably renders the tragic conflict between Wang Ch'iang's external role—an involuntary barbarian queen—and her internal allegiance to Chinese civilization.

Poems 78 and 79 are linked together even more closely than 75 and 76. Liu Pei, the hero of Poem 78, and his loyal minister Chu-ko Liang, the subject of Poem 79, were close associates, and the latter already appears in Poem 78, which speaks of the union that keeps them together beyond death. They are admired by Tu Fu and other Chinese literati for their nobility of character and their valiant though unsuccessful efforts to reunite China. Their personal tragedy is combined in the two poems with reflections on the ephemerality of all human lives and endeavors. The transience of human grandeur is forcefully expressed in lines 4–5 of Poem 78: the only visitors to the former imperial palace are the cranes nesting there and a few village elders who attend the semiannual festivals. As the crane is a symbol of immortality, line 5 perhaps implies that Liu Pei has won immortal fame. The concepts of "empty," "void," and "deserted" assume additional significance here as they are applied to a Buddhist temple.

In Poem 79, the ubiquitous principle of presenting famous men in pairs rather than singly—the same principle that we have seen at work in Poems 75–76 and 78–79—is evident in lines 5 and 6, and the pairs in turn match each other. In lines 3 and 4, the juxtaposition of numerals—triple, single, and thousand (literally ten thousand)—combines parallelism within the line with parallelism in neighboring lines, recalling a similar pattern in Poem 77. At the same time, the juxtaposition enhances the force of each individual numeral as they bring out, in turn, the tragic division of China ("triple division"), the uniqueness of Chu-ko Liang ("a single feather"), and the eternity of his fame ("a thousand ages").

We will add a few observations on the cycle as a whole. All five poems deal with personalities of the past who engaged Tu Fu's admiration and sympathy. All of them, except Sung Yü, were uprooted from their home regions under circumstances that had something in common with Tu Fu's own experiences. (He probably wrote the cycle in 766 at K'uei-chou, in modern Szechuan, far from home and from the imperial court.)[35] Three of the historical persons became famous through their poems, and Tu Fu specifically acknowledges the first two as his masters and models. He makes the words of Sung Yü his own by direct quotation (76.1), and those of Yü Hsin by borrowing and adaptation, as noted above. The evocation of the historical figures and their fate is combined with reflections on the vanity and brevity of all human lives. Yet the influence of great persons such as those celebrated in these poems extends beyond the normal limitations of space and time, and their universality is emphasized in both spatial and temporal terms. As Yü Hsin's poetry stirred all China, "the rivers and passes" (75.8), so "Chu-ko's great name hangs across the world" (79.1). Sung Yü is remembered "across a thousand autumns" (76.3), and Wang Ch'iang "for a thousand years" (77.7), while Chu-ko Liang is a unique phenomenon in "a thousand ages" (79.4). Tu Fu was aware, no doubt, that by writing these poems he was helping to perpetuate the memory of his heroes.

To conclude this chapter, we will consider a poem by Wang An-shih.

Poem 80[36]

Wang An-shih

Form: *tz'u*; tune pattern: "The Cassia Twigs Are Fragrant"

I climb up and look down, letting my eyes wander.
Just now it's late autumn in the old capital,
The weather is turning severe.
For a thousand miles, the clear river is like silk   4
And the green peaks are like bamboo shoots.
The homebound sailboat rests its oars in the setting sun
And turns its back to the west wind.
The wineshop flag slants high;   8
Above the painted boat the clouds are pale;
On the River of Stars an egret rises.
It would be hard to do justice to this in a painting.

I think of the past,   12
Successive dynasties vying for glory.
I lament what happened outside the gate and upstairs,
Continuous sorrows and pain.
For a thousand years, leaning on lofty railings,   16
Facing this scene, people have sighed over glory and shame.
Past events of the Six Dynasties have flowed away with the river,

---

王安石 〈桂枝香〉 登臨送目　正故国晚秋　天氣初肅　(4)千里澄江似練　翠峰如簇　歸
帆去棹殘陽裡　背西風　(8)酒旗斜矗　綵舟雲淡　星河鷺起　畫圖難足　(12)念往昔
繁華競逐　歎門外樓頭　悲恨相續　(16)千古憑高　對此漫嗟榮辱　六朝舊事隨流水

There's only chilly mist
And fragrant grasses stiff with frost.   20
Even now, singing girls
From time to time still sing
The old song of blossoms in the rear court.

Like many of the poems analyzed throughout this study, this one consists of two parts. The first stanza describes the scene around Chin-ling (modern Nanking), the old capital of the Six Dynasties (A.D. 222–589), as seen from an unspecified point of elevation. The second stanza contemplates the past in conjunction with the present. The two parts are closely coordinated. The first stanza, though limited to what is visible at the present moment, contains many images conventionally associated with meditating on the past: looking down from a height, late autumn, sunset, a river, mountain peaks, clouds, boats, and returning home which implies homesickness.

An interesting aspect of the description is the intermingling of terrestrial and celestial features (cf. above, Poems 8–9). The colorful boat is juxtaposed with the paling clouds (line 9), and the Yangtze River (lines 4 and 18) is confounded with the Milky Way ("the River of Stars," in line 10). Or, if you prefer a more realistic reading, the egret in its flight links the earthly with the heavenly river.

Though the second stanza is primarily devoted to reflections on the past, it continues the description of the autumn scene in a way that brings out its relation to the suffering and decay wrought by the passage of time: there is chilly mist, the green grass stiffening, and the river representing the relentless flux of time, as expressed in the magnificent line 18. The regret of the transience of past glory, extending over "a thousand years," is expressly linked to the contemplation of this particular scene from an elevated point (lines 16–17).

Lamenting the passing of the Six (Southern) Dynasties, the second stanza concentrates on the last of them, the Ch'en dynasty, which fell in 589 to the conquering armies of Sui. Line 14 recalls the climax of the conquest in the words of a poem by Tu Mu which contains the following couplet: "Outside the gate, Han Ch'in-hu; / Upstairs, Chang Li-hua."[37] (See appendix 2.) In his pregnant allusion, Wang An-shih condenses Tu Mu's two lines of five syllables each into just four syllables, juxtaposing the two critical locations, the battleground

---

但寒煙　(20)芳草凝綠　至今商女　時時猶唱　後庭遺曲

("outside the gate") and the scene of oblivious pleasure ("upstairs").
In this process of compression, parallelism within the line replaces
parallelism of neighboring lines.

Ch'en Shu-pao, the last Ch'en emperor (vanquished in 589),
was a talented poet. While his empire was crumbling, he composed a
cycle of poems entitled "The Jade Tree Blossoms in the Rear Court."
One of them is extant,[38] and from another, we have the fragment:

> The jade tree blossoms in the rear court,
> When the blossoms open they won't last long.

The official *History of the Sui Dynasty*, which preserves this fragment,
adds: "People at the time considered it a prophetic song; it was an
omen that he would not last long."[39] It is an open question whether
the Emperor, in composing this couplet, had in mind the impending
collapse of his own rule or whether he was merely reformulating a
conventional poetic image. What matters is that later generations of
Chinese literati, including Wang An-shih, saw in these lines a predic-
tion of the fall of the Ch'en dynasty. Wang delays a direct mention of
"The Jade Tree Blossoms in the Rear Court" until the very end of his
poem. Here again he adapts a poem by Tu Mu, just as he had done
in line 14. The relevant portion of Tu Mu's poem reads:

> The singing girls don't know the ruined dynasty's grief,
> Looking down on the river they still sing "Blossoms in the
>   Rear Court."[40]

The song plays a crucial and complex role in Wang An-shih's poem.
Ch'en Shu-pao in creating it is seen as predicting and simultaneously
defying the imminent disaster. The girls in their ignorance continue
to sing it as though the tragedy had not happened. And the present
poet perpetuates the same song, not out of defiance or ignorance,
but with the knowledge that poetry has the power to recreate the
past.

Significant in this connection may be the poet's remark (line 11)
on the inability of painting to do justice to the scene. On the surface,
this line merely emphasizes the extraordinary beauty of the view at
this particular moment. But it also implies, I suggest, that poetry can
do what painting is unable to do, namely, view past scenes in conjunction with the visible present. Thus the poet, like the Ch'en emperor
and the singing girls, manages to counteract the ravaging effects of

time. In poetry and song the glorious past survives and continues to live forever.

We have not yet exhausted the complexities of the role of the song in Wang's poem. In the traditional Chinese view, shared by Wang An-shih and by literary critics down to modern times, prophetic songs tend to be composed in times of moral decay, predicting the downfall of the ruling house. Ch'en Shu-pao, as noted above, was believed to have been such a prophet, and Wang An-shih here casts himself in the same role. By pointing out that the same song which presaged the fall of the decadent Ch'en dynasty is being sung today, he hints that the present decadence may lead to a similar disaster.[41] (We may note incidentally that the same tune title, "The Cassia Twigs Are Fragrant," was used by more than thirty of Wang's contemporaries for poems contemplating the past;[42] unlike the tune titles of most *tz'u* poems, it fits the poem's content, using the same flower symbol that had been employed in Ch'en Shu-pao's couplet quoted above.) Thus Wang An-shih makes use of a historical theme to drive home a moral lesson, following in the long poetic tradition that we have observed from the beginning of this chapter.

10

The Past: A Legend and a Satire

(Poems 81–84)

The following poem deals with two events widely separated in time:
a personal experience of the immediate present and a legend of the
remote past.

Poem 81, "Myriad Mountain Pool"[1]
Meng Hao-jan
Form: *ku-shih*

On a flat stone I sit and fish.
The water is clear, my mind at ease.
Fish swim beneath the pool's trees,
Apes hang among the island's vines.
Wandering maidens once took off their pendants,
Tradition says it was in these mountains.*
I seek them but cannot find them.
Following the moon and chanting a boat song I return.

The present and the past are clearly set apart in this poem, yet they
also blend into each other. The simultaneous separation and fusion
of past and present is one of the marvels of Chinese poetry. As is well
known, the Chinese language does not indicate tense morphologi-
cally; the verb "sit" in line 1 is indistinguishable from "sat," and
"took off" (line 5) as an unmodified single word is the same as "take
off." But in this case, "take off/took off" is preceded by a time
marker, *hsi* "formerly, once," which squarely puts the statement in
the past. A Chinese poet is always free to keep time indefinite (an

---

*See appendix 2, "Cheng Chiao-fu."

孟浩然 「萬山潭作」 垂釣坐盤石　水清心亦閑　魚行潭樹下　猿挂島藤間　游女昔解佩
傳聞於此山　求之不可得　沿月櫂歌還

inestimable advantage in poetry), but he also has means to specify an absolute or relative point in time. In this instance, the poet indicates that with the beginning of the second half he is stepping back into the past. But having taken this step, he proceeds at once to link the past with the present. As his link he uses the locality, which is the same for both events: "Tradition says it was in these mountains." (A more prosaic and "logical" order would be: It was in these very mountains, tradition says, that the wandering maidens once took off their pendants.)

Despite the neat division of the poem into two equal halves and the delayed introduction of the legend at the beginning of the second half, the legendary figures are not presented abruptly but gradually. The poet leads up to them through four images, strategically placed at the beginning of the first four lines: angling—water—fish (living creatures in the water)—apes (anthropoids). All four are relevant to the evocation of the water nymphs. From the evocation, the poem proceeds at once to an active search: "I seek them but cannot find them." ("Them" in the original is ambiguous and vague; it may refer to the maidens, or to the pendants, or to both.) This line recalls a passage in the first poem of the *Shih ching* anthology.

> A refined, good lady,
> Awake and asleep he seeks her,
> He seeks her but cannot find her,
> Awake and asleep he thinks of her.

It also recalls the opening of the ninth poem of the *Shih ching*, which is the oldest reference to the legend of the Han River maidens:

> In the South there are tall trees,
> One cannot rest under them.*
> At the Han River there are wandering maidens,
> One cannot seek them.

Thus it was an essential part of the legend already in this earliest version that an attempt to find the maidens could never succeed. In Meng Hao-jan's poem, the legendary past and the actual present (a tranquil fishing trip) come close together, without catching up with one another. The two events interact, and each becomes more meaningful through its association with the other.

---

*Because they offer no shade.

The last line winds up the travel motif that had begun with the fish and led to the wandering fairies. Even the still moon is in motion. Always ahead of the boat, it eludes the angler as much as the fairies had eluded him and Cheng Chiao-fu before him, and as the legend itself eludes the poet who tries to recapture it. The last word, "return," is a sign of conclusion and marks the return from the fairy world to actuality.

The remainder of this chapter will be devoted to a long poem written in early T'ang times—the seventh century—which purports to recreate the atmosphere of the western capital, Ch'ang-an, as it was under the Han dynasty (206 B.C.–A.D. 220). As will become apparent in our discussion, however, it is actually a satire on the contemporary state of affairs in the capital. The title "old-time poem" is already familiar to us from a previous instance (Poem 74).

Poem 82, "Ch'ang-an: An Old-Time Poem"[2]
Lu Chao-lin (635–84)
Form: ku-shih

1

Ch'ang-an's broad streets connect with narrow lanes;
Black oxen, white horses, chariots of fragrant wood,
Jade-inlaid sedan chairs, go all over town, past princesses'
    homes;
Golden saddles head continuously toward noblemen's
    mansions.   4
Dragons hold in their mouths costly chariot parasols that
    glitter in the morning sun;
Phoenixes* spit forth tassels that shine beneath the
    evening clouds.
Gossamer threads, a thousand feet long, compete to wind
    around the trees;
A whole flock of gorgeous birds chorus among the
    blossoms.   8

2

They chorus among the blossoms, with flirting butterflies
    by the thousand palace gates;

---

*Embroidered on the saddle blankets.

盧照鄰「長安古意」 長安大道連狹斜　青牛白馬七香車　玉輦縱橫過主第　(4)金鞭絡繹
向侯家　龍銜寶蓋承朝日　鳳吐流蘇帶晚霞　百丈遊絲爭繞樹　(8)一群嬌鳥共啼花　啼花
戲蝶千門側

Emerald trees, silver terraces, myriad colors.

The palace galleries alternating with windows form acacia
    leaves;

The ridge tiles linking the paired watch towers are
    drooping phoenix wings.   12

The Liang family's painted halls rise to the sky,*

The Han Emperor's Golden Stems go straight beyond the
    clouds.†

People in front of the tall houses don't know the folk they
    see,

Those who meet on the streets fail to recognize each
    other.   16

3

Let me ask about her who plays the flute facing the
    purple mist.

In her fragrant years she became an expert dancer.

She longs for a mate—like a pair of fish with one eye
    each—then she wouldn't mind death,

Or a couple of mandarin ducks, then she wouldn't envy
    the immortals.   20

4

The couples of fish and the mandarin ducks are truly to
    be envied,

In pairs they go, in pairs they come, don't you see them
    there?

How hateful! A solitary pheasant embroidered on the
    curtain.

How lovely! A pair of swallows affixed to the door screen.   24

5

The paired swallows fly together around the painted
    ridgepole,

Silk curtains, kingfisher-green covers, "rich gold" incense.

---

*Liang Chi (died A.D. 159) built a luxurious family residence in Ch'ang-an.

†Bronze pillars were erected by Emperor Wu of Han (reigned 141–87 B.C.) to hold
receptacles designed to catch the dew of immortality.

碧樹銀臺萬種色　複道交牕作合歡　(12)雙闕連甍垂鳳翼　梁家畫閣天中起　漢帝金莖雲
外直　樓前相望不相知　(16)陌上相逢詎相識　借問吹簫向紫煙　曾經學舞度芳年　得成
比目何辭死　(20)願作鴛鴦不羨仙　比目鴛鴦眞可羨　雙去雙來君不見　生憎帳額繡孤鸞
(24)好取門簾帖雙燕　雙燕雙飛繞畫梁　羅幃翠被鬱金香

On layers of "drifting cloud" hair she fixes a "cicada-
    wing" coiffure;
Above the thin, thin "new moon" eyebrows she applies
    yellow powder.   28

6

Wearing yellow and white powder she goes out in the
    chariot,
Coquettish and flirtatious, she often changes expression.
Handsome lads on valuable horses with coin-shaped metal
    adornments,
Courtesans with "coiled dragon" coiffures and "bent
    knee" golden hairpins.   32

7

Inside the Censorate, ravens caw at night,
In front of the gate of the Hall of Justice, sparrows are
    eager to perch.
Grand, grand, the vermilion city overlooks the jade-
    bright road;
Far, far, the green carriage curtains sink behind the
    metal barriers.   36
Clasping pellet-shooters, men go hawking north of the
    Tu-ling Plateau;
Assassins draw pellet-lots west of the Wei River Bridge.
Dandies with "lotus" swords welcome each other,
Together they follow the beaten path to the courtesans'
    peach and plum blossoms.   40

8

The courtesans at sunset in purple silk skirts
With clear voices sing gentle tunes.
At the Northern Halls* each night men stay as long as
    the moon,
At the Southern Road each morning horses gather like
    clouds.   44

---

*The courtesans' quarter.

片片行雲着蟬鬢　(28)纖纖初月上鴉黃　鴉黃粉白車中出　含嬌含態情非一　妖童寶馬鐵
連錢　(32)娼婦盤龍金屈膝　御史府中烏夜啼　廷尉門前雀欲棲　隱隱朱城臨玉道　(36)
遙遙翠幰沒金堤　挾彈飛鷹杜陵北　探丸借客渭橋西　俱邀俠客芙蓉劍　(40)共宿娼家桃
李蹊　娼家日暮紫羅裙　清歌一囀口氛氳　北堂夜夜人如月　(44)南陌朝朝騎似雲

9

The Southern Road and the Northern Halls are linked to
   the Northern Quarter,
Five-way crossroads and three-lane streets lead to the
   Three Markets.
Supple willows and green locust trees droop, sweeping the
   ground;
Balmy air and red dust rise in the darkening sky.   48

10

Here you come, metropolitan police of the Han dynasty, a
   thousand horse strong,
To drink "kingfisher" wine in nautilus-shell cups.
Silk jackets and jeweled belts are removed for you,
Songs from Yen and dances from Chao are performed
   for you.   52

11

Then there are nobles, calling themselves generals and
   ministers;
They turn the sun and the sky around, they yield to
   none,
So arrogant they could push a Kuan Fu* aside,
So arbitrary they will not tolerate a Hsiao Wang.†   56

12

Arbitrary, arrogant—such are noble lords:
Black Dragon and Purple Swallow‡ stir a breeze even
   when they sit.
They claim their singing and dancing will last a thousand
   years,

---

*A very straightforward general (d. 131 B.C.) who often got drunk. He did not like to
yield place to men of higher rank and would insult them, but showed respect to those
who ranked below him.

†A chief minister (106–47 B.C.). Stern and incorrupt, he ran afoul of enemies at court
and committed suicide.

‡Famous horses.

南陌北堂連北里　五劇三條控三市　弱柳青槐拂地垂　(48)佳氣紅塵暗天起　漢代金吾千
騎來　翡翠屠蘇鸚鵡杯　羅襦寶帶爲君解　(52)燕歌趙舞爲君開　別有豪華稱將相　轉日
囘天不相讓　意氣由來排灌夫　(56)專權判不容蕭望　專權意氣本豪雄　青虯紫燕坐生風
自言歌舞長千載

They say their proud extravagance surpasses the Five
    Lords'.*   60

13

In the cycle of seasons, scenes change without delay;
In a twinkling a mulberry orchard becomes an emerald
    green sea.†
Where once there were golden steps and white jade halls
Today there are only green pines.   64

14

Quiet and austere is Master Yang's life,
Year in and year out a couch full of books.
There are only the cassia flowers blooming on South
    Mountain,
Flying to and fro they invade his robes.   68

Let us begin our discussion of this poem by noting a few facts
about its structure. It is divided into fourteen stanzas by the use of a
separate rhyme for each stanza. The rhyming words are always at
the end of the first line of the stanza, and at the end of each even-
numbered line. Most stanzas consist of four lines; the only exceptions are stanzas 1, 2, and 7, which number eight lines each. A
majority of the stanzas are linked to the preceding and to the following stanza by the *ting-chen t'i* ("thimble design") device, which
we observed in another "Old-Time Poem" (Poem 74). The absence
of this linkage at the beginning of six stanzas (3, 7, 10, 11, 13, and
14) marks in each instance a shift to a different scene and (except in
stanza 13) the appearance of new persons. In all but one of the places
where the *ting-chen t'i* linkage is lacking, we have instead a topical
linkage. Thus at the transition from stanza 2 to stanza 3, people's
ignorance of each other leads to the question about the flute player;[3]
the dust at the end of stanza 9 heralds the approach of the equestrian
police at the opening of stanza 10; the behavior of the police in
stanza 10 is similar to that of the nobles in stanza 11; the noblemen's
presumption of longevity in stanza 12 contrasts with the swift and

---

*Five powerful courtiers of the Former Han dynasty; one of them was the Hsiao Wang
of line 56.

†See appendix 2, "Ma-ku."

(60)自謂驕奢凌五公　節物風光不相待　桑田碧海須臾改　昔時金階白玉堂　(64)即今惟
見青松在　寂寂寥寥揚子居　年年歲歲一牀書　獨有南山桂花發　(68)飛來飛去襲人裾

radical changes described in stanza 13; and the desolation of ruins and tombs at the end of stanza 13 goes well with the solitude of Yang Hsiung at the beginning of stanza 14. The only place where there is no linkage of either kind is between stanzas 6 and 7, and this is the point where the poem's first major theme—prostitution—gives way to the second—corrupt officials. The two themes are connected inasmuch as these two groups of people mingle in both parts. While each of the two major parts takes up six stanzas, the two final stanzas are reserved for other subjects.

Parallelism between the two lines of a couplet is maintained through most of the poem (the exceptions are lines 1–2, 21–22, 25–26, 29–30, 41–42, 49–50, 53–54, 57–58, 61–64, 67–68), and there is also much parallelism within single lines (lines 1, 2, 11, 12, 15, 16, 22, 25, 26, 30, 45, 46, 51, 52, 54, 58, 62, 63, 65, 66, 68). (Parallelism is discussed fully in chapter 11.)

Further remarks on noteworthy details will take the form of a running commentary. The first line simultaneously conveys three different meanings. Taken literally, it states that the capital boasts a splendid network of streets connecting all parts of the city with each other. But "narrow lanes" is also a euphemism for "houses of prostitution," thus the line implies that such houses are frequented by rich and noble men, who live on "broad streets." Finally, the term *ta tao*, translated here as "broad streets," means literally "great way," and this is sometimes used in a moral sense, corresponding to what we, by way of a different metaphor, call "the straight and narrow." And the term *hsia hsieh*, here translated as "narrow lanes," may also mean "crooked ways, immoral behavior." Hence the line suggests that in the capital are found side by side the Great Way of morality, emanating from the imperial court, and the illicit actions of the citizens. A literary antecedent of line 2 will be cited below in the discussion of lines 33–34.

In the course of the first two stanzas, the description progresses from the network of streets to the numerous, richly adorned carriages, sedan chairs, and riding horses, and to the size and number of luxurious dwellings, producing a vivid picture of a prosperous, crowded, busy metropolis. Enhancing this sense of abundance, each of the first twelve lines contains at least two different objects or phenomena, and this same crowding can be observed in a remarkably long passage later in the poem (lines 23–52). There is in the opening portion a nice balance of the two sexes, with ladies riding in sedan chairs and

chariots, and men on horseback. Lines 5 and 6 are an instance of
hu-wen: the chariots and the horses (i.e., the ladies and the gentlemen)
are on the move morning and evening, that is to say, constantly.

In lines 7–14, imagery is used again to convey multiple meanings.
The gossamer threads, the flowering trees, the singing birds, the
gracefully fluttering butterflies, the magnificent buildings—all these
are visible objects, forming part of the grand scene; but they are also
poetic symbols, representing the continuous visiting and party-
going, the gay music, singing, and dancing, the extravagant living,
the shameless pursuit of illicit pleasures.

Stanza 3 marks a shift from the general to the specific. The woman
singled out for attention in stanzas 3–6 is a prostitute looking for a
lover. Though she remains nameless, she is associated with a legendary figure for reasons to be explained shortly. In line 17, the combination of "playing the flute" and "purple mist" suggests the story
of Nung-yü (see appendix 2). The phrase "purple mist" indicates the
realm of the immortals, Hsiao Shih's original home, to which he and
his wife Nung-yü eventually return. The same phrase is used with
reference to their flight in several earlier poems, including one by
Chiang Tsung (518–90):

> Nung-yü is the daughter of the house of Ch'in,
> Hsiao Shih is a lad from the land of the immortals,
>
> . . . .
> They fly toward the purple mist.[4]

The identification of women of loose morals with legendary princesses and Taoist immortals is not uncommon in the literature of the
T'ang period (in prose fiction as well as poetry). Such women are
conceived as being superior in beauty to ordinary women, and they
are free from the conventions restricting the behavior of women in
contemporary society. They are accomplished in music and dancing,
they live in luxuriously furnished apartments, they fix their hair and
makeup with consummate skill, and of course they are unsurpassed
in the art of coquetry.

Comparable to the multiple use of imagery noted in lines 7–14, we
find in this passage a shift from paired animals as amatory ideals
(lines 19, 22) to birds as decorations (lines 23–24, 26), to live birds
(line 25). Similarly, "drifting cloud" and "new moon," primarily
technical terms denoting fashions of coiffure and makeup, serve the

additional poetic function of conjuring up the nocturnal scene of the courtesan plying her trade.

Stanza 7 introduces, as already mentioned, the poem's second major theme: the failure of public officials to perform their duties. Lines 33 and 34 contain a number of allusions that are combined in an artful and complex manner. By considering them in some detail we will gain an insight into Lu Chao-lin's craftsmanship. Two of the sources are biographies of Han-dynasty officials. Line 33 alludes to the following passage from the biography of Chu Po: "During the reign of Emperor Ai [reigned 7–1 B.C.], at the offices of the Censorate, which consisted of more than a hundred buildings, the water of the wells was not used, and inside the compound cypresses were planted. Several thousand wild ravens constantly perched there; they left in the morning and returned in the evening, and were called 'morning-evening ravens.'"[5] In line 34 there is an allusion to a portion of the historian's critique at the end of the biography of Chi Cheng: "When Duke Ti of Hsia-kuei was Superintendent of Justice, guests thronged his gate. When he was dismissed, one could place nets to catch sparrows outside the gate. Later he was reappointed Superintendent of Justice, and guests were again eager to come."[6]

Every single word in lines 33–34 has an antecedent. From the first of the two biographies just cited are taken the words "inside," "censorate," "ravens," and "perch"; from the second biography, "[hall] of Justice," "gate," "sparrows," and "eager." Most of the borrowings from the first biography occur in the first line of the couplet, but the word "perch" is saved for the conclusion of line 34. The phrase "outside the gate" in the second biography turns into "in front of the gate" in line 34. The phrase "ravens caw at night" comes from a different source: it is the title of a *yüeh-fu* song, said to have originated in the middle of the fifth century. Eight anonymous poems bearing this title, consisting of four five-syllable lines each and dating probably from the fifth century, are extant today.[7] Men of letters also wrote poems with this title, using different meters;[8] the earliest one we have is by Hsiao Kang, the author of "The Flowering Plum" (Poem 1 above). The theme of most of the anonymous songs, as well as those of the literati, is the separation of two lovers. The ravens become symbols of the husband who travels to distant parts and the wife who stays behind, and the nocturnal cawing expresses the sorrow of separation. Not all of these poems mention ravens in the body of the poem. One of them that does is the following, which may serve as a sample of the group.

> Poem 83, "Ravens Caw at Night"[9]
> Anonymous (fifth century A.D.?)
> Form: *yüeh-fu*

> Ravens from birth are eager to fly;
> When two of them fly, each goes by itself.
> Separated in life, their minds are not at ease;
> All night they caw until day breaks.

The association of ravens cawing at night, symbolizing the separation of a married couple, with the office of the Censorate is already to be found in two *yüeh-fu* poems by Yü Hsin, both titled "Ravens Caw at Night."[10] The second of these contains the following lines:

> In the Censorate, where shall I spend the night?
> On the walls of Lo-yang, how can they perch?
>
> . . . .
>
> How can I help being startled and shedding long tears?
> Everywhere the cawing ravens caw all through the night.

Here the ravens obviously represent a man who is separated from his wife while serving as a censor in the capital. A different kind of husband is symbolized by a perching raven in the following poem by Hsiao Kang (whose "Ravens Caw at Night" was mentioned a few lines above).

> Poem 84, "Song of the Perching Raven"[11]
> Hsiao Kang
> Form: *yüeh-fu*

> Black oxen, red wheels, chariots of fragrant wood,
> What a pity—tonight he stays at the singing-girl's house.
> In the tall tree the raven is eager to perch;
> The gauze curtain and kingfisher-embroidered screen are
>   lowered for you.

The speaker is a wife who complains that her husband, like a perching raven, strays from home and spends the night with a singing-girl. It is clear beyond doubt that Lu Chao-lin had this poem in

「烏夜啼」 烏生如欲飛　二飛各自去　生離無安心　夜啼至天曙

蕭綱 「烏棲曲」 青牛丹轂七香車　可憐今夜宿倡家　高樹烏欲棲　羅幃翠帳向君低

mind. Not only did he use the image of "ravens at night" for philandering gentlemen in line 33 and the phrase "eager to perch" in line 34 but he also took over Hsiao Kang's first line and made it line 2 of his own poem, with only one change, from "red wheels" to "white horses," referring as in Hsiao Kang's poem to men on their way to houses of prostitution.

We can now set down the various implications inherent in the verbal and thematic allusions in lines 33–34 of Lu's poem. The references to the biographies of Chu Po and Chi Cheng suggest that judicial functions are being neglected and justice is not being carried out. In this connection, it may be relevant that in the anecdotes surrounding the *yüeh-fu* song "Ravens Caw at Night," the cawing of the ravens is interpreted as an omen of an impending amnesty.[12] In the context of our poem, this may mean that punishments are not being meted out as they should be. This is perhaps too speculative. More definite implications of the *yüeh-fu* title "Ravens Caw at Night" are the themes of wandering males, illicit lovemaking, and wives complaining of being temporarily deserted by their husbands. The combination of this thematic complex with the lack of human activity at the Censorate and the Hall of Justice suggests that the censorial and judicial officials are neglecting their duties and spending their time on illicit pleasures. These men, like the ravens and sparrows, perch where they are not supposed to perch. Since birds figure prominently in augury—in China as well as in other cultures— the unusual behavior of the birds in lines 33–34 should perhaps be taken as an ill omen. At the very least, it indicates a serious deviation from the normalcy of law and order.

In lines 35–52, the beauty and grandeur of the scene and the luxury of precious objects are set against the baseness of human behavior. This strategy is in evidence in other parts of the poem as well. Line 38 refers to illegal killings in private vendettas, such as are reported in the official histories of the Han dynasty. Professional assassins drew lots in the form of pellets to distribute victims among them. This line indicates the failure of the law-enforcement officials to prevent serious crimes. Line 40 alludes to a proverb that is cited in the historian's critique following the biography of the Han-dynasty general Li Kuang (died 119 B.C.): "The peach tree and the plum tree do not speak, but beneath them a path forms naturally."[13]

At the end of stanzas 7, 8, and 9 we find the same kind of multiple imagery as we observed in stanzas 1–5: the flowering peaches and plums and the willows and locust trees are part of the visible scene, but they are also metaphors for the courtesans; conversely, the moon and the clouds are brought in as similes, but they are also fitting components of the nocturnal setting.

Lines 45–46 hark back to the theme struck at the poem's opening: all streets of the metropolis interconnect, and they all serve the pursuit of licentious pleasures.

Stanza 13, as mentioned earlier, reasserts Nature's supreme law of continuous change in the face of haughty men's vain expectations of permanence. The "green pines" that replace the "golden steps" and the "white jade halls" (lines 63–64) are another instance of multiple imagery: on the one hand, the constancy of the evergreens contrasts with the inevitable decay of man's costliest constructions; on the other hand, pine trees are traditionally associated with death, as they are often planted around tombs.

In the final stanza, Yang Hsiung (53 B.C.–A.D. 18) is held up as a model Confucian, with a minimum of social life and full-time devotion to his studies. The phrase "quiet and austere" is adapted from a line in Yang Hsiung's "Rebuttal of Ridicule,"[14] and ultimately derives from Lao Tzu, *Tao-te ching*, sec. 25.[15]

The cassia blossoms represent the life of the recluse, since cassia trees appear in the opening line of the *Ch'u tz'u* anthology piece "Summons for a Gentleman Who Became a Recluse."[16] "South Mountain" is traditionally associated with longevity,[17] and this implication may be intended here, contrasting with the impermanence of human endeavors that had been emphasized in the preceding stanza. The phrase "flying to and fro," more literally "flying they come, flying they go," is reminiscent of a phrase that was used in line 22: "in pairs they go, in pairs they come." The similarity is perhaps a deliberate maneuver to bring out the difference between the evildoers, who viewed natural phenomena as *contrasting* with their own situation, and Yang Hsiung, who lived in *harmony* with nature.

While in the poems discussed in the preceding chapter we saw the past intermingling with the present, Lu Chao-lin's poem uses a different strategy. Unlike those poems, it does not indulge in admiration or melancholy contemplation of the past as available in visible remains or in written records; it does not articulate points of contact, similarity, or contrast between the past and the present; nor does it move back and forth between the two. On the contrary, the poem carefully refrains from any overt allusion to contemporary affairs while specifically naming seven personalities and institutions of the Han dynasty (206 B.C.–A.D. 220) in lines 13, 14, 49, 55, 56, 60, and 65. By this ostensible concentration on the Han period, and by choosing the title "old-time poem," Lu Chao-lin makes it appear that he is dealing exclusively with the past, without any regard to the present. Actually, the opposite is true. As critics have long recognized, the poem is a scathing satire of the moral depravity which the stern Confucian poet saw all around him in Ch'ang-an, the western capital. The Han scene is merely a disguise, and a very transparent disguise at that. Poets of the T'ang period established the convention of speaking of their own time in terms of the Han dynasty. The Han was a natural choice for this substitution because, like the T'ang, it brought strong rule and a measure of prosperity to a united China, it had expansionist ambitions abroad, and its capitals were, as in T'ang times, Ch'ang-an and Lo-yang.

The substitution is used particularly in poems that imply criticism of governmental policies or social conditions. Tu Fu's "Ballad of the Army Carts"[18] and Po Chü-i's "Song of Everlasting Sorrow"[19] are famous examples. It is not so much a question of "security" for the poet. If the authorities wanted to punish him for his criticism, the disguise would have given him little protection. It is rather a matter of making the satire more palatable and saving face by pretending that another age, not one's own, is the butt of the strictures.

One theme that Lu's poem (from line 59 on) shares with those considered in the preceding chapter is its concern with the rapid changes and the constant decay that are inherent in the flow of time. But again there is a difference. In the other poems, the destructive flow of time was viewed as continuing right up to the speaker's own present, for example: "How many worthies and sages have perished!" (Poem 71); "Human lives succeed each other and decay, / They come and go, becoming past and present" (Poem 72). Lu Chao-lin, however, confines the continuing process of decay within the historical limits of the Han period, for the reasons stated above.

Some other aspects of Lu's poem are revealed in its artful use of imagery. We note, first, the sustained emphasis on the capital's fabulous wealth and luxury: "chariots of fragrant wood," "jade-

inlaid sedan chairs," "golden saddles," "costly chariot parasols,"
"silver terraces," "Golden Stems," "embroidered . . . curtain,"
"painted ridgepole," " 'rich gold' incense," "valuable horses with
coin-shaped metal adornments," " 'Bent knee' golden hairpins,"
" 'lotus' swords," "nautilus-shell cups," "jeweled belts," "golden
steps," "white jade halls."

Other conspicuous groups of images involve birds, trees, and blossoms. In addition to the "gorgeous birds" occurring in line 8, eight
different species of birds are named: phoenixes, mandarin ducks,
pheasants, swallows, kingfishers, ravens, sparrows, and hawks. Of
specific trees, there are willows, locusts, pines, mulberries, and
acacias. Of blossoming trees, there are peach, plum, and cassia.
Blossoms in general are found in lines 8 and 9, and trees in general
in lines 7 and 10.

Of animals other than birds, there are oxen, horses, dragons, fish,
butterflies, and cicadas.

The singing birds and the blossoming trees in many instances
symbolize attractive women. The paired animals represent lovemaking and togetherness, and the single ones loneliness and frustrated desire. (This becomes explicit in lines 19–24). But again we
find many images serving multiple purposes. The majority of the
animal and plant images contribute to the general atmosphere of
beauty, wealth, and luxury. The blossoms, singing birds, dallying
butterflies, and drifting gossamer threads belong to the vernal scene
of burgeoning life and spring fever. The horses and oxen enhance
the impression of busy traffic. Together with the birds, the blossoms,
the butterflies, the gossamer threads, and the clouds, they create a
sense of continuous motion.

While some of the images represent *horizontal* movement—the
comings and goings of men and women pursuing wicked pleasures—
others involve *upward* motion, which suggests overbearing ambition.
In this sense, the soaring birds go together with passages such as
these: "The Liang family's painted halls rise to the sky, / The Han
Emperor's Golden Stems go straight up beyond the clouds"; "tall
houses"; "facing the purple mist"; "Balmy air and red dust rise in
the darkening sky." Finally, the *downward* movement implicit in the
falling of blossoms conventionally represents the decay of human
vigor and beauty, as we have seen previously. Pointing in the same
direction are the following phrases: "drooping phoenix wings";

"Far, far, the green carriage curtains sink behind the metal barriers"; "Supple willows and green locust trees droop, sweeping the ground."

The immorality of those who go against the natural order of the universe is expressed in line 54, "They turn the sun and the sky around, they yield to none," which contrasts with the model figure of Yang Hsiung, who lives in harmony with Nature and accepts whatever she brings, even the falling blossoms (stanza 14).

Before leaving this poem, I would like to point out its use of a poetic device that will be discussed in the next chapter, namely, the rendering of a concept through a pair of terms which together make up the whole or a significant portion of the concept. This device often adds vivid, concrete details to what might otherwise be a flat, prosaic statement. Here are the pairs: "broad streets . . . narrow lanes"; "black oxen, white horses"; "jade-inlaid sedan chairs . . . golden saddles"; "past princesses' homes . . . toward noblemen's mansions"; "the morning sun . . . the evening clouds"; "a pair of fish with one eye each . . . a couple of mandarin ducks"; "in pairs they go, in pairs they come"; "yellow and white powder"; "coquettish, flirtatious"; "handsome lads . . . courtesans"; "inside the Censorate . . . in front of the gate of the Hall of Justice"; "ravens . . . sparrows"; "dandies . . . courtesans"; "at the Northern Halls . . . at the Southern Road"; "each night . . . each morning"; "supple willows and green locust trees"; "balmy air and red dust"; "silk jackets and jeweled belts"; "songs from Yen and dances from Chao"; "generals and ministers"; "they turn the sun and the sky around"; "Black Dragon and Purple Swallow"; "singing and dancing"; "golden steps and white jade halls"; "year in and year out"; "flying to and fro."

This device enjoys widespread use in Chinese poetry and prose for the purpose of stating a single generality by means of two particulars. In the pairs just cited (to spell it out in three instances), "the morning sun . . . the evening clouds" is a poetic way of saying "at all times, constantly"; "generals and ministers" signifies "all kinds of officials, military as well as civil"; "Black Dragon and Purple Swallow" means "fine horses"; and the like.

11

Parallelism and Antithesis

(POEMS 85–91)

The importance of parallelism and antithesis as organizing principles in Chinese poetry has become apparent in many of the poems considered so far. In this and the next chapter, these principles will be examined in some detail. But before doing so, it will be useful to look at some linguistic devices used to form compounds in Chinese because, as we shall see, the same principles are employed there as in the joining of poetic phrases and ideas.

A common device for forming compounds of nouns, verbs, or adjectives, is to join two near-synonyms. This has been in operation from the earliest texts down to the modern spoken language. I will give some examples from poetry, with references to the poems discussed: *wei-chang* "curtains" (Poem 38, Line 2), *pieh-li* "to be parted" (poem 27, line 4). Since the members of each pair are nearly synonymous, each of these compounds can be reversed. This reversibility is deliberately exploited in Poem 10 which uses *shih-chia* "home, family" at the end of the first stanza, and *chia-shih* at the end of the second stanza.

Another type of coordinating compound consists of two antonyms or members of a set which are combined to signify a collective or abstract concept. Examples are *ch'in-shou* "birds and beasts," i.e., "animals";[1] *ts'ao-mu* "grasses and trees," i.e., "vegetation";[2] *shan-shui* "mountain(s) and water(s)," i.e., "landscape";[3] *chü-ma* "carriages and horses," i.e., "traffic";[4] *tan-ch'ing* "red and green," i.e., "color painting";[5] *ssu-chu* "silk and bamboo," i.e., "strings and flutes, instrumental music";[6] *hsing-chih* "to move and stop," i.e., "to travel";[7] *jih-hsi* "day and night," i.e., "continually, always";[8] *jih-yüeh* "days and months," i.e., "passing time";[9] *kuang-yin* "light and shade," i.e., "time" (Poem 50, line 116); *feng-yü* "wind and rain," i.e., "climate";[10] *feng-ch'en* "wind and dust," i.e., "hardships of travel."[11]

In these two types of compound formation we observe the principle of simply joining two words without any cement. It is left to the reader (or listener) to determine whether AB means "A plus B" (as in *ssu-chu*); or "of the several meanings of A, the one which coincides with B" (as in *pieh-li*); or "the common denominator of A and B" (as in *tan-ch'ing*); or "the total entity of which A and B are constituents" (as in *ch'in-shou*); or "the abstract concept suggested by the concrete instances A and B" (as in *feng-ch'en*).

This kind of shorthand is not limited to the production of compound words. It is also at work in the juxtaposition of coordinated statements, particularly in poetry, since poetry often ignores the normal relations of cause and effect, of distribution in space and time, and of resemblances and contrasts. Thus a poet may make two bald statements in succession, without any explanatory connectives, which could mean "A is the case, and B is also the case"; or else "because (in spite of) A, B happened"; or "A is (un)like B"; or "first there was A, then there came B"; or "in one place there is A, and somewhere else there is B"—to spell out just a few of the many possibilities. The advantages of this procedure are many: it makes for brevity and force (letting the facts speak for themselves), it involves the reader in the thought process, it dispenses with normal restrictions of logic, chronological sequence, orderliness, and the like, and it leaves room for multiple meanings.

In poetry, syntactic and semantic parallelism is likely to be coordinated with the prosodic structure. Parallelism (combined with antithesis) of successive lines is a well-known feature of Chinese verse. There is also parallelism within the line, and occasional parallelism between larger prosodic units. We shall take up these various phenomena in turn, beginning with the parallelism of neighboring lines.

A striking and perhaps unique feature of Chinese poetry is its predilection for the couplet as a structural unit. From the earliest times to the present, the majority of Chinese verse has been organized in *pairs* of lines, usually of equal length. Each line is normally a grammatically complete unit, a sentence. (The same Chinese term, *chü*, is used to denote both a grammatical sentence and a line of verse.) Yet each line usually forms part of a larger unit, the couplet.

That is to say, every odd-numbered line tends to be in closer juncture with the following line than with the preceding line. The fact that the rhyme normally comes at the end of every even-numbered line reinforces the function of the couplet as a prosodic unit.

Several factors coming together favor the occurrence of parallelism. (1) Each line of verse is normally a grammatically complete statement. (2) Two lines usually combine to form a couplet. (3) The lines of a given poem, or at least of a couplet, tend to be of equal length. (4) As literary Chinese is predominantly monosyllabic, an equal number of syllables means an equal number of words. (5) Caesuras normally occur at fixed positions. (6) The genius of the Chinese language favors the coordination of successive statements.

Thus, when two poetic statements, equal in overall length, in prosodic structure, and in the size of their constituent parts, are placed side by side and coordinated, it is natural that they should closely match. But too exact a correspondence would lead to monotony. Chinese poetry has therefore worked out a balancing system of similarities and differences, operating on the three levels of sound, grammar, and meaning.

On the acoustic level, the listener's ear readily perceives the identity of rhythmic structure in the two lines of each couplet, independently of the syntactic and semantic parallelism. In some poetic forms (excluding the strictest form, Regulated Verse), complete acoustic (and semantic) matching is occasionally brought about by the use of identical words in corresponding positions. As may be expected, this phenomenon occurs particularly in those poetic genres which originated from songs, namely, the *Shih ching* (*Classic of Songs*), *yüeh-fu*, *tz'u*, and *ch'ü*. I will give a few examples.

> Like one standing on tip-toe, so reverent,
> Like an arrow, so swiftly-moving,
> Like a bird, so spreading the wings,
> Like a pheasant, so flying—
> Thus is the lord where he ascends.[12]

> One layer of mountains,
> Two layers of mountains. . . .[13]

> The splendor of the mountain is like indigo,
> The splendor of the lake is like dressed silk.[14]

Such repetitions of words in neighboring lines are a rather rare phenomenon, since the prevailing tendency is to keep corresponding syllables in the two lines of a couplet phonetically distinct from each other. This tendency also affected the tones, in a long development which began about the third century A.D. and culminated in the Regulated Verse that was established in the seventh century. For prosodic purposes, the four tones of literary Chinese were grouped in two categories, with the level tone constituting one category, and the other three tones forming the second category. We may note in passing that prosody generally favors binary rather than multiple distinctions. In languages where length of syllable or stress are metrically significant, versification makes a single distinction between long and short syllables, or between stressed and unstressed syllables, reducing the multiple gradations of length and stress to a simple binary system.[15] In Chinese poetry, the principle is that each syllable should differ in its tonal category from the corresponding syllable in the neighboring line, with the modification that certain positions within the line are more sensitive to this rule than others. (See also *Lü-shih*, in appendix 1.)

Summing up the acoustic features of parallelism and antithesis, we may say that the prevailing trend is to establish rhythmic identity and phonetic dissimilarity between the lines of a couplet.

Turning to the grammatical level, we find that parallelism demands maximum similarity: a noun must be matched by a noun, a verb by a verb, a numeral by a numeral, a particle by a particle, and so forth. This follows also for sentence structure: a subject must be matched by a subject, a predicate by a predicate, an object by an object, a modifier by a modifier. Furthermore, a two-syllable compound must be matched by a two-syllable compound, a reduplication by a reduplication, and the like. One can easily see that grammatical parallelism goes hand in hand with the rhythmic parallelism we mentioned earlier.

On the semantic level, we find a neat balance of similarity and difference. The governing principle is that matching words should belong to the same category, but they should differ in meaning. They may be synonyms, antonyms, or members of the same set in some other way. Thus it happens that word pairs which tend to be combined into compounds (examples were given earlier in this chapter) are likely to occur in parallelistic couplets in matching positions. That is to say, the same principles that govern the formation of words are also at work in the poetic juxtaposition of phrases and concepts. Some of the matching pairs do not even have to belong to the same semantic category, provided they are established in the language as constituents of a phrase or compound. Examples are *lao-ping* "old age and sickness" and *shih-chiu* "poetry and wine."[16]

To show how parallelism and antithesis work, I will cite a few parallel couplets from the poem discussed in previous chapters.

> No lined robe in winter,
> No light clothes in summer.
>
> . . . .
> Few are those who help me,
> Many are the melon eaters.
>> [Poem 47, ll. 30–31, 42–43]

> Once he was a lord in the northern region,
> Now he is a commoner in the Southeast.
>> [Poem 24, ll. 7–8]

> The flowing waves go, carrying the moon;
> The tide water comes, bringing the stars.
>> [Poem 8, ll. 3–4]

> Fish swim beneath the pool's trees,
> Apes hang among the island's vines.
>> [Poem 81, ll. 3–4]

> The bright moon shines among the pines,
> The clear fountain flows over the stones.
>> [Poem 4, ll. 3–4]

> Falling petals, a man stands alone,
> Light rain, swallows fly in pairs.
>> [Poem 30, ll. 4–5]

Also, Wang Wei's "High Plateau" (Poem 3) consists completely of parallel couplets, as does Yang Kuang's "Feasting in the Eastern Hall" (Poem 5) with the exception of the final couplet.

The poetic form known as *lü-shih* ("regulated verse") has parallelism and antithesis in each of the two middle couplets as one of its obligatory features. Poems 85 and 86 illustrate this.

Poem 85, "Seeing Off My Younger Cousin Tsung-i"[17]
Liu Tsung-yüan (773–819)
Form: *lü-shih*

Wandering in distraction, our bereft souls double their gloom,
We both shed tears of parting on the Yüeh River bank.
A whole lifetime away from home six thousand miles,
Dying a thousand deaths in the wilderness twelve years.
At Kuei-ling, when the miasma comes, the clouds look like
   ink;
At Tung-t'ing, when spring ends, the water resembles the sky.
If you want to know where from now on my dreams of
   longing will take me,
It'll always be to Ching-men and Ying among the misty trees.

The region of Ching-men and Ying, in modern Hupei, must have
been cousin Tsung-i's destination.

Poem 86, "Inscribed at the Water Pavilion of the K'ai-yüan
   Temple in Hsüan Prefecture; There Were Residential
   Houses on Both Sides of the Winding Stream Below
   the Pavilion."[18]
Tu Mu
Form: *lü-shih*

Where the Six Dynasties flourished, grass joins the sky.
Heaven is placid, clouds are lazy, present and past unite.
Birds come, birds go within the mountain scene;
People sing, people weep amidst the water's sound.
Deep autumn, screens and curtains, a thousand houses, rain;
Setting sun, towers and terraces, a single flute, wind.
Alas, there is no way of seeing Fan Li*
Along the zigzag line of misty trees east of the Five Lakes.

We can see that the categories shared by matching words are some-

*See appendix 2.

柳完元 「別舍弟宗一」 零落殘魂倍黯然 雙垂別淚越江邊 一身去國六千里 萬死投荒
十二年 桂嶺瘴來雲似墨 洞庭春盡水如天 欲知此後相思夢 長在荊門郢樹煙

杜牧 「題宣州開元寺水閣閣下宛溪夾溪居人」 六朝文物草連空 天澹雲閑今古同 鳥去
鳥來山色裏 人歌人哭水聲中 深秋簾幕千家雨 落日樓臺一笛風 惆悵無因見范蠡 參
差煙樹五湖東

times broad, sometimes narrow. Instances of word pairs that have little in common beyond being members of the same word class are "ink" and "sky," and "houses" and "flute." But on closer inspection, we find that the two pairs are well matched. "Ink" and "sky" in the context both denote colors, and they are preceded by two synonymous verbs. "Houses" and "flute," though normally far apart, come together in this case because they are both parts of the same scene. They are further linked and contrasted by their modifiers, which are both numerals, just as "ink" and "sky" were linked by the synonymous verbs of which they were the grammatical objects.

Instances of narrow categories are "home" and "wilderness" (85.3–4); "mountain" and "water" (86.3–4); "Kuei-ling" and "Tung-t'ing" (85.5–6), place names consisting of two nouns each; and "screens and curtains," matched by "towers and terraces" (86.5–6). In the last juxtaposition, we have in both cases two co-ordinated nouns, each pair in common use as a phrase, each element fairly close in meaning to its mate, and both phrases related to the concept "house."

As far as grammatical structure is concerned, the parallelism of the middle couplets is fairly close, which will come through, I hope, in the translations. Note, for example, the peculiar effect achieved by the matching repetition of "birds" and "people" (86.3–4). Note also the pivotal positions of "away from home" and "in the wilderness" (85.3–4): both phrases go with what precedes and with what follows in the same line.

Parallelistic couplets are to be found in Western poetry, too, though with less frequency than in Chinese. Of the examples I have found, it will suffice to quote the following, from each of four languages.

> segunda invidia de Marte,
> primera dicha de Adonis.[19]
> [Mars' second envy,
> Adonis' first delight.]

He gave to Misery all he had, a tear,
He gained from Heaven ('twas all he wished) a friend.[20]

> Der Tod, das ist die kühle Nacht,
> Das Leben ist der schwüle Tag.[21]

> [Death is the cool night,
> Life is the sultry day.]

Il n'avait pas de fange en l'eau de son moulin,
Il n'avait pas d'enfer dans le feu de sa forge.[22]
[He had no filth in the water of his mill,
He had no hell in the fire of his forge.]

While the parallelistic couplet is the most common form of parallelism and antithesis in Chinese poetry, it is not the only one. There is also parallelism within a single line, as noted earlier. We had an instance in Tu Mu (Poem 86): "Birds come, birds go . . . / People sing, people weep . . ." (lines 3–4). We note that the internal parallelism is taken into account in the parallelistic structure of the couplet.

Whereas the parallelistic couplet exploits the structural identity of neighboring lines, parallelism within the line must come to terms with the internal structure of a single line. A simple solution offers itself in the case of the four-syllable line, which unlike most other meters consists of two equal halves, with a caesura between the second and the third syllable. I will give two examples from the *Shih ching* and one from a *fu*.

> I cut it, I boil it,
> I make fine cloth, I make coarse cloth.[23]

> Oh sun, ah moon![24]

> With light diffused and shadows mingled,
> Twigs abound and trunks are everywhere.
> [Poem 1, ll. 5–6]

The five-syllable line, with the caesura following the second syllable, consists of two unequal segments. Parallelism may be achieved in five different patterns. I will give a definition and two examples for each pattern, indicating the order of the Chinese syllables by superscript numbers. A hyphen will link the members of a compound corresponding to a single Chinese syllable (e.g., "ten-thousand" for *wan*).

In Pattern 1, syllable 1 matches syllable 4, syllable 2 matches syllable 5, syllable 3 has no match.

¹Southern ²branches ³cross [with] ⁴northern ⁵leaves,
¹New ²shoots ³mingle [with] ⁴old ⁵twigs.²⁵

[At the] ²pass [of] ¹Ch'in [I] ³look [at the] ⁵road [to] ⁴Ch'u,
[On the] ²bank [of the] ¹Pa [I] ³think [of the] ⁵deeps
      [of the] ⁴River.²⁶

We note that in both instances the internal parallelism features also in the parallelism of the couplet.

In Pattern 2, syllable 1 matches syllable 3, syllable 2 matches syllable 5, syllable 4 has no match.

¹Winter ²comes, ³autumn [has] ⁴not-yet ⁵departed.²⁷

¹Heaven [is] ²eternal, ³earth [is] ⁴naturally ⁵long-lasting.²⁸

In Pattern 3, syllable 1 matches syllable 3, syllable 2 matches syllable 4, syllable 5 has no match.

[A] ¹thousand ²autumns, ³ten-thousand ⁴years [his]
      ⁵fame [will last].²⁹

¹Three ²Gorges: ³one ⁴thread [of] ⁵sky,
¹Three ²Gorges: ³ten-thousand ⁴cords [of] ⁵springs.³⁰

In Pattern 4, syllable 1 matches a compound formed by syllables 3 and 4, syllable 2 matches syllable 5.

¹One ²strum, ³two [or] ⁴three ⁵sighs.³¹

[The] ¹country [is] ²broken, [the]
      ³mountains [and] ⁴rivers ⁵remain.³²

In Pattern 5, syllable 1 matches syllable 3, syllable 2 matches a compound formed by syllables 4 and 5.

[His] ¹body ²died, [his] ³soul ⁵soared [in] ⁴flight.³³

[I] ¹left [the] ²capital [and] ³returned [to my]
      ⁴native ⁵village.³⁴

A few general remarks on parallelism in the five-syllable line may be appropriate here. As noted earlier, the five-syllable line consists of two unequal segments, separated by the caesura, which nearly always comes between the second and the third syllable. When the poet wishes to match the two segments with each other, he has to compensate for the imbalance between them. He achieves this either by leaving one of the three syllables in the second half unmatched (Patterns 1, 2, and 3) or by combining two of the three syllables into a compound (Patterns 4 and 5). Of the five patterns, Pattern 1 is by far the most common.

The six-syllable line is a rather rare meter and has two caesuras which divide it into three equal segments of two syllables each. While internal parallelism is not *required* in this meter—any more than in any other meter—we often do find the third and the fourth syllable matching either the two preceding or the two following syllables. Examples of both occur in these two poems.

Poem 87
"The Three Terraces Inside the Palace"[35]
Wang Chien (*chin-shih* 775)
Form: *yüeh-fu*

North of the pond, south of the pond, grass is green;
In front of the palace, behind the palace, flowers are red.
The Son of Heaven: a thousand autumns, ten thousand years;
The Wei-yang Palace—bright moon, clear wind.

Poem 88 "The Three Terraces South of the River"[36]
Wang Chien
Form: *yüeh-fu*

In the trees, blossoms fall, blossoms open;
On the road, people go, people come.
Sad in the morning, sad in the evening, so we grow old;
In a hundred years, how many times passing the
  Three Terraces?

In the seven-syllable line, the possibilities for internal parallelism are far more numerous than in the shorter meters. I will give examples of twenty-two different patterns. It should be remembered that the seven-syllable line normally has a major caesura following the fourth syllable, and a minor one following the second syllable. In the first seven patterns, there will be three parallel phrases; in the remaining patterns, there will be two.

王建 「宮中三臺詞」 池北池南草綠 殿前殿後花紅 天子千秋萬歲 未央明月清風
王建 「江南三臺詞」 樹頭花落花開 道上人去人來 朝愁暮愁即老 百年幾度三臺

In Pattern 1, syllable 1 matches syllables 3 and 5; syllable 2 matches syllable 4 and a compound formed of syllables 6 and 7.

[The] [1]night [is] [2]long, [the] [3]wine [is] [4]plentiful, [the]
[5]music [is] [6]not-yet [7]over.[37]

[1]Spring [2]blossoms, [3]autumn [4]moon, [5]winter [6]ice [and] [7]snow.[38]

In Pattern 2, syllable 1 matches syllable 3 and a compound formed of syllables 5 and 6; syllable 2 matches syllables 4 and 7.

[The] [1]snowfall [has] [2]stopped, [the] [3]clouds [have]
[4]scattered, [the] [5]north [6]wind [is] [7]cold.[39]

[1]Willow [2]lake, [3]pine [4]island, [5]lotus [6]blossom [7]temple.[40]

In Pattern 3, syllable 1 matches syllables 3 and 5; syllable 2 matches syllable 4; syllables 6 and 7 have no match.

[1]Ten-thousand [2]grasses [and a] [3]thousand [4]flowers [7]open
[in the space of] [5]one [6]mealtime.[41]

[1]Ten-thousand [2]rivers, [a] [3]thousand [4]mountains, [7]all [5]one
[6]color.[42]

In Pattern 4, three compounds match each other; they are formed by syllables 1 and 2, syllables 3 and 4, and syllables 6 and 7; syllable 5 has no match.

[1]Barbarian [2]zithers, [3/4]guitars, [5]and [6]Tibetan [7]flutes.[43]

[1/2]Light, [3/4]carefree, [5]and [6/7]slanting.[44]

(In the original, each of the three adjectives in the second line is reduplicated.)

In Pattern 5, syllable 1 matches syllables 3 and 6; syllable 2 matches syllables 4 and 7; syllable 5 has no match.

[1]Nephrite [2]gates [and] [3]jade [4]steps [lead] [5]up [to the]
[6]pepper [-scented] [7]apartment;

[On] [1]patterned [2]windows [and] [3]ornamented [4]doors
[5]hang [6]silk-gauze [7]curtains.[45]

[The] [1] Southern [2]Road [and the] [3]Northern [4]Halls [are]
[5]linked [to the] [6]Northern [7]Quarter,

¹Five [-way] ²crossroads [and] ³three [-lane] ⁴streets ⁵lead
[to the] ⁶Three ⁷Markets.

[Poem 82, ll. 45–46]

In Pattern 6, syllable 1 matches syllables 3 and 5; syllables 2, 4, 6,
and 7 have no match.

¹Red ²phoenixes, ³crimson ⁴walls, [the] ⁵white ⁶sun ⁷setting;

¹Greenish ²oxen, ³purple ⁴carriage-curtains, ⁵red ⁶dust
⁷passing.⁴⁶

[In] ¹ eight ²directions [for] ³ten-thousand ⁴miles
[stretches]⁵one ⁶blue ⁷sky.

[Poem 16, l. ll]

In Pattern 7, syllable 1 matches syllables 3 and 6; syllables 2, 4, 5,
and 7 have no matches.

[A] ¹purple ²flute [and a] ³white ⁴crane ⁵ascend [to the]
⁶blue ⁷sky.⁴⁷

This pattern is used in the last two lines in the following poem.

Poem 89,
"Seeing Azaleas at Hsüan-ch'eng"⁴⁸
Li Po
Form: *chüeh-chü*

In the country of Shu I used to hear the nightjar;
In the city of Hsüan-ch'eng I see again the azaleas in
bloom.
¹One ²call, ³one ⁴turn, ⁶one ⁷broken ⁵heart;

[In the] ¹third ²spring [moon, in the] ³third ⁴month, [I]
⁵remember [the] ⁶three [lands of] ⁷Pa.

This poem calls for some commentary. The city of Hsüan-ch'eng
is in modern Anhwei Province. Shu and Pa are in modern Szechuan, Li Po's home. The poet is homesick. The nightjar of Shu is
linked to the azaleas through the legend of Tu Yü (see appendix 2).
The nightjar's call in late spring suggests nostalgia.

李白 「宣城見杜鵑花」 蜀國曾聞子規鳥 宣城還見杜鵑花 一叫一回腸一斷 三春三月
憶三巴

In addition to the internal parallelism there is parallelism between lines 1 and 2, and also between lines 3 and 4.

In Pattern 8, a compound formed by syllables 1 and 2 matches a compound formed by syllables 5 and 6; a compound formed by syllables 3 and 4 matches syllable 7.

[1]Lo-[2]yang [3/4]youths, [5]Han-[6]tan [7]girls.[49]

[1]P'eng-[2]lai [3/4]writings, [5]Chien-[6]an [7]bones.[50]

P'eng-lai, the name of a Taoist fairyland, was applied to the imperial library of the Han dynasty. The Chien-an era (196–220) was famous for the excellence of the literature it produced. "Bones" is a technical term in literary criticism, signifying vigor and substance.

In Pattern 9, a compound formed by syllables 1 and 2 matches syllable 5; syllable 3 matches syllable 6; syllable 4 matches syllable 7.

> [The] [1/2]cherries' [3]red [4]calixes, [the] [5]orchids' [6]purple [7]shoots.[51]

> [The] [1/2]lotuses [3]resembled [her] [4]face, [the] [5]willows [6]resembled [her] [7]eyebrows.[52]

In Pattern 10, syllable 1 matches syllable 5; syllable 2 matches syllable 6; a compound formed by syllables 3 and 4 matches syllable 7.

> [1]Nine [2]days [3]hustling [and] [4]bustling, [5]one [6]day [at] [7]leisure.[53]

> [The] [2]time [of] [1]parting [is] [3/4]easy [to get], [the] [6]time [of] [5]meeting [is] [7]hard.[54]

In Pattern 11, syllable 2 matches syllable 5; syllable 3 matches syllable 6; syllable 4 matches syllable 7; syllable 1 has no match.

> [She] [1]only [2]has [3]frost's [4]splendor, [she] [5]lacks [6]frost's [7]integrity.[55]

> [They do] [1]not [2]value [3]having [4]sons, [they] [5]value [6]having [7]daughters.[56]

In Pattern 12, syllable 1 matches syllable 5; syllable 3 matches syllable 6; syllable 4 matches syllable 7; syllable 2 has no match.

> [In the] [1]East [2]there-is [a] [3]green [4]dragon, [in the] [5]West [a] [6]white [7]tiger.[57]

[The] [1]pear [2]blossoms [are] [3]pale [4]white, [the] [5]willows [are] [6]dark [7]green.[58]

In Pattern 13, syllable 1 matches syllable 5; syllable 2 matches syllable 6; syllable 4 matches syllable 7; syllable 3 has no match.

[The] [2]day [of] [1]parting—[3]how [4]easy! [The] [6]day [of] [5]meeting [is] [7]hard.[59]

This line is very similar to Li Yü's verse cited above under Pattern 10.

[1]One [2]slice [of] [3]lonely [4]town, [5]ten-thousand [6]feet [of] [7]mountain.[60]

In Pattern 14, syllable 1 matches syllable 5; syllable 2 matches syllable 6; syllable 3 matches syllable 7; syllable 4 has no match.

[As a] [1]young [2]boy [I] [3]left [4]home, [as an] [5]old [6]man [I] [7]return.[61]

[On the] [1]east [2]side [the] [3]sun [4]rises, [on the] [5]west [6]side [7]rain.[62]

In Pattern 15, a compound formed by syllables 1 and 2 matches syllable 5; a compound formed by syllables 3 and 4 matches a compound formed by syllables 6 and 7.

[The] [1]sky's [2]color [is] [3]pure [and] [4]clean, [the] [5]air [is] [6]pleasantly [7]gentle.[63]

[The] [1]green [2]mountain [is] [3/4]secluded, [the] [5]river [is] [6/7]remote.[64]

In Pattern 16, syllable 3 matches syllable 6; syllable 4 matches syllable 7; syllables 1, 2, and 5 have no match.

[The] [1]amnesty [2]letter [in] [3]one [4]day [5]traveled [a] [6]thousand [7]miles.[65]

[I] [1]saw [2]flowers [at the] [3]southern [4]patch [and] [5]again [at the] [6]eastern [7]road.[66]

In Pattern 17, syllable 3 matches syllable 5; syllable 4 matches syllable 6; syllables 1, 2, and 7 have no match.

[1]Suddenly [2]there-were [3]white [4]hair [and a] [5]gray [6]mustache [7]growing.[67]

[For] [1]ten [2]miles, [3]yellow [4]clouds [and a] [5]white [6]sun [in
   the] [7]twilight.[68]

In Pattern 18, a compound formed by syllables 3 and 4 matches
a compound formed by syllables 5 and 6; syllables 1, 2, and 7 have
no match.

[The] [1]sage [2]ruler [3]day [after] [4]day, [5]night [after]
   [6]night [was] [7]brooding.[69]

[1]Surrounding [the] [2]temple, [3]thousands [and] [4]thousands,
   [5]myriads [and] [6]myriads [of] [7]peaks.[70]

In both examples, all the compounds are formed by reduplication.

In Pattern 19, syllable 1 matches syllable 6; syllable 2 matches
syllable 7; syllables 3, 4, and 5 have no match.

[2]Outside [the] [1]city, [the] [3]green [4]mountain [is] [5]as-if
   [7]inside [the] [6]house;
[From the] [1]eastern [2]house, [the] [3]running [4]water [5]enters
   [the] [6]western [7]adjoining [property].[71]

[The] [1]old [2]monk, [3]now [4]dead, [has] [5]become [a] [6]new
   [7]pagoda.[72]

In Pattern 20, syllable 1 matches syllable 5; syllable 2 matches
syllable 6; syllables 3, 4, and 7 have no match.

[A] [1]thousand [2]miles [to] [3]Chiang-[4]ling: [in] [5]one [6]day [I]
   [7]return.[73]

[1]This [2]year's [3]blossoms [4]match [5]last [6]year's [in] [7]beauty;
[1]Last [2]year's [3]people [4]by [5]this [6]year [have grown] [7]old.[74]

Noteworthy here is the chiasmus of the repetitive pattern in the
couplet.

In Pattern 21, syllable 1 matches syllable 3; syllable 2 matches
syllable 4; syllables 5, 6, and 7 have no match.

[In the] [1]morning [they] [2]come, [in the] [3]evening [they]
   [4]go [at] [5]I-[6]yang [7]Creek.[75]

[1]Orioles [2]call, [3]swallows [4]speak, [5]announcing [the]
   [6]New [7]Year.[76]

In Pattern 22, a compound formed by syllables 1 and 2 matches a compound formed by syllables 3 and 4; syllables 5, 6, and 7 have no match.

> 1/2Quiet [and] 3/4austere [is] 6Master 5Yang's 7life,
> 1/2Year-in [and] 3/4year-out 5a 6couch [full of] 7books.
>
> [Poem 82, ll. 65–66]

In the original, the four terms "quiet," "austere," "year in," and "year out" are each formed by reduplication.

> 1Wind, 2wind, 3rain, 4rain—5again 6spring [is] 7gone.
> 1White, 2white, 3red, 4red—5already 7no 6sights [are left].77

"White" and "red" refer to the flowers of spring.

Some general observations on internal parallelism and antithesis in the seven-syllable line may be useful here. This phenomenon, as we have seen, grows out of the general tendency to make two or more closely coordinated statements which through similarity or contrast, or a combination of both, enhance the poignancy of the poetic communication. This feature produces an aesthetically pleasing sense of balance and order. It also serves to bring out the internal structure of the seven-syllable line. Patterns 1–7 emphasize the tripartite nature of the line, with its caesuras after the second and fourth syllables. In some of the examples given for these schemes, a single line contains three statements or three separate objects, neatly coordinated. Patterns 8–15, on the other hand, divide the line into two unequal segments—syllables 1–4 and 3–7—and play the two segments against each other. To equalize the two segments, the same devices are used as in the five-syllable line, namely, two syllables are combined into a compound and matched with a single syllable (Patterns 8–10, 15), or one of the first four syllables remains unmatched (Patterns 11–14). In Patterns 16–18, the first two syllables remain outside the parallelistic pattern, and syllables 3–4 are matched with syllables 5–7. The resulting schemes are therefore the same as those encountered in the five-syllable line. In Patterns 19 and 20, syllables 3 and 4 are unaffected by the matching scheme. Finally, in Patterns 21 and 22, it is the last three syllables that are ignored, which makes possible perfect parallelism between syllables 1–2 and 3–4.

Internal parallelism within a single line is also used as a literary device by some Western poets, for example, Luis de Góngora in his *Soledades*. I will give four out of many possible examples from that poem:

> borró designios, bosquejó modelos (I, 98)
> [Erased designs, sketched models]

> su orgullo pierde y su memoria esconde (I, 211)
> [He loses his pride and hides his memory]

> calzada abriles y vestida mayos (I, 577)
> [Shod with Aprils and dressed in Mays]

> apenas hija hoy, madre mañana (I, 834)
> [Barely a daughter today, a mother tomorrow]

Another poet who conspicuously uses parallelism within the line is Alexander Pope (1688–1744). His "Epistle to Dr. Arbuthnot,"[78] for example, contains forty-two such lines, including these four:

> If foes, they write, if friends, they read me dead   [l. 32]

> Damn with faint praise, assent with civil leer   [l. 201]

> Nor dared on oath, nor hazarded a lie   [l. 397]

> By nature honest, by experience wise   [l. 400]

Victor Hugo, whose penchant for parallelistic couplets was noted earlier in this chapter, also has many lines with internal parallelism and antithesis. Here are a few examples from his poem "L'expiation":[79]

> On s'endormait dix mille, on se réveillait cent   [l. 39]
> [Ten thousand went to sleep, a hundred awoke]

> Roulant dans les fossés, se cachant dans les seigles   [l. 137]
> [Rolling in the ditches, hiding in the rye]

> Ou le consul de marbre ou l'empereur d'airain   [l. 232]
> [Either the consul in marble or the emperor in bronze]

Algernon Charles Swinburne (1837–1909) uses the same pattern in nearly a third of the fifty-six lines of a chorus (beginning "When the hounds of spring are on winter's traces") in his *Atalanta in Calydon*.[80]

Some of the most striking lines are the following:

> With lisp of leaves and ripple of rain   [l. 4]

> And time remembered is grief forgotten,
> And frosts are slain and flowers begotten   [ll. 29–30]

> And fruit and leaf are as gold and fire   [l. 37]

> Follows with dancing and fills with delight   [l. 43]

> To the limbs that glitter, the feet that scare
> The wolf that follows, the fawn that flies.   [ll. 56–57]

Though the most common occurrences of parallelism in Chinese verse are within the line and within the couplet, it is also found occasionally in larger prosodic units. There are cases where successive couplets match each other, as in Poem 92 below. Here are two other examples.

> Though the noble deem themselves noble,
> He considered them as dust and dirt.
> Though the humble deem themselves humble,
> He esteemed them as a thousand weight.[81]

> Dark hair is like an autumn garden,
> Once cut it does not grow again.
> Youth is like a hungry flower,
> After you catch a glimpse it does not shine again.[82]

"Hungry flower" is a striking phrase of which I have found no other occurrence.

Proceeding to a larger prosodic unit, we come to consider parallelism between stanzas. As we have seen, most poetic forms in Chinese poetry are not organized into stanzas. Among those which are, we find occasional parallelism. Some examples may be found in poems already cited. One of the processes of composition in the *Classic of Songs* is to have each stanza repeat the words of the preceding stanza, with only slight changes. (See Poems 10, 35, 45, and 103–105.) In the *tz'u* genre, many poems are divided into two stanzas, which are not always metrically identical. When they are, this prosodic symmetry is sometimes exploited for poetic purposes (see Poem 27). A striking example is the following poem.

Poem 90[83]
Hsin Ch'i-chi
Form: *tz'u*; tune pattern: "The Ugly Slave"

When I was young I did not know the taste of grief.
I loved to climb tall buildings,
I loved to climb tall buildings,
Composing original poems that artificially spoke of grief.

Now I fully know the taste of grief.
I want to speak of it but don't,
I want to speak of it but don't,
I just say, "What a nice cool autumn day!"

Though on the semantic level the poem displays much less parallelism than in its prosody, it uses the symmetry to good advantage to bring out the contrast between youth and experience, between utterance and emotion.

To conclude this chapter, I mention a poetic device which deliberately violates the norm of strict parallelism in consecutive lines. It may be called "oblique parallelism," and consists in arranging the matching words in such a way that they occupy *different* positions in their respective lines. This phenomenon has been pointed out by Chinese theoreticians.[84] To the examples given by them I will add three more.

[1]Young [and] [2]strong, [he] [3]left [4]home [and] [5]went
[away];
[1]Exhausted [and] [2]old, [he] [3]returned [and] [4]entered [the]
[5]gate.[85]

The matching words are: "young" (1.1) and "old" (2.2), "strong" (1.2) and "exhausted" (2.1), "left home" (1.3–4) and "entered the gate" (2.4–5), "went away" (1.5) and "returned" (2.3).

Poem 91, "The Princely Friend's Travels"[86]
Hsieh T'iao
Form: *ku-shih*

[The] [1]green [2]grass [3]spreads [4]like [5]silk-floss,
[On the] [1]forest [2]trees, [3]red [4]blossoms [5]open.

辛棄疾 〈醜奴兒〉 少年不識愁滋味 愛上層樓 愛上層樓 爲賦新詞强說愁　　而今識
盡愁滋味 欲說還休 欲說還休 卻道天涼好箇秋

謝朓 「王孫遊」 綠草蔓如絲 雜樹紅英發

¹No ²matter [if] ³you ⁴don't ⁵return—
[If] ¹you ²return, [the] ³fragrance [will] ⁴already [be] ⁵gone.

"Green grass" corresponds to "red blossoms," and "you don't return"
to "you return."

²Before [my] ¹eyes, ³a ⁴cup [of] ⁵wine;
¹Who [wants to] ²speak [of] ⁵fame ³after ⁴life?[87]

"Before [my] eyes" matches "after life," more literally, "after body."

Oblique parallelism is far less common than the straight variety.
Like other deviations from normal poetic practice, it is used to single
out certain phrases for special emphasis.

One more syntactic phenomenon that deserves consideration in
this chapter is the use of particles in the *fu* form. While literary
Chinese employs a large number of particles to indicate syntactic
relationships between sentences and between parts of sentences, most
of these particles are used primarily in prose. Poets, as we have
observed on numerous occasions, tend to place two statements side
by side, leaving it to the reader (or listener) to determine their
precise mutual relationship. An important deviation from this trend
is found in the *fu* form, which in other respects too exhibits some prosaic features in its verse portions. A new section of a *fu* is often
introduced by an initial particle, or a phrase containing one or more
particles. Since such an initial phrase constitutes an intrusion of a
prosaic element into a poetic composition, the head phrase is excluded from the line's syllabic count. For example, if a two-syllable
head phrase is used to introduce a section written in lines of four
syllables each, the first line of that section will consist of six syllables.
Two such supernumerary head phrases are used in "The Seven
Stimuli" (Poem 106 below), one of the oldest extant *fu*, namely, *yü
shih* "thereupon" (lines 112, 169, 227, 256, 292, and 355) and *yü
shih shih* "thereupon let (there be)" (lines 142, 175, and 187). In
Hsiao Kang's "The Flowering Plum" (Poem 1), *yü shih* is employed
just once, to mark the poem's divison into two parts. In Chiang Yen's
"Parting" (Poem 50), there is a greater variety of such supernumerary head phrases: *shih i* "thus" (lines 7 and 119), *ku* "therefore" (line 27), *chih jo* "such as" (line 29), *nai yu* "then there are"
(line 41), *huo nai* "or else" (line 55), *chih ju* "now consider" (line 67),
yu jo "again, suppose" (line 79), *t'ang yu* "if there is" (line 93), *hsia yu*

無論君不歸　君歸芳已歇

"in the world below there are" (line 105), *chih nai* "as for" (line 113), and *shih jen* "as a result, men('s)" (line 123). Note that only one of these phrases (*shih i*) is used more than once.

Another use of particles in the *fu* form is related to the principle of pairing. When two corresponding statements are juxtaposed, they are sometimes headed by a pair of coordinating particles, comparable to the Greek particles μέν . . . δέ "on the one hand . . . on the other hand." Several such pairs occur in "The Flowering Plum" (Poem 1), namely, *huo* . . . *cha* "now . . . now" (lines 15–16), also reversed as *cha* . . . *huo* (lines 29–30); *huo* . . . *huo* "either . . . or" (lines 41–42); and *chi* . . . *ch'ieh* "as . . . so" (lines 19–20). In the *fu* "Parting" (Poem 50) we have again *huo* . . . *cha* (lines 5–6), which in the context may be rendered as "now . . . then," juxtaposing a spring scene and an autumn scene.[88]

12

Special Parallelistic Phenomena

(Poems 92–105)

As we have seen in the preceding chapter, the tendency to arrange statements in parallel and antithetical units looms large in Chinese poetry. In this chapter we will consider some special phenomena arising out of this tendency. One of them we have already encountered. The ballad "Mu-lan" (Poem 49), it may be recalled, contains two instances of the pattern known as *hu-wen*, which literally means "reciprocal phrasing." A more explicit equivalent would be "two-part statement with mutual relevance." In other words, two parallel statements are so arranged that the statement made about the first topic is also applicable to the second, and vice versa. The two instances of *hu-wen* in "Mu-lan" are:

> Generals die in a hundred battles,
> Stout soldiers return after ten years.

> The he-hare's feet go hop and skip,
> The she-hare's eyes are muddled and fuddled.

The following *Shih ching* poem contains additional examples.

> After days of summer,
> After nights of winter,
> After a hundred years*
> I shall join him in his abode.†
> After nights of winter,
> After days of summer,
> After a hundred years,
> I shall join him in his chamber.[1]

---

*At the end of life.
†I shall remain faithful to him until death, and be buried with him in his grave.

"Days of summer" tacitly includes the *nights* of summer, and "nights of winter" includes the winter *days*. The poem's restrictive distribution is appropriate because summer is naturally associated with day, and winter with night.

The verbs "to go" and "to come" are paired, with mutual applicability, in the following passage (line 51 of Poem 106):

> Going by chariot and coming by sedan chair.

The idea being expressed here is that the prince travels always by one or the other of these conveyances, without getting any exercise. The movements are artificially differentiated and distributed among different modes of transportation.

Another instance of the same pattern occurs in the account of a battle in an anonymous ballad of Han times:

> They fought south of the walls,
> They died north of the ramparts.[2]

As "walls" and "ramparts" are near synonyms which could easily change places, so "south" and "north" are meant to be interchangeable, and likewise "fought" and "died." In other words, there was fighting and dying everywhere.

Let us try now to state more explicitly what is involved in the phenomenon of *hu-wen*. Parallelism, by imposing the same pattern on two separate statements, forces the reader to consider them in conjunction with each other. In the extreme case, represented by *hu-wen*, the association is so close that the normal boundaries between the two discrete statements are transgressed, and the predicate of one statement becomes simultaneously also the predicate of the other. We may consider this device as a triumph of poetic brevity. We may also view it as a process of redistribution. The elements of a given situation are removed from their normal context and rearranged to form startling new combinations which are not necessarily logical and realistic but eminently satisfying poetically. Thus "days" is separated from its complement, "nights," and coupled with "summer," and "nights" with "winter"; one mode of transportation is associated with "going," and another with "coming"; "fighting" is located in one part of the battlefield, and "dying" in another. A similar principle of unrealistic redistribution for aesthetic purposes may be seen in lines 17–20 of "Mu-lan" (Poem 49), where the purchase of four articles needed for war is distributed over four different markets.

The following examples of *hu-wen* are somewhat more complex.

> The flower path had not been swept for visitors,
> The overgrown gate is only now opened for you.[3]

The two parallel lines make sense only when taken in conjunction with each other: there had been no visitors for a long time, hence the path had not been swept, and the gate, overgrown, remained closed; now at last, on the occasion of your arrival, the path has been swept and the gate opened.

> The wind holds the green bamboo, graceful and clean;
> The rain envelops the red lotus, tender and fragrant.[4]

The first line speaks not only of the wind but also of the rain ("clean"), and the second line implies the action of the wind ("fragrant").

The following instance was perhaps inspired by the couplet just cited.

> Green splendor: the wind stirs the wheat;
> White fragments: the sun upsets the pond.[5]

Again, the agent of the second line ("sun") is involved in the first line as well ("splendor"), and the agent of the first line ("wind") affects the second line ("fragments," "upsets").

Two poems discussed earlier are also likely to contain instances of *hu-wen*. In the anonymous ballad "The Orphan" (Poem 47), I take the couplet

> At dawn they send me to draw water,
> At sunset, fetching water, I come home

to mean: from dawn to sunset they keep me running back and forth, going to the well and bringing back water. In discussing a poem by Hsieh Ling-yün (Poem 7) I proposed to see in each of the two opening couplets an instance of *hu-wen*, with the terms used in one line also applicable to its twin. Here and elsewhere, recognition of the *hu-wen* pattern enhances the understanding of the passages in question.

Hu-wen is a characteristic Chinese phenomenon with no exact counterpart in other literatures as far as I know. However, in Western poetry, too, phrases are sometimes paired in such a way that each of them becomes fully significant only in conjunction with the other. A typical baroque conceit, for instance, consists in juxtaposing two objects (or persons) and endowing each with a quality properly belonging to the other. (In Greek rhetoric, this is known as enallage.) Note the reversal of colors in the following description of the Titan Oceanus by Luis de Góngora:

> del padre de las aguas, coronado
> de blancas ovas y de espuma verde.[6]
> [Of the father of the water, crowned
> With white seaweeds and green foam.]

The exchange of essential properties is sometimes seen as a dynamic process; for example, the effect of a fisherman's song is said by Góngora to be:

> ondas endurecer, liquidar rocas.[7]
> [To harden waves, to liquefy rocks.]

Pairs of objects, persons, animals, or plants may also be made to exchange location. The elements, for instance, in which two different animals live may be switched around:

> Delphinum silvis adpingit, fluctibus aprum.[8]
> [He paints a dolphin in the forest, a wild boar
>   in the water.]

> que siendo brutos del viento,
> siendo aves de la tierra . . .[9]
> [Being beasts of the wind,
> Being birds of the earth . . .]

> . . . por seis hijas, por seis deidades bellas,
> del cielo espumas y del mar estrellas.[10]
> [By six daughters, by six beautiful goddesses,
> Foam of the sky and stars of the sea.]

The same sort of parodoxical reversal of location can be found in Chinese as well:

> Would you gather the wild-fig in the water?
> Or pluck the lotus-flower in the tree-tops?[11]

For an exchange of occupation we can again quote Góngora, who reverses the activities of two goddesses:

> cazar a Tetis veo
> y pescar a Diana con dos barquillas.[12]
> [I see Thetis hunting
> And Diana fishing with two little boats.]

The roles of poet and painter are exchanged in a sonnet by Lope de Vega (1562–1635):

> Marino, gran pintor de los oydos,
> y Rubens, gran poeta de los ojos.[13]
> [Marino, a great painter for the ear,
> And Rubens, a great poet for the eye.]

Such a belief in the affinity and mutual convertibility of poetry and painting is also common in China, particularly from the eleventh century on.[14]

In Chiang Yen's "Parting" (Poem 50, line 124) two verbs in parallel statements are made to change places:

> Hearts are splintered, and bones dismayed.

A closely related poetic device is the bringing together of two quite distinct objects and describing each in terms normally applicable to the other, to bring out their similarity. Lope de Vega makes such a reciprocal comparison of birds and flowers:

> Las aves parecen flores,
> entre las hojas las alas;
> las flores, aves que mezclan
> con sus colores las ramas.[15]
>
> [The birds resemble flowers,
> Their wings among the leaves;
> The flowers are like birds that mingle
> The branches with their colors.]

A related poetical figure brings together two things or concepts (often opposites) and converts each into the other:

> Tant loin sois-tu, toujours tu es présente:
> Pour près que soye, encore suis-je absent.[16]

[No matter how distant you are, always you're present;
However close I am, still am I absent.]

Le jour sera la nuit, la nuit sera le jour
Plutôt que je m'enflamme au feu d'un autre amour.[17]
[Day will be night, night will be day
Before I burn with the fire of another love.]

The concept of the affinity of opposites is forcefully expressed by
Christian Hofmann von Hofmannswaldau (1617–79) in the following passage, where contrasting objects are brought together by
the compelling power of love:

Ich weiss/das meine Gluth sich denckt zu hoch zu heben/
und dass mein Kieselstein zu Diamanten wil.
Doch die Erfahrung wird vor mich die Antwort geben/
der Stände Gleichheit ist der Liebe Possenspiel;
sie bindet Gold an Stahl und Garn zu weisser Seyde/
macht das ein Nesselstrauch/die edle Rose sucht/
zu Perlen legt sie Gras/zu Kohlen legt sie Kreyde/
und pfrofft auf wilden Baum offt eine süsse Frucht.
Sie lachet/was die Welt von Blutverwandnüss saget/
dis/was man Ehlich heist/hemmt ihre Pfeile nicht/
der Kayser wird ihr Knecht/der Jäger wird erjaget/
man spührt/wie ihre Macht/in Stock und Closter
    bricht.[18]

[I know that my ardor plans to rise too high,
And that my pebble longs for diamonds.
But experience will provide the answer for me,
The equality of ranks is Love's tomfoolery:
He binds gold to steel, and yarn to white silk,
He makes a nettle bush seek the noble rose,
With pearls he puts grass, with coals he puts chalk,
And on a wild tree he often grafts sweet fruit.
He laughs at what the world says of blood relationship;
That which is called marriage does not stop his arrows.
The emperor becomes his servant, the hunter is hunted
    down;
One feels his might breaking into stockades and
    cloisters.]

Still another poetic strategy consists in juxtaposing two sets of relationships, each of which is the reverse of the other. This strategy is pushed to an extreme by the Mexican poet Sor Juana Inés de la Cruz (1651–95) in some of her sonnets, of which I will cite one.

Al que ingrato me dexa, busco amante;
al que amante me sigue, dexo ingrata.
Constante adoro a quien mi amor maltrata;
maltrato a quien mi amor busca constante.

Al que trato de amor, hallo diamante;
y soy diamante, al que de amor me trata.
Triunfante quiero veer al que me mata,
y mato a quien me quiere veer triunfante.

Si a éste pago, padece mi deseo;
si ruego a aquél, mi pundonor enojo:
de entrambos modos infelix me veo.

Pero yo, por mejor partido escojo,
de quien no quiero, ser violento empleo,
que de quien no me quiere, vil despojo.[19]

[Him who ungratefully leaves me, I seek lovingly;
Him who lovingly pursues me, I leave ungratefully.
With constancy I adore the one who maltreats my love;
I maltreat the one who seeks me with constancy.

Him whom I treat with love, I find a diamond;
And a diamond I am to him who treats me with love.
Triumphant I want to see him who kills me,
And I kill him who wants to see me triumphant.

If I reward this one, my desire suffers;
If I beg that one, I vex my sense of honor;
Both ways I find myself unhappy.

But I choose, as the better part,
To be the violent object of the one I love not,
Rather than the vile spoils of the one who loves me not.]

A Chinese poet who uses this pattern repeatedly is the Buddhist monk Han-shan, the author of Poems 92–94.

Poems 92–94
Han-shan (early seventh century?)
Form: *ku-shih*

Poem 92[20]

When an old man takes a young wife
His hair is white, she can't stand it.
When an old woman marries a young man
Her face is sallow, he doesn't love her.
When an old man takes an old wife
Neither rejects the other.
When a young woman marries a young man
Both have tender feelings for each other.

Poem 93[21]

In the house to the east lives an old woman,
She's been rich these three to five years.
She used to be poorer than I,
Now she laughs at me for having no money.
She laughs at me for being behind her,
I laugh at her for being ahead of me.
We laugh at each other as if we'd never stop,
One in the east, the other in the west.

Poem 94[22]

If you want to know a simile for life and death,
Take ice and water for comparison.
When water congeals it becomes ice,
When ice melts it again becomes water.
What has died is bound again to live,
What is born must revert to death.
Ice and water do not hurt each other,
Life and death in turn are both beautiful.

The reversal of a relationship is sometimes connected with a

寒山　老翁娶少婦　髪白婦不耐　老婆嫁少夫　面黃夫不愛　老翁娶老婆　一一無棄背
少婦嫁少夫　兩兩相憐態

東家一老婆　富來三五年　昔日貧於我　今笑我無錢　渠笑我在後　我笑渠在前　相笑儻
不止　東邊復西邊

欲識生死譬　且將冰水比　水結即成冰　冰消返成水　已死必應生　出生還復死　冰水不
相傷　生死還雙美

comparison: A = B, B = A. An example is the following couplet from a poem by Chang Yüeh (667–730):

> Last year in South Ching the plum trees resembled snow,
> This year in North Chi the snow is like plum trees.[23]

Reversibility in such paired comparisons serves as an indication of similarity and contrast. In other contexts, it is employed to express mutual need, as in this couplet from an anonymous Chinese ballad of the Northern Dynasties, dating from the fifth or sixth century:

> A stout lad needs a swift horse,
> A swift horse needs a stout lad.[24]

The same pattern of reversibility can also be used to render an intellectual puzzle. It is so used by Johann Scheffler (Angelus Silesius, 1624–77):

> Ich weiss nicht, was ich bin; ich bin nicht, was ich weiss,
> Ein Ding und nit ein Ding, ein Stüpfchen und ein Kreis.[25]
> [. . . I know not what I am; I am not what I know,
> A thing and not a thing, a little dot and a circle. . . .]

While the principle of pairing is ubiquitous in Chinese poetry, parallelism is not necessarily binary. Each of the three kinds of parallelism may occasionally involve more than two members. A passage of three successive lines paralleling each other in form and content occurs in Poem 106 (lines 434–36); the literal translation given here shows the parallelism clearly:

> The birds don't get to fly away,
> The fish don't get to turn around,
> The beasts don't get to run off.[26]

Another *fu*, written at about the same time as the one from which I have just quoted, contains the following passage, speaking of the Emperor:

> He roams through the Park of the Six Arts,
> He speeds along the road of kindness and righteousness,
> He contemplates the grove of the *Spring and Autumn* [*Annals*].[27]

Among the nine poetic forms represented in this study, the only one in which triple parallelism is not extremely rare is the *san-ch'ü*.

But even here it is far less common than binary parallelism. We find both parallelism between three successive lines and triple parallelism within a single line in *san-ch'ü*, as the following examples will show. In the first poem, the last three lines are parallel.

Poem 95[28]

Liu Shih-chung (flourished late thirteenth century)

Form: *san-ch'ü*; tune pattern: "Four Pieces of Jade"

Floating in a colored boat,
Holding her red sleeve,
A new tune for the song about Yi-chou.
Facing the cup there is still more: a friend aloof from
    the world.
Above the waves a gull,
Beneath the blossoms a dove,
Beside the lake a willow.

Parallelism in the last three lines is a frequent (but not obligatory) feature of this tune pattern. The following poem is another instance.

Poem 96, "Enjoying Leisure"[29]

Chang K'o-chiu (ca. 1270–ca. 1350)

Form: *san-ch'ü*; tune pattern: "Four Pieces of Jade"

I keep away from gossip,
I seek the unconventional.
The earth is warm: in the South the time is ripe for
    swallows to nest;
Man is at leisure: north of the river spring is priceless.
Seven kinds of tea,
Five-colored melons,*
Four seasons of flowers.

We may note, incidentally, that this tune pattern tends to combine triple parallelism with the much more common and familiar binary parallelism: line 2 parallels line 1, and line 4 parallels line 3.

In the next poem, three parallel lines are placed at the beginning.

---

*Such melons, grown by a certain Shao P'ing in the third century B.C., were said to be particularly tasty. Whether the "five colors" were on the outside or inside I do not know.

劉時中 〈四塊玉〉 泛綵舟 携紅袖 一曲新声按伊州 尊前更有忘機友 波上鷗 花底
鳩 湖畔柳

張可久 〈四塊玉〉 「樂閒」 遠是非 尋瀟灑 地暖江南燕宜家 人閒水北春無價 七品
茶 五色瓜 四季花

Poem 97, "In Lu-ch'ing's Cottage"[30]
Chang K'o-chiu
Form: *san-ch'ü;* tune pattern:
"The Sky Is Clear Like Gauze"

Green moss, old trees—gloomy.
Dark clouds, autumn river—distant.
Red leaves, mountain cottage—small.
Who ever came here?
A man in search of plum trees crossed the creek bridge.

In the next poem (by the same author as the last two examples)
there will be two series of triple parallelism: lines 3–5 and lines 6–8.

Poem 98, "Spring Evening"[31]
Chang K'o-chiu
Form: *san-chü;* tune pattern:
"People and Moon Are Complete"

Lush growth of fragrant grasses, a scattering of spring clouds,
Sadness in the evening sun.
In the low pavilion, farewell wine;
On the smooth lake, a painted boat;
By the drooping willow, a spirited piebald.

One sound of a calling bird,
One spell of evening rain,
One fit of easterly wind.
The peach blossoms are all blown down.
The fair one, where is she?
The gate is closed on fallen red blossoms.

The poem laments the absence of a beloved woman, and is filled
with the conventional images of separation that we encountered in
chapter 9: grass, clouds, sunset, a farewell banquet in a pavilion,
a boat, a willow, a horse, a bird, rain, wind, a closed gate, and fallen
blossoms. The two series of parallel lines are artfully arranged. In
the first series (lines 3–5), each line consists of two symmetrical halves,
and each half is made up of a noun preceded by a modifier. The
first noun is a locus of separation, and its modifier describes its

張可久 〈天淨沙〉「魯卿庵中」 青苔古木蕭蕭 蒼雲秋水迢迢 紅葉山齋小小 有誰
曾到 探梅人過溪橋

張可久 〈人月圓〉「春晚」 萋萋芳草春雲乱 愁在夕陽中 短亭別酒 平湖畫舫 垂柳
驕驄 一声啼鳥 一番夜雨 一陣東風 桃花吹盡 佳人何在 門掩殘紅

appearance and shape. The second noun is, as it were, an instrument
of departure. While this first series of three parallel lines recalls the
day of parting, the second series (lines 6–8) describes three natural
phenomena occurring at the moment of recollection. Each of the
three phenomena sharply drives home the painful sensation of
separation. The parallelism between the three lines receives maximum audibility through the repetition of the initial word "one."
This word, furthermore, by contrast draws attention to the multi-
plicity of the painful perceptions. There is an additional implied
contrast between the shortness of each phenomenon and the length
of the separation. Still another contrast is provided by the tune title,
which verbalizes the wish whose unfulfillment is the burden of the
poem.

The following poem, cast in the same tune pattern, exhibits the
same feature of triple parallelism in lines 3–5 and again in lines 6–8.

Poem 99,
"Longing for the Past at Sweet Dew Temple"[32]
Hsü Tsai-ssu (born ca. 1280?, died before 1330)
Form: *san-ch'ü;* tune pattern:
"People and Moon Are Complete"

A tall monastery on the river bank: a temple from a
   bygone age.
The aspect of autumn enters the Ch'in-huai Valley.
Crumbling walls, fragrant grasses,
Empty verandahs, fallen leaves,
Hidden steps, green moss.

The distant friend is going south,
The evening sun is setting in the west,
The river water is coming east.
The magnolia flowers are here,
The mountain monk wonders:
Who knows for whom they blossom?

We have here a contemplation of the past in a manner reminiscent of poems considered in chapter 9. The poet's reflections are
occasioned by his visit to Sweet Dew Temple on Mount Pei-ku,

徐再思 〈人月圓〉「甘露懷古」 江皋樓觀前朝寺　秋色入秦淮　敗垣芳草　空廊落葉
深砌蒼苔　遠人南去　夕陽西下　江水東來　木蘭花在　山僧試問　知爲誰開

near Chen-chiang, in modern Kiangsu Province, overlooking the Yangtze River. The temple was so named because sweet dew (a manifestation of divine favor) was said to have come down from heaven when it was built in the third century A.D. Here, as in other poems considered, evocation of the past is combined with longing for a distant friend whose identity remains vague. The images relevant to contemplation of the past and simultaneously to separation are familiar ones: the river flowing east and its bank, autumn, sunset, fallen leaves, grass, moss, blossoms, an ancient building in ruins, emptiness and solitude.

The two series of parallel lines are as artfully structured as in the preceding poem. The first series (lines 3–5) even duplicates its structure. The first noun in each line is a part of the ruined building, and the second noun always belongs to the plant kingdom. The second series (lines 6–8) has a modifier as the first word of each line, the second word is always a noun, the third is an adverb indicating a point of the compass, and the last word is a verb of motion. The three directional adverbs in conjunction with the three verbs of motion dynamically expand the scope of the scene, moving it outward in three different directions. Yet the effect of this threefold expansion is not exhilarating but depressing, since all three movements signify disappearance and loss; the friend moves farther away, the sun is about to set, and the river's eastward flow represents, as we have seen repeatedly, the irretrievable loss of the past. In sharp contrast with this sustained emphasis on disappearance stands the word *tsai*, "are here," at the end of line 9. But this positive note is followed by a negative conclusion: the presence of the beautiful flowers is frustrated by the absence of those who might enjoy it.

We have seen five poems of the *san-ch'ü* genre exemplifying parallelism between three successive lines. In the next two poems we will find triple parallelism within single lines.

Poem 100, "Autumn"[33]
Pai P'u (born 1226, died in or after 1291)

Form: *san-ch'ü*; tune pattern: "The Sky Is Clear Like Gauze"

> Lone village, setting sun, remnants of colored clouds,
> Light mist, old tree, jackdaw.
> A single dot—a flying goose—casts a shadow below.

白樸　〈天淨沙〉　「秋思」　孤村落日殘霞　輕烟老樹寒鴉　一點飛鴻影下

Blue mountains, green water,
White grass, red leaves, yellow flowers.

Here we have internal parallelism in every line except the third. In addition, lines 1 and 2 parallel each other. (The phrase *ts'an hsia*, "remnants of colored clouds," consists of an adjective and a noun; "jackdaw" is literally "cold crow.") Line 3 is the only complete sentence (in the prose sense of the term) in the entire poem. It is flanked on both sides by strings of two-syllable phrases, each made up of an adjective and a noun. But on closer inspection, we do not find just a series of uniform phrases on either side of the middle line. Rather, the adjective-plus-noun phrases fall into groups, and each group coincides with a line of verse. The clouds are colored by the sun as it sets over the village. The jackdaw perches on a tree chilled by the evening mist of autumn. The mountains are matched with water, forming a conventional pair that we have encountered several times, while the last line, with its three botanical nouns, resumes the pattern of triple parallelism. Of the six adjectives in the first two lines, all except one ("light") suggest decline and solitude; they fit the autumn mood. In the final couplet, all the adjectives denote colors, and those of the last line are colors associated with autumn.

The following poem, written in the same tune pattern, employs similar techniques and was perhaps intended to surpass Pai P'u's. It will be our last example of the *san-ch'ü* genre.

Poem 101, "Autumn Thoughts"[34]
Ma Chih-yüan (ca. 1260–ca. 1325)
Form: *san-ch'ü*; tune pattern:
"The Sky Is Clear Like Gauze"

Withered creepers, old tree, crow at dusk.
Small bridge, flowing water, flat sand.*
Old road, west wind, skinny horse.
The evening sun sets in the West.
A heartbroken man at the edge of the sky.

Here we have triple internal parallelism in each of the first three

---

*Variant: "a human dwelling" in place of "flat sand."

青山綠水　白草紅葉黃花

馬致遠　〈天淨沙〉「秋思」　枯藤老樹昏鴉　小橋流水平沙　古道西風瘦馬　夕陽西下

斷腸人在天涯

lines, and these three lines also parallel each other. As in the preceding poem, each line constitutes a unit, and again, there is no predicate in these three lines, just a succession of two-syllable phrases, each consisting of a noun preceded by a modifier. Most of the modifiers have again to do with decline and old age. In addition, we have the conventional complexes of time passing (evening, autumn, senescence, flowing water) and separation. (The latter becomes clear only at the very end of the poem.) The images are all taken from nature and, in the customary manner, form part of the visible scene. The appearance of a human figure is delayed until the last line.

At this point we may recall our earlier examination of internal parallelism in the seven-syllable line. Though binary matching turned out to be most common, we also found seven types of triple internal parallelism. (See chapter 11, Patterns 1–7.)

As for multiple coordination on a larger scale, we have already encountered some instances in the poems studied in previous chapters. Poem 47 told of *three* trips taken by the orphan. Poem 7 involved *three* places. The folk song cycle "Nine Looms" from which we considered two excerpts (Poems 18–19) consisted of *nine* songs, each organized in a similar structure. Many of the songs in the earliest extant anthology, *The Classic of Songs*, are divided into stanzas, and there is often only slight variation from stanza to stanza. Several poems from that anthology have already been discussed, and we will consider three more now.

Poem 102, *Shih ching*, no. 77
Anonymous
Form: *Shih ching*

Shu is in the fields,
Nobody lives in our street.
It's not that nobody lives there
But they're not as good as Shu,
He is truly handsome and kind.

Shu is in the hunting fields,
Nobody drinks wine in our street.
It's not that nobody drinks wine

詩經77 「叔于田」 叔于田 巷無居人 豈無居人 不如叔也 洵美且仁 叔于狩 巷無
飲酒 豈無飲酒

But they're not as good as Shu,
He is truly handsome and good.

Shu went to the countryside,
Nobody drives horses in our street.
It's not that nobody drives horses
But they're not as good as Shu,
He is truly handsome and brave.

The pattern of variation is clear. Changes occur only at the end of the first, second, third, and fifth line of every stanza; otherwise the stanzas are identical. This organizing principle of repetition with only slight variations at fixed places in successive stanzas informs a large portion of *The Classic of Songs*. It is akin to the kind of variation to be found in music and dance. (All pieces in this classical anthology are known to have been songs, and many were probably accompanied by a dance.)

A charming feature of this poem is the psychology of the woman in love, who feels that nobody exists except her lover. Also interesting psychologically is the reversal, in the third line of each stanza, of the statement made in the preceding line, being a juxtaposition of the subjective and the objective view. A similar reversal, again associated with being in love, occurs in each stanza of the following song.

Poem 103, *Shih ching*, no. 64
Anonymous
Form: *Shih ching*

She gave me a quince,
I requite her with a fine jade pendant.
It is not a requital
But a token of eternal love.

She gave me a peach,
I requite her with a fine jasper pendant.
It is not a requital
But a token of eternal love.

She gave me a plum,
I requite her with a fine black-jade pendant.

不如叔也　洵美且好　叔適野　巷無服馬　豈無服馬　不如叔也　洵美且武

詩經64 「木瓜」 投我以木瓜　報之以瓊琚　匪報也　(4)永以爲好也　投我以木桃 報之
以瓊瑤　匪報也　(8)永以爲好也　投我以木李　報之以瓊玖

> It is not a requital
> But a token of eternal love.

Here the changes are even fewer: only the last syllable of the first and of the second line varies from stanza to stanza.

Poem 104, *Shih ching*, no. 48
Anonymous
Form: *Shih ching*

Where do I pick dodder?
South* of Mei.
Who is on my mind?
The beautiful eldest daughter of the Chiangs.   4
She made a date with me in the mulberry grove,
She invited me upstairs,
She saw me off on the bank of the Ch'i.

Where do I pick wheat?   8
North of Mei.
Who is on my mind?
The beautiful eldest daughter of the Yis.
She made a date with me in the mulberry grove,   12
She invited me upstairs,
She saw me off on the bank of the Ch'i.

Where do I pick turnips?
East of Mei.   16
Who is on my mind?
The beautiful eldest daughter of the Yungs.
She made a date with me in the mulberry grove,
She invited me upstairs,   20
She saw me off on the bank of the Ch'i.

The town of Mei and the Ch'i River are located in what is now northeastern Honan Province. According to some commentators, *sang-*

---

*This interpretation of *hsiang* is suggested by Karlgren; others take it to mean "in the countryside."

匪報也　（12）永以爲好也

詩經48「桑中」　爰采唐矣　沫之鄉矣　云誰之思　（4）美孟姜矣　期我乎桑中　要我乎上宮
送我乎淇之上矣　（8）爰采麥矣　沫之北矣　云誰之思　美孟弋矣　（12）期我乎桑中　要我
乎上宮　送我乎淇之上矣　爰采葑矣　（16）沫之東矣　云誰之思　美孟庸矣　期我乎桑中
（20）要我乎上宮　送我乎淇之上矣

chung, which I have rendered "in the mulberry grove," and *shang-kung,* translated as "upstairs," are also place names. (See Poem 50, lines 107–08.) Lines 6, 13, and 20 in my interpretation imply intimacy. Following the precedent set by this poem, the mulberry grove became a symbol for amorous trysts in later poetry.

The poem presents a puzzling situation. According to the old commentaries, the girls to whom the three stanzas refer are three separate persons. One would have to suppose, then, that the singer proclaims his love of three girls in a single song; that each of the three is the eldest daughter of her family; and that each of them meets him in a mulberry grove, becomes intimate with him, and goes with him to the bank of the Ch'i River. To eliminate these absurdities, some modern scholars have suggested that the same girl is referred to in every stanza.[35] But this interpretation creates another difficulty: How can one woman bear three different surnames? A helpful note is supplied by Hsü Po-cheng (eighteenth century). He states that names such as "eldest daughter of the Chiangs," "eldest daughter of the Yis," and "eldest daughter of the Yungs" are type names for a beautiful girl.[36] This assertion is borne out by another poem of the *Classic of Songs* (no. 8) which speaks of "the beautiful eldest daughter of the Chiangs." But if one accepts Hsü's suggestion, one may still wonder: why *three* type names?

To solve the dilemma, we must stop looking at the poem as though it were a real life happening. We are faced with a man imagining an ideal situation and expressing it in the form of a song with a conventional metric pattern. The resulting poem works out the imaginary situation in three different ways, presenting three alternatives, all equally pleasant to contemplate. Conforming to the metric requirements of the genre, the three parts differ only at a few fixed points— in this case, the third syllable of the first, second, and fourth line of each stanza—and these syllables rhyme with each other in each stanza: *t'ang* "dodder" rhymes with *hsiang* "south" and with *Chiang,* and correspondingly in the other two stanzas. To those who object that this interpretation is too artificial for a genuine love poem, the reply would be that all poetry is artificial to a certain extent. In real life, an emotional outburst would not employ measured lines, rhyme, or stanzas.

From these early anonymous songs we turn now to a later imitation similar in form but different in spirit.

Poem 105, "Four Sorrows"[37]
Chang Heng (78–139)
Form: *ku-shih*

My love is at Mount T'ai.
I want to go and be with her but Mount Liang-fu blocks
  the way.
I turn and look east, tears moisten my gown.
She gave me a knife inlaid with gold,
What shall I give her in return? A precious jade.
The road is far, no one takes me there—I fret.
How much I grieve! My heart is troubled and bothered.

My love is at Kuei-lin.
I want to go and be with her but the Hsiang River is deep.
I turn and look south, tears moisten my robe.
She gave me a jade zither ornament,
What shall I give her in return? A double jade dish.
The road is far, no one takes me there—I worry.
How much I grieve! My heart is troubled and hurt.

My love is at Han-yang.
I want to go and be with her but the Lung Slope is long.
I turn and look west, tears moisten my clothes.
She gave me a sable cloak,
What shall I give her in return? A "bright moon" pearl.
The road is far, no one takes me there—I pace to and fro.
How much I grieve! My heart is troubled and twisted.

My love is at Yen-men.
I want to go and be with her but it's snowing heavily.
I turn and look north, tears moisten my scarf.
She gave me a set of embroidered brocade,
What shall I give her in return? A green jade table.
The road is far, no one takes me there—I sigh.
How much I grieve! My heart is troubled and unhappy.

張衡 「四愁詩」 我所思兮在太山 欲往從之梁父艱 側身東望涕霑翰 美人贈我金錯刀
何以報之英瓊瑤 路遠莫致倚逍遙 何爲懷憂心煩勞 我所思兮在桂林 欲往從之湘水深
側身南望涕霑襟 美人贈我琴琅玕 路遠莫致倚惆悵 何以報之雙玉盤 何爲懷憂心煩傷
我所思兮在漢陽 欲往從之隴阪長 側身西望涕霑裳 美人贈我貂襜褕 何以報之明月珠
路遠莫致倚踟躕 何爲懷憂心煩紆 我所思兮在雁門 欲往從之雪紛紛 側身北望涕霑巾
美人贈我錦繡段 何以報之青玉案 路遠莫致倚增歎 何爲懷憂心煩惋

The poem is clearly indebted to two poems from the *Classic of Songs*: nos. 48 and 64 (Poems 104 and 103 above). From the former it has borrowed the pattern of four parallel stanzas devoted to four different girls on the speaker's mind; from the latter it has taken the idea of a series of gifts and requitals. The artificial nature of Chang Heng's construct is obvious. The phrases that sounded fresh and spontaneous in the original songs have a hollow, contrived ring in his imitation.

Whether or not the poem was intended as a love poem is by no means certain. Possibly the speaker's longing for distant girls is an allegory for the poet's frustration in his failure to achieve some moral or political purpose, on the model of the allegories of Ch'ü Yüan's "Li sao" ("The Sorrow of Parting"), which has inspired so many Chinese poets. Such an interpretation is suggested in a preface to Chang Heng's poem which, though probably not written by Chang Heng himself, is worth quoting.

> Chang Heng did not enjoy spending much time on his official mysterious work.* During the Yang-chia era (132–36), he was [therefore] transferred to a provincial post as Chief Administrator of [the fief of the Prince of] Ho-chien. The Prince was at that time haughty and extravagant, without any respect for the law, and there were also [in his fief] many powerful and grasping men. From the moment that Heng arrived at his post he governed with severity. He managed to investigate all the districts of the fief, secretly noted the names of those who committed wicked and cunning crimes, and had them arrested by constables. None of them offered resistance. He also seized vagabonds. All tramps became frightened and left the territory. Peace and order reigned in the fief, lawsuits ceased, and the prisons were empty. At that time, the Empire was gradually becoming more corrupt. [Chang Heng] felt sad and frustrated, and wrote the poem "Four Sorrows." Following Ch'ü Yüan's model, he used fair women to represent the ruler, precious objects to represent humaneness and righteousness, and deep water and heavy snow to represent inferior men. His idea was to requite the reigning emperor's favor with this moralistic

---

*He held the office of Court Astrologer, in charge of probing the mysteries of the celestial constellations.

work and to offer it to him, but he was afraid that slanderous, evil courtiers would not let it pass.

Chang Heng's poem may not appeal to the modern reader, but it did meet with response in his own time, and was imitated repeatedly. Two extant imitations are by Fu Hsüan (217–78) and Chang Tsai (flourished late third century), both entitled "Imitation of 'Four Sorrows.' "[38] In their pattern and even in their wording they follow Chang Heng's poem quite closely.

13

An Early *Fu*: "The Seven Stimuli"

(POEM 106)

This final chapter will be devoted to a longer work, partly in prose but largely in verse, titled "The Seven Stimuli." It consists of seven sections, each dealing with a separate stimulus, plus an introductory section. I do not know why the author, Mei Sheng (his name may also be read Mei Ch'eng), chose the number seven; perhaps because it is a magic number in China, as elsewhere.* The text is preserved in the sixth-century anthology *Wen hsüan*, which is arranged by genres. The anthology sets up *ch'i* "sevenses" as a separate genre, and gives three instances, Mei Sheng's and two imitations. (An excerpt from one of these will be quoted later in this chapter.) "The Seven Stimuli" was in fact imitated many times. The late Hsü Shih-ying lists no less than fifty-four "sevenses" by fifty-one authors from the second century of our era to the nineteenth; twenty-one of these pieces have survived complete.[1] All stick closely to Mei Sheng's pattern, and even to his ideas. But as far as generic classification is concerned, "The Seven Stimuli" is often considered as an early instance of the *fu*, and that is how it will be treated here.

Poem 106, "The Seven Stimuli"[2]
Mei Sheng (died 140 B.C.)
Form: *fu*

[Introduction]
[*Prose lines 1–7*] The Heir Apparent of Ch'u was ill, and a

---

*It may or may not be significant that in "The Seven Stimuli" there are three lists of seven items, along with many lists of larger and smaller numbers: two lists of seven dishes each in the Second Stimulus (ll. 134–39, 144–51) and a list of seven "beautiful people" in the Fourth Stimulus (l. 229).

枚乘 「七發」 楚太子有疾

186

visitor from Wu came to inquire after his health. "I have heard," he said, "that your Royal Highness's precious body has not been well. Has there been any relief?" The Heir Apparent replied: "I feel weak. I respectfully thank you for your concern." The visitor continued:

"At present the whole world is at peace,   8
The Four Quarters are in harmony.
Your Highness now has a full life before you.
But in my opinion,
You have long been addicted to comforts and
   pleasures,   12
Day and night you never stop.
Evil ether has invaded you,
Your chest seems to be blocked.
Listless and without a will of your own,   16
You sigh and suffer from hangovers.
Troubled and frightened,
You find no sleep when you lie down.
You hear things where there is no noise   20
And detest the sound of human voices.
Your vital spirits disperse and scatter,
And all the hundred diseases develop.
Hearing and sight are blurred and dimmed,   24
Joy and anger are not normal.
If the illness lasts long without being stopped,
Your great life will be ruined.

[*Prose lines 28–34*] Isn't that Your Royal Highness's condition?" The Heir Apparent replied: "I respectfully thank you for your concern. Owing to our sovereign's strength, though the symptoms appear from time to time, my illness has not gone to that extent." "Nowadays," the visitor said,

"The young men of the best families
Invariably live in palaces, reside in sheltered
   quarters.   36

而吳客往問之曰　伏聞太子玉體不安　(4)亦少閒乎　太子曰　憊謹謝客　客因稱曰　(8)今時天下安寧　四宇和平　太子方富於年　意者　(12)久耽安樂　日夜無極　邪氣襲逆　中若結轖　(16)紛屯澹淡　嘘唏煩醒　惕惕怵怵　臥不得暝　(20)虛中重聽　惡聞人声　精神越渫　百病咸生　(24)聰明眩曜　悅怒不平　久執不廢　大命乃傾　(28)太子豈有是乎太子曰　謹謝客　賴君之力　(32)時時有之　然未至於是也　客曰　今夫貴人之子　(36)必宮居而閨處

With protective nurses within
And magisterial tutors without
There is no chance for social mingling.
Drinks and foods are pleasantly flavored, sweet   40
    and crisp,
Meat and wine are fat and strong.
Clothes are of many kinds and plentiful, light yet
    warm,
Melting hot, sweltering and scorching.

[*Prose lines 44–95*] Even one who had the firmness of metal or
stone would melt and dissolve, break and disintegrate under
these circumstances. How much more one built around sinews
and bones! Therefore it is said: He who gives in to the desires
of ear and eye, who indulges in the comforts of body and limbs,
will hurt the harmony of blood and vessels. Indeed, going by
chariot and coming by sedan chair has been called 'an omen of
paralysis.' Secluded apartments and cool palaces have been
called 'go-betweens of chills and fevers.' Gleaming teeth and
moth-like eyebrows have been called 'axes that cut vitality.'
Sweet, crisp, fat, strong food and wine have been called 'drugs
that rot the intestines.'³ At present Your Royal Highness's
complexion is pale, your four limbs are numb, your sinews and
bones are disintegrating, your blood vessels are enlarged, your
hands and feet are inert. Girls from Yüeh serve you in front,
beauties from Ch'i wait on you in back. Always coming and
going from one amusement and feast to another, yielding to
pleasures in secluded rooms and private apartments—this is
swallowing poison voluntarily, and playing with the claws and
teeth of wild beasts. By now this has gone quite far. There is a
chronic congestion which does not come out into the open.⁴
Even if you had Pien Ch'üeh as a physician and Wu Hsien as a
shaman, nothing could be accomplished. Now in the case of an
illness like Your Royal Highness's, the only proper thing to do is

內有保母　外有傅父　欲交無所　(40)飲食則溫淳甘膬　腥醲肥厚　衣裳則雜遝曼煖　燀
爍熱暑　(44)雖有金石之堅　猶將銷鑠而挺解也　況其在筋骨之間乎哉　故曰　(48)縱耳
目之欲　恣支體之安者　傷血脈之和　且夫出輿入輦　(52)命曰蹷痿之機　洞房清宮　命
曰寒熱之媒　皓齒蛾眉　(56)命曰伐性之斧　甘脆肥膿　命曰腐腸之藥　今太子膚色靡曼
(60)四支委隨　筋骨挺解　血脈淫濯　手足惰窳　(64)越女侍前　齊姬奉後　往來遊讌　縱
恣乎曲　房隱間之中　(68)此甘餐毒藥　戲猛獸之爪牙也　所從來者至深遠　淹滯永久
而不發　(72)雖令扁鵲治內　巫咸治外　尚何及哉　今如太子之病者　(76)獨宜世之君子

to have gentlemen outstanding in this age for their broad experience and retentive memory seize the opportune moment to speak to you of the things they know, to reform your thoughts and change your views, constantly at your side, like the wings that lift a bird. Then neither the joy of immersion in pleasures nor the idea of colossal licentiousness nor the intention of idle indulgence will be able to reach you." "All right," said the Heir Apparent, "when my illness is gone, I propose to do what you have said." "Now," said the visitor, "Your Royal Highness's illness can be cured without drugs, acupuncture, or cauterization. It can be made to vanish by the persuasive force of essential words and marvelous doctrines. Don't you want to hear them?" "Yes," replied the Heir Apparent, "I would like to hear them."

[First Stimulus]

The visitor said: 96
"The paulownia of Mount Lung-men
Has no branches up to a height of a hundred feet.
In its trunk, revolving rings collect;
Its roots spread out far apart.   100
Above there is an eight-thousand-foot peak,
Below it looks down on a thousand-foot gorge.
Rushing waves and countercurrents
Strike and burst through, back and forth.   104
Its roots are half alive, half dead.
In winter it is stirred by violent winds, driving sleet,
    and flying snow;
In summer it is shaken by the claps and crashes of
    thunder.
At dawn the oriole and the *ko-tan* birds cry there.   108
At dusk deserted female and stray birds perch there.
A lone crane at sunup calls above it;
A *k'un* fowl mournfully cries, fluttering below it.

博見強識　承間語事　變度易意　(80)常無離側　以爲羽翼　淹沈之樂　浩唐之心　(84)
遁佚之志　其奚由至哉　太子曰諾　病已　(88)請事此言　客曰　今太子之病　可無藥
石針刺灸療而已　(92)可以要言妙道說而去也　不欲聞乎　太子曰　僕願聞之

(96)客曰　龍門之桐　高百尺而無枝　中鬱結之輪菌　(100)根扶疏以分離　上有千仞之峯
下臨百丈之谿　湍流遡波　(104)又澹淡之　其根半死半生　多則烈風漂霰飛雪之所激也
夏則雷霆霹靂之所感也　(108)朝則鸝黃鳱鴟鳴焉　暮則羈雌迷鳥宿焉　獨鵠晨號乎其上
鵾雞哀鳴翔乎其下

Thereupon, as the season turns its back on autumn
    and passes into winter,   112
Let Zither-master Chih chop it down to make a
    zither;
Take the cocoons of wild silkworms to make the
    strings;
Take an orphan's belt hook to make the adornment;
Take the earrings of a widow with nine children to
    make the frets,   116
Then let Master T'ang* play the tune 'Ch'ang,'
And let Po Tzu Ya† sing to it a song.
These are the words of the song:
'The grain ears have sharp points, the pheasant flies
    at dawn.   120
Bound for the empty valley, he turns his back on the
    withered locust tree.
Close to the sheer cliff, he looks down on the winding stream.'

[*Prose lines 123–132*] When the flying birds hear this, they fold
their wings and cannot go on. When the wild beasts hear this,
they droop their ears and cannot move on. When the crawling
chih, chiao, mole crickets, and ants hear this, they open their
mouths and cannot advance. This surely is the saddest music in
the world. Can Your Royal Highness force yourself to rise and
listen to it?" The Heir Apparent said: "I'm too sick, I can't."

              [Second Stimulus]
The visitor said:
"The fat meat of a calf's belly
Is cooked with the shoots of bamboos and rushes.
A soup made from a fatted dog   136
Is stewed with mountain lichens.
Rice from Mount Miao in Ch'u
And *an-hu* cereal

---

*A zither teacher who had Confucius as one of his disciples.
†See appendix 2, "Po Ya and Chung Tzu-ch'i."

(112)於是背秋涉冬　使琴摯斫斬以爲琴　野繭之絲以爲絃　孤子之鈎以爲隱　(116)九寡
之珥以爲約　使師堂操暢　伯子牙爲之歌　歌曰　(120)麥秀蔪兮雉朝飛　向虛壑兮背槁
槐　依絕區兮臨廻溪　飛鳥聞之　(124)翕翼而不能去　野獸聞之　垂耳而不能行　蚑蟜
螻蟻聞之　(128)拄喙而不能前　此亦天下之至悲也　太子能彊起聽之乎　太子曰　(132)
僕病未能也　客曰　犓牛之腴　菜以筍蒲　(136)肥狗之和　冒以山膚　楚苗之食　安胡
之飯

Are rolled into balls that don't fall apart   140
But melt at once when sucked into the mouth.
Thereupon let Yi Yin cook
And Yi Ya* spice these dishes:
Bear's paws well done   144
With perfect-blend sauce;
Roasted thin-sliced dorsal meat
With fresh carp slivers;
Autumn-yellowed thyme   148
And legumes laden with early fall's white dew.
Orchid blossom wine
Is poured to rinse the mouth.
Then a dish of wild pheasant hen   152
And the unborn young of a tame leopardess.
Eat little and drink much:†
It's like hot water poured on snow.

[*Prose lines 156–159*] This surely is the most delicious food in
the world. Can Your Royal Highness force yourself to rise and
taste it?" The Heir Apparent said: "I'm too sick, I can't."

                    [Third Stimulus]
The visitor said: 160
"Stallions from Chung and Tai
Of the right age are harnessed to a chariot.
The front horses are like flying ducks,
The rear horses resemble *chü-hsü*.‡   164
With wheat grown in rice fields as their fodder,
They are impetuous in the stable and abroad.
Bridled with firm reins,
They hold to the level road.   168

---

*Yi Yin and Yi Ya are famous cooks of antiquity.

†You will not overeat, and the meal is easily washed down and digested. Or, if line 154
is taken as *hu-wen*, you can eat and drink as much (or as little) as you like without ill
effects.

‡A fabulous, speedy animal, variously described, e.g., "with the rear of a rat and the
front of a hare" (Li Shan's commentary to this line in Hsiao T'ung, *Wen hsüan* [Ssu-pu
ts'ung-k'an], 34.7a, citing a no longer extant passage in *Lü shih ch'un-ch'iu*).

(140)搏之不銷　一啜而散　於是使伊尹煎熬　易牙調和　(144)熊蹯之臑　勺藥之醬　薄
耆之炙　鮮鯉之鱠　(148)秋黃之蘇　白露之茹　蘭英之酒　酌以滌口　(152)山梁之餐　豢
豹之胎　小飰大歠　如湯沃雪　(156)此亦天下之至美也　太子能彊起嘗之乎　太子曰　僕
病未能也　(160)客曰　鍾岱之牡　齒至之車　前似飛鳧　(164)後類距虛　稻麥服處　躁
中煩外　轡堅轡　(168)附易路

Thereupon Po Le* decides from their appearance
    which will be in front and which behind;
Wang Liang and Tsao Fu† serve as charioteers,
With Ch'in Ch'üeh and Lou Chi‡ as guards on
    the right.
These two men   172
Can stop the horses should they bolt,
And right the chariot should it overturn.
Thereupon let there be a wager of twenty thousand taels
And a race of a thousand miles.   176

[*Prose lines 177–180*] These surely are the finest horses in the
world. Can Your Royal Highness force yourself to rise and take
a ride?" The Heir Apparent said: "I'm too sick, I can't."

[Fourth Stimulus]
The visitor said:
"Having climbed to the terrace of Ching-i,
To the South you look out on Mount Ching,
To the North you look out on the Ju Sea;   184
To the left the Yangtze River, to the right Lake
    Tung-t'ing:
The joy of it—there is nothing like it.
Thereupon let learned and eloquent men
Explain the origins of mountains and rivers   188
And name the various plants and trees,
Classifying and arranging them
All in correct order.
You roam and wander, enjoying the view.   192
Then you descend, and a banquet is served in
    the Palace of the Gratified Heart.
A continuous verandah runs around its four sides.
Lookouts tower on the walls,

---

*An expert on horses.
†Two famous charioteers of antiquity.
‡Two famous runners of antiquity.

於是伯樂相其前後　王良造父爲之御　秦缺樓季爲之右　(172)此兩人者　馬佚能止之
車覆能起之　於是使射千鎰之重　(176)爭千里之逐　此亦天下之至駿也　太子能彊起乘
之乎　太子曰　僕病未能也　(180)客曰　旣登景夷之臺　南望荆山　(184)北望汝海　左
江右湖　其樂無有　於是使博辯之士　(188)原本山川　極命草木　比物屬事　離辭連類
(192)浮游覽觀　乃下置酒於虞懷之宮　連廊四注　臺城層構

Black and green in mingled profusion. 196
Sedan chair routes run crisscross,
A moat twists and turns.
Colorful *hun-chang* birds and snowy egrets,
Peacocks and *yün-ku* fowl, 200
Wan-ch'u birds and night herons,
Green crests and purple necks,
Female and male with ornate heads and bellies,
In chorus they sing. 204
Virile fishes frisk and frolic,
Flap their fins and shake their scales.
Thick covers, heavy layers
Of spreading, fragrant aquatic plants. 208
Girlish-soft mulberry trees and river tamarisks,
White leaves and purple stems,
Pines from Mount Miao and camphor-laurel,
Branches reaching up to the sky; 212
Wu-t'ung trees and palms,
As far as the eye can see they stand in groves.
Copious scents of heavy fragrance
Are spread by the winds in all directions. 216
In leisurely, graceful motion they sway,
Making light and darkness vanish and appear.
The company sits down and indulges in wine,
Exciting music delights the heart. 220
Ching Ch'un* serves the wine,
Tu Lien† plays the music.
Many savory foods are mixed and prepared,
Assorted delicacies are mingled and set out. 224
Choice beauties delight the eye,
Sensuous melodies please the ear.
Thereupon is heard the finale of 'Whirling Ch'u'[5]
And rousing tunes from Cheng and Wei.[6] 228

---

*A rhetorician of antiquity.
†A famous zither player of antiquity.

(196)紛紜玄綠　輦道邪交　黃池紆曲　湓章白鷺　(200)孔雀鵷鶵　鵁鶄鴗鶬　翠鬣紫纓
螭龍德牧　(204)邕邕羣鳴　陽魚騰躍　奮翼振鱗　淀瀿壽蓼　(208)蔓草芳苓　女桑河柳
素葉紫莖　苗松豫章　(212)條上造天　梧桐并閭　極望成林　衆芳芬鬱　(216)亂於五風
從容猗靡　消息陽陰　列坐縱酒　(220)蕩樂娛心　景春佐酒　杜連理音　滋味雜陳　(224)
肴粻錯該　練色娛目　流声悅耳　於是乃發激楚之結風　(228)揚鄭衛之皓樂

Let beautiful people like Hsi Shih, Cheng Shu, Yang
    Wen, Tuan Kan, Wu Wa, Lü Tsou, and Fu Yü,*
With colorful robes and flowing hair,
Flirt with their eyes and dally with their hearts:
A flow of sparkling waves,   232
A medley of fragrant herbs.
They wear bright powder
And orchid hair-ointment.†
In casual clothes they wait on the guests.   236

[*Prose lines 237–240*] This surely is the most luxurious, extrava-
gant, and lavish enjoyment in the world. Can Your Royal
Highness force yourself to rise and go on this excursion?" The
Heir Apparent said: "I'm too sick, I can't."

[Fifth Stimulus]

The visitor said:
"Let us do *this* for Your Royal Highness:
    outstanding horses are trained
And hitched to a flying-railing chariot,‡
So that you may ride in a vehicle drawn by
    strong, swift steeds.   244
On your right, powerful arrows from the quiver
    of Yü,
On your left, the carved bow 'Crow Call.'**
You roam the Cloud Forests,
Ride around the Orchid Marshes,   248
Stop at the bank of the Yangtze River.
You have mats spread on the green sedge
And face the pure breeze;
You enjoy the vital force of spring   252

---

*The commentators do not agree whether these seven are all women or women and men.

†The Chinese orchid (*lan*) is fragrant.

‡A hunting chariot on which the hunter stands behind a curved railing.

**The name of the Yellow Lord's bow. The Yellow Lord, like Yü, is one of the legendary rulers of the Golden Age of antiquity.

使先施徵舒陽文段干吳娃閭娵傅予之徒　雜裾垂髾　目窕心與　(232)揄流波　雜杜若　蒙
清塵　被蘭澤　(236)嬿服而御　此亦天下之靡麗皓侈廣博之樂也　太子能彊起游乎　太
子曰　(240)僕病未能也　客曰　將爲太子馴騏驥之馬　駕飛輪之輿　(244)乘牡駿之乘　右
夏服之勁箭　左烏號之雕弓　游涉乎雲林　(248)周馳乎蘭澤　弭節乎江潯　掩青蘋　游
清風　(252)陶陽氣

And bathe your heart in the vernal essence.
You pursue the wily beasts
And collect the nimble birds.
Thereupon you use to the full the power of dogs
    and horses   256
To wear out the wild beasts' legs;
You exhaust the knowledge and skill of guides
    and drivers
To frighten tigers and leopards,
To terrify birds of prey.   260
Horses in pursuit sound the bells on the bridles,
The fish jump, the deer butt.
You run down roebucks and hares,
Trample on one-horned deer.   264
Sweat flows, froth drips,
The hunted flee and cower in distress.
Those that die without wounds
Quite suffice to fill the carriages following
    behind.   268

[*Prose lines 269–277*] This is the most spirited of all hunts. Can Your Royal Highness force yourself to rise and go to it?" The Heir Apparent said: "I'm too sick, I can't." But a sign of vitality appeared on his forehead; it slowly increased and rose, filling almost his whole face.

When the visitor saw that the Heir Apparent looked pleased, he pushed the theme further by saying:

"Fires in darkness press to the sky,
War chariots thunder and move;
Banners and flags flutter aloft,   280
Bird feathers and buffalo tails in copious array.
Men race and compete,
With their minds on the taste of meat they vie to
    be first.

蕩春心　逐狡獸　集輕禽　(256)於是極犬馬之才　困野獸之足　窮相御之智巧　恐虎豹
(260)慴鷙鳥　逐馬鳴鑣　魚跨麋角　履游麀兔　(240)蹈踐麏鹿　汗流沫墜　宪伏陵窘　無
創而死者　(268)固足充後乘矣　此校獵之至壯也　太子能彊起游乎　太子曰　(272)僕病
未能也　然陽氣見於眉宇之間　侵淫而上　幾滿大宅　(276)客見太子有悅色也　遂推而
進之曰　冥火薄天　兵車雷運　(280)旌旗偃蹇　羽旄蕭紛　馳騁角逐　慕味爭先

The hunting ground that has been burned black
    extends far,   284
You can barely see its end.
Game of pure color and perfect shape
Is saved for sacrifice at court."

[*Prose lines 288–291*] The Heir Apparent said: "Good, I want
to hear more." "I haven't finished yet," said the visitor and
continued:

"*Thereupon* in dense forests and deep bogs,   292
From mist and clouds, hazy and gloomy,
Rhinos and tigers rise together.
Bold warriors, extremely fierce,
Strip and press close to them.   296
Bright swords do their sharp work,
Lances and halberds crisscross.
Each man's catch is reckoned,
To be rewarded with gold and silk.   300
Mats of fragrant grass are spread on the sedge
To feast the hunters.
Fine wine and choice morsels,
Delicacies are cooked, meat slices are roasted   304
To be offered to the guests.
With wine poured into their cups, all rise and cheer,
Stirring the heart and startling the ear.
Their devotion is without reservation,   308
Resolutely they decide to accept their tasks.
Their show of sincere loyalty
Is shaped into music played on metal and stone.
The community sings loudly: 312
'Ten thousand years without decline for our lord!'

[*Prose lines 314–319*] This surely is something Your Royal
Highness will enjoy. Can you force yourself to rise and go to it?"
The Heir Apparent said: "I would like very much to go along,

---

(284)徹墨廣博　觀望之有圻　純粹全犧　獻之公門　(288)太子曰善　願復聞之　客曰　未
既　(292)於是榛林深澤　煙雲闇莫　兕虎並作　毅武孔猛　(296)袒裼身薄　白刃磑磑
矛戟交錯　收獲掌功　(300)賞賜金帛　掩蘋肆若　爲牧人席　旨酒嘉肴　(304)羞炰膾炙
以御賓客　涌觴並起　動心驚耳　(308)誠必不悔　決絕以諾　貞信之色　形於金石　(312)
高歌陳唱　萬歲無斁　此眞太子之所喜也　能彊起而游乎　(316)太子曰　僕甚願從

I only fear it would inconvenience my courtiers." But he was beginning to look better.

[Sixth Stimulus]

[*Prose lines 320–333*] The visitor said: "Let us do *this*: on the fifteenth day of the eighth moon, you go, accompanied by nobles, friends, and relatives from afar, to view the bore of the Winding River at Kuang-ling. When you arrive, before you behold the bore itself, just seeing how far the water's power extends is fearsome enough to terrify you. Viewing its overtaking, its pulling up, its stirring up, its converging, its washing —even one who has in his mind a general conception of the phenomenon and the ability to articulate it in words, really cannot give a detailed sequential account of it.

> Blurred and obscure,
> Terrible and frightening,
> Crests converging and roaring,   336
> Obscure and blurred,
> Special and extraordinary,
> Grandly deep and broad,
> Blurredly vast.   340
> You fix your attention on the Southern Mountains,
> And your gaze is carried all the way to the
>   Eastern Sea.
> Vast and loud, it joins the blue sky;
> You strain to the utmost to perceive its limits,   344
> But wherever you look there is no end,
> And your attention is taken to the place where
>   the sun rises.*
> The rapid flow descends downstream,
> Nobody knows where it stops.   348
> Now it splits into many winding flows,

---

*The bore moves from west to east.

直恐爲諸大夫累耳　然而有起色矣　(320)客曰　將以八月之望　與諸侯遠方交游兄弟　並
往觀濤乎廣陵之曲江　(324)至則未見濤之形也　徒觀水力之所到　則邮然足以駭矣　觀
其所駕軼者　(328)所擢拔者　所揚汩者　所溫汾者　所滌汔者　(332)雖有心略辭給　固
未能縷形其所由然也　怳兮忽兮　聊兮慄兮　(336)混汨汨兮　忽兮慌兮　俶兮儻兮　浩
瀁瀁兮　(340)慌曠曠兮　秉意乎南山　通望乎東海　虹洞兮蒼天　(344)極慮乎崖涘　流
覽無窮　歸神日母　汩乘流而下降兮　(348)或不知其所止　或紛紜其流折兮

Suddenly it twists and proceeds upstream
　without returning.
It goes to the Vermilion Bank and vanishes in the
　distance,
Inside you feel empty, upset, and exhausted.　　　352
In the evening it disperses and starts again
　in the morning.
In your heart you keep and hold it.
Thereupon it bathes the breast,
Washes the five organs,　　　　　　　　　　　356
Cleanses hands and feet,
Rinses the hair and teeth.
It does away with indolence,
Purges impurities,　　　　　　　　　　　　　360
Clears up suspicions and doubts,
Sharpens ears and eyes.

[*Prose lines 363–374*] At this time, though men have chronic
illnesses and lingering diseases, this will straighten hunchbacks,
make the lame get up, open the eyes of the blind, and unlock the
ears of the deaf as they observe it. How much more is this true
of those who only suffer from minor mental upsets and excessive
eating and drinking! Therefore it is written: 'It clears up dullness and resolves delusions without any difficulty.' "[7] The
Heir Apparent said: "Good, but what kind of a phenomenon
is the bore?" The visitor said: "This is not recorded; but I have
heard my teacher say, There are three things about it that seem
supernatural but are not:

A sudden thunder is heard a hundred miles;
The river's water flows upstream,　　　　　　376
As does the sea's rising tide;
The mountains give forth clouds and take them
　back,
Day and night without ceasing.

忽繆往而不來　臨朱汜而遠逝兮　(352)中虛煩而益怠　莫離散而發曙兮　內存心而自持
於是操檓胸中　(356)灑練五藏　澹澉手足　頮濯髮齒　揄棄恬怠　(360)輸寫淟濁　分決
狐疑　發皇耳目　當是之時　(364)雖有淹病滯疾　猶將伸傴起躄發瞽披聾而觀望之也　況
直眇小煩懣醒醲病酒之徒哉　故曰　(368)發蒙解惑　不足以言也　太子曰善　然則濤何
氣哉　(372)客曰不記也　然聞於師曰　似神而非者三　疾雷聞百里　(376)江水逆流　海
水上潮　山出內雲　日夜不止

The water flows in fullness with rapid speed;   380
It gushes up, and the bore begins.
When it first begins,
The drops come down in a vast descent,
Like snowy egrets swooping down.   384
A little farther on,
It's splendid, towering, and bright,
Like pale-silk chariots with white horses and
    canopies spread on top.
When the billows swell and spread like clouds,   388
It's as jumbled as the piled baggage of the Three
    Armies.
When it swells at the sides, rising on top,
It glides like a light command chariot directing
    the troops.
Six dragons harnessed to the chariot   392
Take orders from the Great White River God,
Halting and rushing on, always high,
Front and rear, always joined.
Lofty and tall,   396
Freely expanding at the sides,
Billows flowing over each other.
A fortress many-layered and strong,
A mixed multitude, like army columns.   400
Booming and crashing,
Crushing and gushing,
Absolutely irresistible.
As you observe its two edges,   404
They stir with wrath
In vast agitation.
Striking above, rolling below,
Like brave warriors   408
Rushing out angry and fearless,

---

(380)衍溢漂疾　波涌而濤起　其始起也　洪淋淋焉　(384)若白鷺之下翔　其少進也　浩
浩澄澄　如素車白馬帷盖之張　(388)其波涌而雲乱　擾擾焉如三軍之騰裝　其旁作而奔起
也　飄飄焉如輕車之勒兵　(392)六駕蛟龍　附從太白　純馳浩蜺　前後絡驛　(396)顚顚
卬卬　椐椐彊彊　莘莘將將　壁壘重堅　(400)沓雜似軍行　訇隱匈礚　軋盤涌裔　原不
可當　(404)觀其兩旁　則滂渤怫鬱　闇漠感突　上擊下律　(408)有似勇壯之卒　突怒而
無畏

Trampling cliffs and bursting across fords,
Filling every bend and cove,
Flooding shores and rising above sandbanks.   412
Whoever meets it dies,
Whoever opposes it is destroyed.
When it first starts at the shore of the Border
    Regions,
Cliffs are twisted, valleys are split,   416
Green-topped revolving carriages,
Gagged horses* zigzagging.
It stops awhile at Wu Tzu Hsü's† mountain,
Then moves on to Hsü's mother's shrine.   420
It encroaches on the Red Shore
And sweeps over the Sunrise Tree.
Perversely it speeds, traveling like thunder.
Truly it bursts forth, that martial spirit,   424
Awesome and wrathful.
Confusion worse confounded,
It looks like galloping horses.
Worse confounded confusion,   428
It sounds like thunder and drums.
In an outburst of wrath it foams at obstacles;
Limpidly swelling it leaps across.
Giant billows, rising in awful majesty,   432
Join battle at the Harbor of Tumult.
There is no time for the birds to fly away,
For the fish to turn around,
For the beasts to run off.   436
Helter-skelter
The billows swell and spread like clouds,
Rush upon the southern hills,
Strike in the rear at the northern shore,   440

---

*Initially the bore is inaudible, thus it resembles a surprise attack with war chariots.
†See appendix 2.

蹈壁衝津　窮曲隨限　(412)踰岸出追　遇者死　當者壞　初發乎或圍之津　(416)涯軫谷
分　廻翔青篾　衡枚檀桓　弭節伍子之山　(420)通厲胥母之場　淩赤岸　篲扶桑　橫奔
似雷行　(424)誠奮厥武　如振如怒　沌沌渾渾　狀如奔馬　(428)混混庵庵　声如雷鼓　發
怒庢沓　清升踰跐　(432)侯波奮振　合戰於藉藉之口　鳥不及飛　魚不及廻　(436)獸不
及走　紛紛翼翼　波湧雲乱　蕩取南山　(440)背擊北岸

Topple hillocks and mounds,
Flatten the western embankment;
Perilously steep they rise
And collapse the sloping banks.   444
Not until the foe is drowned do they halt.
Striking and pushing they roil and roll,
Swelling and rising they splash and dash,
Perverse and cruel in the extreme.   448
Fish and turtles lose their powers,
Upside down and topsy-turvy,
Out of balance and control,
They float and crawl along.   452
The magical phenomena and miracles
Cannot be told in full.
They only make one stumble
In giddy perplexity and fright.   456

[*Prose lines 457–460*] This is the most miraculous and extraordinary sight in the world. Can Your Royal Highness force yourself to rise and view it?" The Heir Apparent said: "I'm too sick, I can't."

[Seventh Stimulus]

[*Prose lines 461–474*] The visitor said: "Let us do *this* for Your Royal Highness: We will present to you experts in philosophy and the occult arts, distinguished and wise, men such as Chuang Tzu and Wei Mou, Yang Chu and Mo Tzu, Pien Chüan and Chan Ho. Let them discuss the subtle mysteries of the world and discriminate between true and false in the myriad phenomena. Confucius and Lao Tzu will display their teachings for you to view. With Mencius moderating the discussion, the chances of error will be less than one in ten thousand. These surely are the most essential words and the most marvelous doctrines in the world. Doesn't Your Royal Highness want to hear them?" Thereupon the Heir Apparent, supporting himself on a low

覆廬邱陵　平夷西畔　險險戲戲　(444)崩壞陂池　決勝乃罷　瀄汩潺湲　披揚流灑　(448)
橫暴之極　魚鱉失勢　顛倒偃側　沈沈湲湲　(452)蒲伏連延　神物怪疑　不可勝言　直
使人踏焉　(456)洄闊悽愴焉　此天下怪異詭觀也　太子能彊起觀之乎　太子曰　(460)僕
病未能也　客曰　將爲太子奏方術之士有資略者　若莊周魏牟楊朱墨翟便蜎詹何之倫　(464)
使之論天下之精微　理萬物之是非　孔老覽觀　孟子持籌而算之　(468)萬不失一　此亦
天下要言妙道也　太子豈欲聞之乎　於是太子據几而起曰

table, rose and said: "My mind has been cleared as if I had just heard the words of the sages and wise men." In a turbid flow, perspiration issued. With a sudden outburst, the illness ended.

The story of this long *fu* is built around the cure of the Heir Apparent's disease. The cure is a kind of psychotherapy, working entirely with words and mental suggestion. As the visitor puts it, "Your Royal Highness's illness can be cured without drugs, acupuncture, or cauterization. It can be made to vanish by the persuasive force of essential words and marvelous doctrines." The visitor cures the patient by stimulating him seven times, describing seven pleasures, including some in which the prince has been indulging and others that he has never experienced. By using fantasy without action, the visitor can carry the pleasures to extremes that would be neither possible nor tolerable in actuality. In the Third Stimulus, for example, the horses are exceedingly swift and impetuous, yet they are firmly controlled at every moment, and even if the chariot should overturn it would be righted at once.

The power of suggestion has implications in this *fu* that go beyond the cure of sick prince. On the one hand, it is linked to a mighty natural phenomenon, the tidal bore. On the other hand, it provides an insight into the poet's conception of his own powers. The description of the tidal bore at Kuang-ling in mid-autumn constitutes the climactic Sixth Stimulus. (There is no agreement among commentators on the location of this Kuang-ling; tidal bores occur at several places on China's southeastern coast.) The bore has a cathartic effect on those who behold it. It cures every imaginable disease and defect (lines 355–69). The troubles plaguing the Heir Apparent are specifically included: "At this time, though men have chronic illnesses and lingering diseases, this will straighten hunchbacks, make the lame get up, open the eyes of the blind, and unlock the ears of the deaf as they observe it. How much more is this true of those who only suffer from minor mental upsets and excessive eating and drinking!" The cure implied in the Sixth Stimulus indicates an elaborate process of double sublimation. At an early stage, I suppose, the healing power was believed to be inherent in the water that washed away defects and impurities. In the next stage—still very much present in our poem—the magic power works on those who simply watch the

---

(42) 渙乎若一聽　聖人辯士之言　言溘然汗出　霍然病已

spectacle. The final stage—suggested in this passage—dispenses not only with physical contact but also with physical presence at the site of the bore. The catharsis is achieved through the ear and the mind, by hearing an aptly worded description of the phenomenon. The magic power of the tidal bore is transformed into the magic power of words. The visitor acts here as a sort of witch doctor. He establishes a connection between the potent, therapeutic flow of the bore and the fluids coursing in the sick prince's body. The cure is achieved when the cleansing liquid flushes out the harmful elements summoned by the visitor's words, and they are expelled from the body when the cumulative effect of his incantations produces the final sweat. The overwhelming power of the bore affects even the narrator in the fiction of this *fu*:

> The magical phenomena and miracles
> Cannot be told in full.
> They only make one stumble
> In giddy perplexity and fright.

The use of well-chosen words to cure an illness of this kind is not just a figment of our poet's imagination. Such cures are attested in the historical records of the period. The following account, for example, reporting the cure of another heir apparent, comes from the official biography of Wang Pao, a man of letters who flourished in the first half of the first century B.C.: "After this, the Heir Apparent's body was in ill health. He became delirious, forgetful, and depressed. The Emperor summoned Pao and others to go to the Heir Apparent's palace to entertain him. Morning and evening they chanted extraordinary writings, including their own compositions. When his health recovered they returned home. The Heir Apparent liked the eulogies 'Sweet Springs' and 'The Flute' by Pao, and had the courtiers and attendants of the rear palace chant them."[8]

For a better understanding of how the poets themselves viewed the magic power of words in this type literature, I will quote a passage from a later composition modeled on Mei Sheng's "Seven Stimuli," namely, "The Seven Openings" by Ts'ao Chih. In this work, a man called Ching-chi Tzu persuades a recluse to return to society. Here is the pertinent passage:

Ching-chi Tzu said: "The fascinating thing about the verbal art is that it can make stagnant bodies of water run fresh, and dead trees sprout new growth, fairly stirring their souls and moving their spirits. How much more, being closer to them, will it work on the feelings of human beings! I am going to tell you of the ultimate pleasures of outings, rehearse for you the bewitching charms of sounds and sights, with music made by beautiful women, discuss for you the ultimate mysteries of transformation, and state to you the vast magnificence of ethics and virtue. Do you want to hear these?"[9]

Further testimony for the notion that a *fu* could function as a magic spell is contained in the preface to "The Dream," a *fu* by Wang Yen-shou (second century A.D.): "When I was young and not yet capped [i.e., under twenty], while I was asleep one night I saw demons fighting with me. I then got a letter from Tung-fang Shuo cursing demons. I then wrote a *fu* to tell of my dream. Thereafter, people who had [similar] dreams chanted [my *fu*] repeatedly with good effect. Thus I dare not keep it hidden."[10] Tung-fang Shuo (154?–93? B.C.) was renowned as one of the early *fu* masters. His "letter" to Wang was presumably part of the dream and helped to inspire the exorcising *fu*.

For their intrinsic interest and for what they reveal about the art of the *fu*, the First, Fifth, and Seventh Stimuli are worth examination also.

The First Stimulus deals with a noble pleasure—music—and specifically with the noblest of all instruments, the zither (*ch'in*). The music of the zither has Orphic powers entrancing all listeners, even animals (lines 123–28). These powers, according to ancient Chinese theories, derive not only from the artisan who makes the instrument and the musician who plays it but also from the elemental forces working on the materials from which the instrument is made. Thus our poet speaks first of the paulownia tree and the musically significant factors of its environment (lines 97–111).[11] The tree's height, shape, and physical location are of course relevant. So are its contacts with winds and other natural elements, with the daily and seasonal cycles of nature. Special emphasis is placed on tall peaks and rushing streams. "Lofty mountains" and "flowing waters" were early associated with zither music through the legend of Po Ya and Chung Tzu-ch'i (see line 118 and appendix 2).

The crucial transformation of the living tree into an instrument begins when nature itself passes through a crisis: the transition from autumn to winter (line 112). There is a practical reason for this timing. The tree is chopped down more easily when the flow of sap slows. But the practice is characteristically in harmony with theory. The change from autumn to winter is the time when *all* cosmic activity halts in preparation for winter. It is a time of destruction and death, looking forward to new life in spring. Formally, this critical point is marked at the beginning of line 112 by the supernumerary phrase *yü shih* "thereupon."

The mournful mood is appropriate to the making of a musical instrument. In our poet's time, and for many centuries thereafter, serious music (like lyric poetry) was predominantly sad. Hence the unhappy birds, the orphan, and the widow with nine children (lines 109–116)—they have faced death and solitude. Birds rather than other animals are chosen because their melancholy is expressed in song. Their music combines with the sounds of torrents, winds, and thunder (lines 103–07).

The Fifth Stimulus describes a royal hunt. Like the other stimuli, it is a mixture of fantasy and reality. Some information on royal hunting in ancient China is relevant here.[12] Building on traditions developed in Chou times, the Han emperors exploited their huge hunting parks on a multiple-use basis, and the various royal courts vied with the imperial model and with each other in a contest of conspicuous consumption. The preserves contained a large variety of wild animals, to be displayed to the members of the court and their guests (a kind of private zoo), to provide sacrificial animals for court rituals, and of course to hunt for food, sport, and the formation of manly skills. Dogs were used for tracking and chasing. The hunters rode in chariots, not on horseback. Fire was used to give light for hunting at night and to clear a large open arena for spectacular chases and combats. The game was driven into such open spaces, which were sometimes enclosed in palisades. Not least important, the art of hunting was viewed in ancient China as akin to the art of war. Hunts served to train men in military skills such as charioteering, archery, swift pursuit, and combat at close quarters, and they produced loyalty to the leader.

Several passages in the Fifth Stimulus reveal a feature already discussed in connection with the Sixth, namely, the cleansing and healing powers emanating from holy places and from magic words.

Before the hunt begins, the Heir Apparent takes a ritual"bath" at a certain river bank. The ritual transfers the rejuvenating power of the spring season to the Prince's body. The "vital force of spring" (*yang ch'i*, line 252) later appears on his forehead as a "sign of vitality" (*yang ch'i*, line 273). This sign encourages the visitor to continue his word magic on the same topic and to prolong a stimulus that had reached an apparent end. During the chase, "sweat flows" from the bodies of the hunters and the hunted, prefiguring the cleansing perspiration at the very end of the *fu*. After the hunt is over, the feast of celebration concludes with a community song, and the words of the song invoke a long and healthy life for the Heir Apparent.

The Seventh Stimulus stands apart from the other six: it is brief and entirely in prose, while the others are prolix and largely in verse; it is moralistic rather than sensuous. These contrasts give the impression that the author enjoyed writing the first six and then unenthusiastically tacked on the seventh in order to give his composition the required moral twist.[13] Actually the last stimulus is not an afterthought but the dramatic conclusion of a planned sequence. The arrangement of the successive stimuli—their order, size, and shape— makes sense artistically and "medically." A buildup in length from the Second and Third Stimulus (about equally short: 26 and 21 lines) through the Fourth (60 lines) and the Fifth (79 lines) to the Sixth (141 lines) is coordinated with a gradual increase in curative power: the first four stimuli have no immediate effect on the patient, but the fifth and sixth produce visible results and are therefore prolonged, with fresh starts. The last stimulus seems to fall out of line, being the shortest by far (14 lines). (At the other end, the First Stimulus is inordinately long—137 lines.) The Seventh Stimulus need not be any longer: the six preceding stimuli have done their work so well that the prince is ready for the decisive stroke. The reader, too, will be grateful to be spared an elaboration of the philosophical doctrines at this point.

The choice of prose, too, shows artistic acumen. Prose is a more suitable medium than poetry for the subject matter at hand, and it is the proper medium here for formal reasons as well. The seventh is, after all, not only the last stimulus but also the conclusion of the *fu*, and therefore resumes the prose form of the Introduction.[14] In the style of this *fu*, prose passages frame the whole piece and mark off divisions between the stimuli and subdivisions within the stimuli.

The Seventh Stimulus also returns to the Introduction in content and even in wording. The "experts in philosophy and the occult arts" conjured up at the end recall the "gentlemen" (or should we read "gentleman"?) mentioned in the beginning, and the "essential words and marvelous doctrines" of the philosophers bring about the cure promised by the visitor. But the "essential words" are never uttered. The mere mention of the sages, without quoting or even summarizing their lectures, is sufficient to exorcise the illness. We recall the magic power of the bore that worked through sheer verbal suggestion. The visitor has mastered the art of words which is the art of the *fu*.

Now a word about the moralistic posture of the Seventh Stimulus, in contrast with the voluptuousness of the other six. If there is any inconsistency here, it is not unique in world literature. Many Western poets—Dante and Milton are among the best known—and their audiences are fascinated by the forces of evil (however "evil" may be defined), and their moral ambivalence is comparable to Mei Sheng's.[15] The conflict between opposite values is the stuff of poetry.

Four characteristic features of "The Seven Stimuli" can also be found in other *fu* of the Han period. The first of these is the tendency to go to extremes. The language is hyperbolical throughout. Each stimulus is a *ne plus ultra*: "the saddest music in the world," "the most delicious food in the world," "the finest horses in the world," "the [most] luxurious, extravagant, and lavish enjoyment in the world," "the most spirited of all hunts," and "the [most] essential words and the [most] marvelous doctrines in the world." The poet conjures up a surfeit of extremes and "feeds" them to the listener. The extremes are often paired: physical height and depth (lines 101–02), spiritual elation and depression (passim), winter and summer (lines 106–07), life and death (line 105). Everywhere, especially in the Sixth Stimulus, the poem dwells on the grandiose, overpowering, magic, and miraculous aspects of nature. In the Fifth Stimulus, the hunters make the fullest possible use of all resources, driving animals and men to the point of exhaustion:

> You use to the full the power of dogs and horses
> To wear out the wild beasts' legs;
> You exhaust the knowledge and skill of guides and drivers.

Related to the first characteristic is the second: prolixity. While

the prevailing trend of Chinese poetry from early times was con-
ciseness, the Han *fu* moved in the opposite direction, perhaps as a
reaction against too much succinctness. Everything is set forth as
fully and completely as possible. The lengthy lists of animals, plants,
foods, entertainments, and the like, used to good effect in "The
Seven Stimuli," become longer and more tiresome in the later *fu*. In
the following passage our poet sums up his own strategy for handling
such compilations (lines 187–91):

> Let learned and eloquent men
> Explain the origins of mountains and rivers
> And name the various plants and trees,
> Classifying and arranging them
> All in correct order.

He does indeed combine erudition with eloquence, though not always in perfect balance. The account of the bore is stated to be
based on written records and the teachings of a scholar (lines 370–
73, written perhaps with tongue in cheek).

In this connection, we may note the *fu* poets' efforts to exploit all
resources of the language. The vocabulary is enormous, and there
are many instances of onomatopoeia and other devices of sound
orchestration. Most of these are lost in translation, but I would like to
call attention to one feature, related to the reversibility of compounds discussed above (in chapter 11). The description of the bore
contains the phrase *huang hsi hu hsi* ("blurred and obscure," line 334),
followed by *hu hsi huang hsi* ("obscure and blurred," line 337). Later
on there is *t'un-t'un hun-hun* ("confusion worse confounded," line
426), reversed as *hun-hun t'un-t'un* ("worse confounded confusion,"
line 428). (*Huang-hu* and *hu-huang* are alliterative compounds, *t'un-
hun* and *hun-t'un* are rhyming compounds.) The device is well suited
to the impression the poet wants to convey.

We move on to the third feature: competition. The whole piece is,
as we have seen, a contest between the visitor and the prince's disease, and in every stimulus, men compete with nature and with
each other. Competition is most conspicuous in the Third Stimulus
(the chariot race), the Fifth (the hunt), and the Sixth (the bore).
The royal chase pits the hunters against animals and against other
men. The latter aspect is explicitly stated in these lines:

Men race and compete,
With their minds on the taste of meat they vie to be first.

. . . .

Each man's catch is reckoned,
To be rewarded with gold and silk.

The view of the hunt as a military exercise is reflected in the language
of the Fifth Stimulus more than once. Note, for instance, the "war
chariots" with flying insignia (lines 279–81) and the "bold warriors"
fighting at close range (lines 292–98). The last-named episode ends
as a confused melee ("lances and halberds crisscross") where the
distinction between human and animal foe is deliberately blurred.
In the account of the bore, martial imagery is prominent in a long
passage (lines 389–445) containing the following key words and
phrases: armies—command chariot directing the troops—fortress—
army columns—absolutely irresistible—brave warriors—whoever
meets it dies, whoever opposes it is destroyed—revolving carriages,
gagged horses—martial spirit—galloping horses—drums—join
battle—not until the foe is drowned [pun] do they halt.

The last stimulus is a contest between true and false and a debate
between rival philosophers. But here conflicts are settled peacefully,
and the *fu* ends on a note of harmony.

The sustained emphasis on competition can be related to the poet's
personal situation. Mei Sheng wrote the "Seven Stimuli" at the
court of Liu Wu, Prince of Liang, in the mid-second century B.C.
Liu Wu surrounded himself with a circle of literati. These men vied
with each other for their patron's favor and for literary fame. Their
new genre, the *fu*, became a vehicle of competitive spirit at this and
other courts. Each writer sought to outdo his colleagues by making
his *fu* more artful and elaborate. As time progressed, *fu* poets exerted
themselves to surpass not only their contemporaries but also earlier
authors who had written on the same topic.

We come to the fourth and final point, the sectioning of this *fu*.
As noted earlier, it is divided into eight coordinated sections (an
introduction and seven stimuli), and some sections are further
divided into subsections. Formal divisional markers, occurring singly
or in various combinations, are change of style (from prose to poetry
or vice versa), change of meter, change of rhyme, and the super-

numerary head phrases *yü shih* "thereupon" and *yü shih shih* "thereupon let (there be)." The successive stimuli are framed by prose
passages that are cut to the same pattern, with many verbatim repetitions. This suggests that the competitive spirit extends to the
stimuli themselves. They are rivals, and each is more effective than
its predecessors. The last one is the winner.

Systematic sectioning can also be observed on a smaller scale. Our
poet likes to break up an object into component parts, and these are
arranged in a structural sequence. The paulownia consists of
branches, a trunk, and roots (lines 98–100). The cleansing bore
affects many parts of the human body, and the parts are listed (lines
355–62). An object, such as the paulownia of the First Stimulus, is
seen from different angles and at different times. From a scenic terrace you look out in four directions: South, North, left, and right
(lines 183–85).

Space is often expanded, in accord with the penchant for extremes
discussed earlier:

> Pines from Mount Miao and camphor-laurel,
> Branches reaching up to the sky;
> *Wu-t'ung* trees and palms,
> As far as the eye can see they stand in groves.
> Copious scents of heavy fragrance
> Are spread by the winds in all directions.
> . . . .
> The hunting ground that has been burned black extends far,
> You can barely see its end.
> . . . .
> And your gaze is carried all the way to the Eastern Sea.
> Vast and loud, it joins the blue sky.
> You strain to the utmost to perceive its limits,
> But wherever you look there is no end.

As space is extended, so is time. We are told of the before and
after, the origins and consequences of the stimuli. We learn where the
rice is grown and how the dishes are prepared for the banquet
(Second Stimulus). The First Stimulus begins with the history of the
tree from which the zither will be cut and ends with the music's
effect on the animal world. The account of the chariot race (Third
Stimulus) first tells from where the horses come and how they are

raised; at the end it looks forward to the bet to be collected after the race.

In these first three stimuli the sequence is temporal, but in the later stimuli it involves both time and space, and the distinction between the two is left vague. We seem to be watching a revolving stage, and as the scene shifts we do not know how far we are being transported in time, or in space, or in both.

Appendix 1: Poetic Forms

Chüeh-chü

(Poems 3, 6, 11–13, 22, 23, 25, 32, 40, 46, 55, 89)

Chüeh-chü (broken-off lines) originated in the fifth and sixth centuries as a special kind of *yüeh-fu*, limited to four lines of either five or seven syllables each. (Examples of this prototype of *chüeh-chü* are Poems 17, 37–39, 58, 83, and 84.) The standard type of *chüeh-chü* developed in the seventh century as one of the three forms of *chin-t'i shih* (modern-style verse), the other two being *lü-shih* and *p'ai-lü*. The standard *chüeh-chü* consists of four lines and obeys rules 2, 3, 4, and 6 of the *lü-shih* form, with two modifications: first, though the rhyme word is usually in the level tone, it may also be in one of the three other tones; second, the pattern of tonal distribution is not observed as strictly as in the *lü-shih*. Parallelism is employed only occasionally (e.g., in Poem 89, where it is used in both couplets).

Chüeh-chü is the most concentrated Chinese poetic form and requires the greatest economy of words. Each of the four lines is a complete grammatical sentence, and each of the two couplets normally forms a unit. The third line tends to introduce a critical turn.

Fu

(Poems 1, 50, 106)

The *fu* (I know of no good English equivalent) is a miscellaneous genre, usually descriptive or philosophical, or both, often quite lengthy and ornate, and frequently intermingled with prose. It became preeminent in the second century B.C., deriving from an earlier type of poetry represented in the anthology *Ch'u tz'u*. The *fu* shows much variety and fluctuation in its prosody. Characteristic features (which need not always be present) are the monosyllable *hsi*, the use of function words in fixed positions, supernumerary initial words and phrases, and pairing particles.

The monosyllable whose modern reading is *hsi* is a kind of exclamatory interjection and marks a break at the end of a line (it often signals the end of the first half of a couplet) or within a line.

A limited number of function words (particles) are sometimes used in a fixed position at or near the center of a line; they were probably unstressed.

The use of supernumerary initial words and phrases and the employment of pairing particles are discussed above (pp. 163–64).

The line length varies in the course of a given *fu*, but individual sections of a *fu* normally consist of lines of equal length. End rhyme generally occurs at the end of every other line.

Ku-shih

(Poems 5, 7–9, 14–16, 20, 26, 29, 31, 33, 34, 41, 67–69, 74, 81, 82, 91–94, 105)

Ku-shih (old-style verse) began to emerge in the second century A.D. and has been a favorite medium of Chinese poetry ever since. A given poem normally consists of lines of uniform length. Most *ku-shih* (including all those that are discussed in this volume) use lines of either five or seven syllables. The lines are nearly always paired syntactically as couplets. Rhyme generally occurs at the end of each couplet. Rhyme may be constant or change in the course of the poem. Parallelism, with antithesis and some repetition, occurs irregularly between the lines of a couplet. There is a caesura in nearly every five-syllable line between the second and the third syllable. In the seven-syllable line, there is a major caesura between the fourth and the fifth syllable, and often a minor caesura between the second and the third syllable. The three syllables following the caesura in both meters are not uniformly structured as far as syntax is concerned: the penultimate syllable may be in closer juncture with the preceding syllable than with the following syllable, or the other way around. This free and unpredictable alternation of two patterns adds a dynamic element to the otherwise somewhat monotonous five-syllable and seven-syllable meters of *ku-shih*.

Lü-shih

(Poems 4, 28, 72, 73, 75–79, 85, 86)

The *lü-shih* (regulated verse) developed in the seventh century A.D. out of the *ku-shih*. It observes the following rules:

1.   The poem consists of eight lines (four couplets).

2.   The line length is constant throughout the poem, either five or seven syllables.

3.   A single rhyme is used. It is nearly always in the level tone, and occurs at the end of the even-numbered lines. In addition, the first line of the poem may end with the same rhyme; it usually does in the seven-syllable form, and occasionally in the five-syllable form.

4.   The distribution of level and deflected tones follows a fixed pattern.

5.   The fourth line parallels the third line, and the sixth line parallels the fifth line.

6.   There is a caesura in the five-syllable form between the second and

the third syllable of every line. In the seven-syllable form, there is a major caesura between the fourth and the fifth syllable, and a minor caesura between the second and the third syllable.

Rules 4 and 5 require further statements. In taking up first the distribution of tones, I will simplify the exposition by speaking of the seven-syllable form only, but my remarks will be equally applicable to the five-syllable form, which as far as prosody is concerned differs from the longer form only in lacking the first two syllables of every line. That is to say, the seven-syllable schema below can be converted into the five-syllable form by omitting the first two syllables of every line. I base this discussion on Downer and Graham, "Tone Patterns in Chinese Poetry," where the principles underlying the distribution of tones have been recognized for the first time as resulting from the meshing of two independent systems. One system governs the alternation of tones in the even-numbered syllables of each line. They will be marked A and B, A representing one tonal category—either level or deflected—and B the opposite tonal category. (For the two tonal categories, see p. 147 above.) The second system governs the alternation of tones in the fifth and seventh syllables of each line. They will be marked x and y, x representing the tonal category of the rhyme word—usually but not necessarily level—and y the opposite tonal category. The poem as a whole can be divided into two equal halves for the purposes of tonal patterning. In each half (quatrain), the two systems combine as follows:

1	2	3	4	5	6	7
	A		B	x	A	y
	B		A	y	B	x
	B		A	x	B	y
	A		B	y	A	x

There is liberty for the tonal category of the first and the third syllable of every line, but they, too, tend to follow a pattern: the first syllable tends to agree in its tonal category with the second syllable, and the third with the fourth. Whenever the first line of the poem shares the rhyme (an optional feature, as mentioned above), x and y change places in the first line but not in the fifth line. In this case, then, the two halves of the poem are not entirely alike in regard to tonal patterning. When a poet sets out to write a *lü-shih*, he either makes A the level tone and B the deflected tone, or he does it the other way around. He also determines the tonal categories for x and y, but the rhyme (x) is nearly always in the level tone; the alternative of making x deflected and y level is seldom chosen.

Parallelism, which is required in each of the two middle couplets, means word-for-word matching. Realized with varying degrees of perfection, it is a combination of sameness, likeness, difference, and antithesis, embracing phonological, grammatical, and semantic features. The phonological feature is the matching of tones just described. Grammatically and semantically, the matching words are supposed to be in the same category, and such words normally perform the same syntactic function. (For further details of grammatical and semantic matching, see chapter 11.)

The three forms *lü-shih*, *chüeh-chü*, and *p'ai-lü* are collectively called *chin-t'i shih* (modern-style verse), as distinct from *ku-shih* (old-style verse).

P'ai-lü

(Poems 70 and 71)

P'ai-lü (regulated couplets) is an extended variation of *lü-shih*. It runs to more than four couplets, without any limitation on its length, and observes rules 2, 4, and 6 of the *lü-shih* form. More than one rhyme may be used. Parallelism of the same type as in *lü-shih* is employed in every couplet except the first and the last.

San-ch'ü

(Poems 95–101)

San-ch'ü (individual songs) originated in the twelfth century A.D. and flourished in the thirteenth and fourteenth centuries. They share many features with the *tz'u* but differ from the latter form in several respects: (1) the language is more colloquial; (2) they cover a wider range of subject matter; (3) they introduce new rhymes, based on the spoken language of their own time, and syllables differing in tones are generally allowed to rhyme with each other. Each poem bears the name of a *san-ch'ü* pattern which determines the number of lines, the number of syllables for each line (the lines of a given pattern are usually of uneven length), the sequence of tonal categories (in some lines even the sequence of individual tones) in each line, and the rhyme. Though the number of syllables is normally fixed for each line, extra words (*ch'en-tzu*) are occasionally inserted at the beginning or in the middle of a line; but this does not happen in the examples chosen in this book. Some *san-ch'ü* are divided into stanzas.

Shih ching

(Poems 2, 10, 35, 36, 45, 102–104)

The *Shih ching* (*Classic of Songs*) forms part of the Confucian canon. The 305 poems of this anthology were composed between the tenth and the sixth century B.C. Many of them probably originated as folk songs, but all seem to have passed through the hands of men of letters at the royal Chou court. Many songs are divided into stanzas of nearly identical metric structure, with many elements of repetition and variation. Line length is not entirely uniform, but the four-syllable line predominates. Most of the lines are paired syntactically as couplets. There is end rhyme and internal rhyme, arranged in varied and fairly complex patterns. Parallelism is employed occasionally, working with a combination of identical and matching words.

Tz'u

(Poems 18, 19, 27, 30, 42–44, 52–54, 56, 57, 63–66, 80, 90)

Tz'u (song words) were originally song words written in fixed patterns to go with new or old musical tunes. The oldest surviving *tz'u* texts are anonymous songs preserved in Tun-huang manuscripts, dating from the eighth century A.D. The early *tz'u* were songs, but eventually they established themselves as a poetic form without music, transforming the musical patterns into metric patterns. After the melodies were forgotten, *tz'u* poems continued to be written, bearing the names and following the patterns of the tunes. This practice has continued down to the present. Each pattern determines the number of lines, the number of syllables for each line, the sequence of tonal categories in each line, and the positions and tone of the end rhyme or rhymes. The lines of a given pattern are usually of uneven length, and the longer patterns feature two or three stanzas.

During the first flourishing of the *tz'u* in the tenth and eleventh centuries, poets felt free to vary the tonal and rhyme patterns of the tunes they were following. But thereafter the patterns became more rigid. The *Ch'in-ting tz'u-p'u* (*Imperial Register of Tz'u Prosody*), completed in 1715, lists 826 tune patterns, illustrated with 2306 varying forms. Naturally, the determination whether two given patterns should be considered separate tunes or variants of one tune is often arbitrary.

Yüeh-fu

(Poems 17, 21, 24, 37–39, 47–49, 51, 58–62, 83, 84, 87, 88)

Yüeh-fu literally means "music bureau." The Music Bureau was established by Emperor Wu of the Han dynasty around 120 B.C. One of its tasks was to collect anonymous folk songs from various parts of China, to be used at the court for ceremonial purposes. These songs became known as *yüeh-fu*, and the same name continued to be used after the abolition of the Music Bureau in 6 B.C. The term *yüeh-fu* was also applied to poems written by men of letters in the style of the anonymous *yüeh-fu* songs.

Each *yüeh-fu* poem bears a title which is frequently (but not always) taken from the opening words of the original song. When a new *yüeh-fu*

was made it often took the title of an older *yüeh-fu* which served as a model
for the music, and possibly also for the content, of the new poem. But
these traditional *yüeh-fu* titles, unlike the tune patterns of *tz'u* and *san-
ch'ü*, do not indicate a fixed metric pattern.

As far as prosody is concerned, we can distinguish two types of *yüeh-fu*
poems. The first type consists of early anonymous songs of the Han period,
composed of lines of uneven length, with end rhyme occurring at about
every second line. The rhyme may change in the course of the poem.
Parallelism is used occasionally. (Poems 47 and 51 are examples of this
type.) The other type is metrically identical with the *ku-shih* form. Some
anonymous four-line *yüeh-fu* songs may be considered forerunners of the
chüeh-chü form. (These *yüeh-fu* are noted under the heading *chüeh-chü*
above.) The remaining *yüeh-fu* of the second type are written in regular
lines of five syllables (Poems 17, 24, 37–39, 47–49, 51, 58, 59, 83, 84), six
syllables (Poems 87 and 88), or seven syllables (Poems 21, 60–62). In
Poem 49, the five-syllable line predominates but a few lines are longer.

Considered from the vantage point of world literature, the *yüeh-fu* may
be called a ballad, predominantly narrative in nature, with occasional
lyric overtones, but without the personal, egocentric thrust of the typical
lyric poem. The narrative tends to focus on one or more key episodes,
with abrupt changes of time and location. The oldest *yüeh-fu* were transmitted orally, and throughout its history this poetic form kept some
features that are bound up with its musical, illiterate origins. The diction
of *yüeh-fu* remained simpler, closer to the spoken idiom, and freer from
learned allusions than *ku-shih*, and in the early poems the language was to
a large extent formulaic. (See Frankel, "The Formulaic Language.")

Appendix 2: Historical and Legendary Figures and Episodes

The Celestial Raft

"According to an old tradition, the Sky River is connected with the sea. In recent times there was a man living on the sea shore. Every year, in the eighth month, a raft came floating by, never missing its schedule. The man conceived a unique project. He placed a high-rising structure on the raft, stocked it with plenty of food, boarded the raft, and departed. For ten-odd days he could still see the stars, the moon, the sun, and the planets. Thereafter it got vague and indistinct; he could not even tell whether it was day or night. When he had traveled another ten-odd days he arrived at a place where there were city walls, houses, and other buildings, all very stately. In the distance he perceived many women weaving in a palace. He saw a man leading a cow to the shore to water it. The cowherd was surprised to see him and asked: 'Where do you come from?' The man then told him his purpose in coming and asked what place this was. The cowherd answered: 'After you return, go to Shu and call on Yen Chün-p'ing, then you will know.' So he did not go ashore after all but returned on schedule. Afterwards he went to Shu and asked Chün-p'ing, who said: 'On such and such a day of a certain month of a certain year, an alien star invaded the constellation of the Cowherd.' Reckoning the year and month it was found to be exactly the time when the man had arrived on the Sky River."

Source: *Po-wu chih*, 10.3a-b. Yen Chün-p'ing was a learned scholar who lived in Shu (in modern Szechuan) in the first century B.C. The Sky River is the Milky Way. The story refers to the legend of the two stars Cowherd (our Altair) and Weaving Woman (Vega) as two lovers, separated by the Sky River but allowed to meet once a year, on the seventh day of the seventh month. For these and other legends, see also Edward H. Schafer, "The Sky River," *Journal of the American Oriental Society* 94 (1974): 401–07.

Chang Li-hua

An attractive and intelligent woman, Chang Li-hua was the favorite of Ch'en Shu-pao (reigned 582–89), the last emperor of the Ch'en dynasty. He gave her the title Kuei-fei, "Precious Consort," and spent much time with her, consulting her even on affairs of state. His rule and his dynasty ended in 589, when General Han Ch'in-hu, in the service of the Sui emperor Wen, conquered Chin-ling (modern Nanking), the Ch'en capital. At the time of the final battle, the Ch'en emperor was in the company of Chang Li-hua and another palace lady. When the military situation became hopeless, the three of them tried to commit suicide by jumping into a well, but they were pulled up with a rope by Sui soldiers and saved. Chang Li-hua was forthwith executed by the conquerors, while Ch'en Shu-pao became a prisoner at the Sui court.

Sources: *Ch'en shu*, 6.16b–17a and 7.8a-b; *Nan shih*, 10.14a-b and 12.9b–11a.

CH'EN P'ING

Ch'en P'ing (died 178 B.C.) eventually became one of the ministers of Kao-tsu, the founder of the Han dynasty. He came from a poor family, and lived in poverty for many years. He dwelled in a hut which used the city wall as one of its walls, and had a mat instead of a door.

Source: *Shih chi*, 56.1a-b.

CHENG CHIAO-FU

During the feudal period of the Chou dynasty, Cheng Chiao-fu was traveling in the Han River valley (in modern Hupei) when he met two river maidens. He dallied with them and asked them to remove their large, egg-sized girdle pendants and to give them to him, which they did. He placed them in his bosom and walked on. After a few steps, he found that the pendants had disappeared, and when he looked back, the maidens had also vanished.

The pendants are apparently pledges of love, and their removal from the girdle has an obvious sexual connotation.

Sources: *Han shih nei-chuan*, quoted by Li Shan in his commentary to Kuo P'u's "Chiang fu," in Hsiao T'ung, *Wen hsüan* (Shih-chieh), 12.173; *Lieh-hsien chuan*, quoted by Li Shan in his commentary to Ts'ao Chih's "Lo-shen fu," in Hsiao T'ung, *Wen hsüan* (Shih-chieh), 19.255.

CHING K'O

Ching K'o (died 227 B.C.), an expert swordsman, was commissioned by Prince Tan of Yen to assassinate King Cheng of Ch'in, who had humiliated Prince Tan when the latter was a hostage at the Ch'in court. Besides, the aggressive might of Ch'in threatened to wipe out Yen and the other feudal states—as it did in fact when Ch'in conquered all the other states, and King Cheng became the ruler of a unified China, styling himself "The First Emperor." Ching K'o's assassination attempt failed, and he was killed. He has been celebrated in the Chinese literary tradition for his brave though unsuccessful attempt on the life of an autocrat who suppressed and destroyed all writings and ideas which conflicted with his totalitarian views.

Source: *Shih chi*, 86.10a–19a. For a scholarly study of Prince Tan and Ching K'o in history and legend, see Franke, "Die Geschichte des Prinzen Tan von Yen."

CHU-FU YEN

Chu-fu Yen did not obtain an official post until about 127 B.C., when he was in his fifties. Up to that time he was despised even by his own parents and brothers.

Source: *Shih chi*, 112.12a–14a.

CHU MAI-CH'EN

Chu Mai-ch'en (flourished late second century B.C.) did not obtain a government post until late in life. When he was in his forties he made his living by selling firewood. His wife felt humiliated by his lowly occupation and left him.

Source: *Han shu*, 64A.11a-b.

CHUAN CHU

Chuan Chu in 515 B.C. assassinated Wang Liao of Wu on orders of Kung-tzu Kuang, who invited Wang to a banquet and had a dagger concealed inside the belly of a cooked fish. Chuan Chu served the fish, pulled out the dagger, and killed Wang Liao.

Source: *Shih chi*, 86.2a–3b.

FAN LI

Fan Li was a minister and general of Kou Chien, king of the southeastern coastal state of Yüeh. He was instrumental in strengthening Yüeh in preparation for the conquest of Wu in 473 B.C. (See also under Hsi Shih.) But soon after that great victory he resigned from Kou Chien's service and disappeared. In the words of the *Wu Yüeh ch'un-ch'iu*, "he traveled in a light boat in and out of the three rivers and the five lakes, and nobody knew where he went." According to the *Shih chi*, he changed his name, settled in the state of Ch'i (in modern Shantung), and amassed great wealth as a merchant. He became a patron deity of boatmen, fishermen, and traders.

Sources: *Wu Yüeh ch'un-ch'iu*, 10.62a–63a; *Shih chi*, 129.3a–5a; Schafer, *Vermilion Bird*, p. 52.

HSI SHIH

Hsi Shih is the prototype of the beautiful woman from Yüeh (approximately modern Chekiang). Kou Chien, King of Yüeh, had been defeated by Fu Ch'a, King of Wu, in 494 B.C. To avenge himself, he trained Hsi

Shih, a simple but extremely attractive peasant girl, in the arts of enter-
tainment and sent her as a gift to the Wu court, escorted by his minister
Fan Li (q.v.), hoping that she would distract Fu Ch'a from affairs of
state. The scheme worked, and led to the conquest of Wu by Yüeh in 473
B.C.

Source: *Wu Yüeh ch'un-ch'iu*, 9.39a–40a.

Li Ssu

Li Ssu (280?–208 B.C.) was a native of the state of Ch'u. He traveled to
the northwestern state of Ch'in and rose high in the favor of King Cheng
of Ch'in. When King Cheng had conquered all of China and proclaimed
himself First Emperor, he made Li Ssu his chief minister.

Source: *Shih chi*, chap. 87. See also Bodde, *China's First Unifier*.

Lu Chung-lien

Lu Chung-lien (flourished mid-third century B.C.), a native of the
state of Ch'i, preferred to live independently without accepting any official post. While he was in the state of Chao, an army from the state of
Ch'in surrounded the capital of Chao in an effort to force Chao to ac-
knowledge the hegemony of Ch'in over all of China. Lu Chung-lien
persuaded Chao not to yield. The commander of the Ch'in army thereupon withdrew his troops.

Sources: *Chan-kuo ts'e*, 6.62b–66b; *Shih chi*, 83.1a–6a.

Ma-ku

Ma-ku is a Taoist fairy. Once she visited the Taoist immortal Wang
Yüan. During her long stay, "Ma-ku said to Wang Yüan: 'Since I have
been entertained [here], I have seen the Eastern Sea change thrice into
mulberry fields. In the direction of P'eng-lai Island, furthermore, the
water is shallower than at the time of my previous visit by about one half.
Will there again come a time when one can walk across there?' Wang
Yüan smiled and said: 'The sages all say, "In the sea, dust is raised." ' "

Source: Ko Hung (284–363?), *Shen-hsien chuan*, 7.4a.

Nieh Cheng

Yen Chung Tzu, while in the service of Marquis Ai of Han (ruled
376–71 B.C.), became an enemy of Hsia Lei, Chief Minister of Han. He
fled to Ch'i and spent a hundred pieces of gold to win the friendship of the
professional assassin Nieh Cheng. Later Nieh Cheng went to Han and
killed Hsia Lei. After the assassination, he mutilated his own body and
gouged out his eyes in order to avoid recognition, then killed himself. His
corpse was displayed in the market place of the Han capital. His elder

sister recognized the body, revealed his identity, and killed herself at the side of his corpse.

Source: *Shih chi*, 86.6b–10a.

NUNG-YÜ

"Hsiao Shih ('Flute Master'?) lived at the time of Duke Mu of Ch'in [ruled 659–21 B.C.]. He excelled in playing the flute. The Duke's daughter Nung-yü loved him, and he married her. He then taught her to play the flute so as to produce the sound of the phoenix's call. For several decades she played phoenix-call music, and phoenixes came to perch at her room. A phoenix terrace was built for them, and the married couple lived there. One morning they both flew away with a phoenix."

Source: *Lieh-hsien chuan*, quoted in *Hou-Han shu*, 83.18a (commentary to biography of Chiao Shen).

PO YA AND CHUNG TZU-CH'I

"Po Ya was a good lute-player, and Chung Tzu-ch'i was a good listener. Po Ya strummed his lute, with his mind on climbing high mountains; and Chung Tzu-ch'i said: 'Good! Lofty, like Mount T'ai!' When his mind was on flowing waters, Chung Tzu-ch'i said: 'Good! Boundless, like the Yellow River and the Yangtse!' Whatever came into Po Ya's thoughts, Chung Tzu-ch'i always grasped it. Po Ya was roaming on the North side of Mount T'ai; he was caught in a sudden storm of rain, and took shelter under a cliff. Feeling sad, he took up his lute and strummed it; first he composed an air about the persistent rain, then he improvised the sound of crashing mountains. Whatever melody he played, Chung Tzu-ch'i never missed the direction of his thought. Then Po Ya put away his lute and sighed: 'Good! Good! How well you listen! What you imagine is just what is in my mind. Is there nowhere for my notes to flee to?'"

Source: Lieh-tzu, 5.7a (sec. 5, "T'ang wen"), as translated by Graham, *The Book of Lieh-tzŭ*, pp. 109–10. Quoted with Professor Graham's permission.

THE SEA GULLS

"There was a man living by the sea who loved sea gulls. Every morning he went to the sea shore and played with the sea gulls; the gulls came by the hundreds without stopping. His father said to him: 'I have heard that all the sea gulls play with you. I want you to attract them so that I can enjoy them.' The following day, at the sea shore, the sea gulls danced in the air but did not alight."

Source: Lieh-tzu, 2.6a (sec. 2, "Huang-ti").

Shih Ch'ung

Shih Ch'ung (249–300) was a military and civil official, socially prominent, and extremely wealthy. He competed with his peers in the display of luxury and conspicuous consumption. He was an influential writer
of poetry and prose, and gathered a circle of men of letters. He owned a
famous estate northwest of Lo-yang, called Chin-ku-yüan, "Gold Valley
Garden."

In 296 or soon thereafter he gave a magnificent farewell party at the
Chin-ku-yüan for General Wang Hsü, who was on his way back to
Ch'ang-an.

Sources: *Chin shu*, 33.10b–13a; Shih Ch'ung's preface to his "Chin-ku
shih," cited by Li Shan in his commentary to P'an Yüeh's "Chin-ku chi
tso shih," in Hsiao T'ung, *Wen hsüan* (Ssu-pu ts'ung-k'an), 20.42b;
Wilhelm, "Shih Ch'ung and His Chin-ku-yüan."

Shu Kuang

Shu Kuang (Su Kuang) was a Confucian scholar, and served as Grand
Tutor to the Heir Apparent during the reign (74–48 B.C.) of Emperor
Hsüan of Han. When he requested retirement because of old age, his re-
quest was granted, and he was given a grand farewell at the East Capital
Gate of Ch'ang-an.

Source: *Han shu*, 71.3b–4b.

Ssu-ma Hsiang-ju

Ssu-ma Hsiang-ju, courtesy name Ch'ang-ch'ing (ca. 179–117 B.C.),
was a native of Ch'eng-tu (in modern Szechuan). Until he came to
Emperor Wu's notice he lived in great poverty. At the imperial court he
became a famous poet.

Sources: *Shih chi*, chap. 117; *Han shu*, chap. 57; Hervouet, *Un poète de
cour sous les Han*.

Su Ch'in

Su Ch'in (died 317 B.C.) was a native of Lo-yang (in modern Honan
Province). He offered his services as a political theorist and adviser to
several states, was turned down by Ch'in but accepted in turn by the
northern states of Yen and Chao, and four other states.

Source: *Shih chi*, chap. 69.

Tu Yü

Tu Yü (Emperor Wang) was a culture hero and legendary ruler of Shu
(in modern Szechuan, southwestern China). He came to Shu from the
sky and taught the people how to plant crops. His minister was Pieh Ling

("Turtle God"). There was a great flood which Tu Yü was unable to stop but Pieh Ling did. While Pieh Ling was away on flood control, Tu Yü had an affair with his wife. Later Tu Yü yielded the throne to Pieh Ling, who ruled as Emperor K'ai-ming. Living in seclusion in the mountains (according to *Hua-yang-kuo chih*) or having died of shame (according to *Shuo-wen chieh-tzu*), Tu Yü was metamorphosed into a nightjar (Chinese *tu-yü*, *tu-chüan*, or *tzu-kuei*). The nightjar sheds bloody tears, which are sometimes identified with azaleas (*tu-chüan*). The nightjar's call reminds the farmers of the work to be done in the fields; its is also mournful, and sometimes nostalgic because it sounds like *pu ju kuei-ch'ü*, "better go home."

Sources: *T'ai-p'ing yü-lan*, 888.2b–3a, quoting "Annals of the Kings of Shu"; *Hua-yang-kuo chih*, 3.1b–2a; *Shuo-wen chieh-tzu*, 4A.5a (s.v. *kuei*); Yüan K'o, *Chung-kuo ku-tai shen-hua*, pp. 232–34.

Tuan-kan Mu

Tuan-kan Mu (late fifth to early fourth century B.C.) was a scholar in the state of Wei. He spurned public office, but Duke Wen of Wei revered him as his teacher. When the King of Ch'in prepared to attack Wei, Ssu-ma T'ang dissuaded him by pointing out that it would be unwise in view of Tuan-kan Mu's high reputation throughout China.

Source: *Lü shih ch'un-ch'iu*, 21.5a–b (sec. "Ch'i hsien").

Wang Ch'iang

Wang Ch'iang, courtesy name Chao-chün, also styled Ming-fei ("Bright Consort"), was a lady in the harem of the Han Emperor Yüan. She was given to the king of the Hsiung-nu (China's powerful nomadic neighbor in the Northwest) when he came to the Han court in 33 B.C. demanding a Chinese lady as his bride. She bore him a son who inherited the throne in 31 B.C. and married his mother, together with his late father's other wives, according to the custom of the Hsiung-nu.

A story included in the *Hsi-ching tsa-chi* says that she refused to bribe the Chinese court painter Mao Yen-shou, who therefore made her portrait ugly. As a consequence, she was not admitted to the imperial presence. Emperor Yüan only saw her after she had been promised to the Hsiung-nu king, and he regretted losing her, but it was then too late to prevent it.

According to another legend, recorded in the *T'ai-p'ing huan-yü chi*, her tomb (in modern Suiyuan Province, Inner Mongolia) always remained green, though surrounded by desert.

Sources: *Han shu*, 94B.7b–11a; *Hou-Han shu*, 89.3a–b; *Hsi-ching tsa-chi*, 2.1a; *T'ai-p'ing huan-yü chi*, 38 .9b.

Wu Tzu Hsü

Wu Tzu Hsü (died 485 B.C.) was a wise statesman and general from the state of Ch'u. He served King Fu Ch'a of Wu but quarreled with him. The King made him commit suicide and had his head cut off. His body was thrown into a river (the identity of the river is not clear) and in revenge, he created a bore in the river. In Later Han times (first to second century A.D.) he was worshipped in temples at several places on the East China coast where bores occurred, and sacrifices to him were intended to mitigate the destructive power of the bores.

Sources: *Wu Yüeh ch'un-ch'iu*, 1.61a–62a; Wang Ch'ung, *Lun heng*, 4.5b–7b (sec. "Shu hsü"); *Liang Han wen-hsüeh shih ts'an-k'ao tzu-liao*, pp. 25–26, n. 60.

Wu Yang

Wu Yang (third century B.C.) from the state of Yen accompanied Ching K'o (q.v.) on his abortive mission to assassinate King Cheng of Ch'in.

"When Ching K'o entered the Ch'in court with Wu Yang, the King of Ch'in had placed halberds on the steps beneath his throne as he received the envoys from Yen; drums and bells sounded at the same time, and all the courtiers shouted, 'Long live the King!' Wu Yang was greatly afraid, and his face turned the color of ash, as if he were dying."

Source: *Yen Tan tzu*, quoted by Li Shan in his commentary to Chiang Yen's *fu* "Parting," in Hsiao T'ung, *Wen hsüan* (Ssu-pu ts'ung-k'an), 16.37b–38a. See also *Shih chi*, 86.16b–17b, which contains the phrase *se pien* "turn pale," used in "Parting," l. 53.

Yü Jang

Having served two masters who treated him shabbily, Yü Jang entered the service of Baron Chih, who rewarded him very generously. When Baron Chih was killed by Lord Hsiang of Chao in 453 B.C., Yü Jang vowed to avenge him. He changed his name, pretended to be a convict, and found work as a mason in Lord Hsiang's palace. He undertook to cement the privy and planned to kill Lord Hsiang there, but he was suspected and arrested. During the interrogation he freely admitted his intention. Lord Hsiang was impressed with his loyalty to his late master and released him. One day Yü Jang hid under a bridge over which Lord Hsiang was going to pass. Again he was discovered before he could carry out the assassination. About to be executed, he requested to be given Lord Hsiang's gown so that he could stab it in an act of symbolic vengeance. Lord Hsiang granted his request. Yü Jang stabbed the gown three times, then hurled himself on his sword and died.

Sources: *Chan-kuo ts'e*, 6.7a–9a; *Shih chi*, 86.4a–6a.

Notes

1 One of the best essays on the latter subject is the first chapter of Graham, *Poems of the Late T'ang*.
2 For classical Chinese versification, see Liu, *The Art of Chinese Poetry*.
3 Edward H. Schafer in numerous publications brings his combined sinological and scientific expertise to bear on historical and literary Chinese texts, with admirable results.
4 See for instance the introduction to Brooks and Warren, *Understanding Poetry*.

CHAPTER 1

1 Hsieh Chen, *Ssu-ming shih-hua*, 3.2b.
2 Text: Chang P'u, *Liang Chien-wen ti chi*, 1.13b–14a; *Ch'üan Liang-wen* (in Yen K'o-chün, *Ch'üan shang-ku*), 8.8b–9a; *Li-tai fu-hui*, 124.1a–b. Incomplete texts: *Ch'u-hsüeh chi*, 28.682; *I-wen lei-chü*, 86.6a. An earlier version of my translation and interpretation was published in "The Plum Tree in Chinese Poetry," *Asiatische Studien* 6 (1952): 99–102. It is used here by permission of Francke Verlag, Bern.
3 The two encyclopedias are *I-wen lei-chü*, compiled by Ou-yang Hsün (557–641) and others, and *Ch'u-hsüeh chi*, compiled by Hsü Chien (659–729) and others. The two versions are fragmentary and overlapping. The quotation in *Ch'u-hsüeh chi* is more extensive, it includes lines 1–28 and 33–52. *I-wen lei-chü* only gives lines 13–16, 23–36, 45–46, and 49–52; moreover, it inserts an extra couplet between lines 32 and 33. This addition is accepted in *Ch'üan Liang-wen* and *Li-tai fu-hui*, but there are several reasons for rejecting it as a spurious interpolation.
4 *Lung-ch'eng lu*, as quoted in Su Shih, *Chi-chu fen-lei Tung-p'o hsien-sheng shih*, 14.19b, note. On the text, see Frankel, "The Date and Authorship of the *Lung-ch'eng lu*."
5 It is accepted, however, without comment in some recent scholarly works such as Yoshikawa, *Shikyō kokufū*, 1: 89, and Takada, *Shikyō*, 1: 93.
6 Waley, *Book of Songs*, p. 60.
7 Karlgren, *Book of Odes*, p. 13.
8 Child, *English and Scottish Popular Ballads*, no. 26 A.
9 Meier, *Balladen*, no. 92 A: broadside, Nuremberg, ca. 1530.
10 In his free translation Ezra Pound caught this point and rendered it beautifully: "Dead as doe is maidenhood" (*The Confucian Odes*, p. 11).
11 Text and commentary: Chao, *Wang yu-ch'eng chi chien-chu*, 14.2a. Previous translations: Payne, *White Pony*, p. 179; Chang and Walmsley, *Poems by Wang Wei*, no. 77 VI.
12 Text and commentaries: Chao, 7.9b–10a; Tsuru, *Ō I*, pp. 118–20; Chiang Shang-hsien, *T'ang Sung ming-chia shih*, pp. 91–92; Yü Shou-chen, *T'ang-*

shih san-pai shou, no. 103. Previous translations: Richard Wilhelm in Gundert, *Lyrik des Ostens*, p. 66; Bynner and Kiang, *Jade Mountain*, p. 192; Chang and Walmsley, no. 99; Tchang Fou-jouei and Jean-Pierre Diény in Demiéville, *Anthologie de la poésie chinoise classique*, p. 248; Yeh Sing-hwa, *Selection of Chinese Poetry*, p. 50.

13   Text: *Ch'üan Sui-shih* (in Ting Fu-pao), 1.1622.

14   Text and commentary: Yang Wan-li, *Ch'eng-chai chi*, 32.15b; Imazeki and Karashima, *Sōshi sen*, p. 239.

15   Text and commentaries: Hsiao T'ung, *Wen hsüan* (Ssu-pu ts'ung-k'an), 26. 35a–b; (Shih-chieh), 26.368; Huang Chieh, *Hsieh K'ang-lo shih chu*, 2.21b–22a; Yeh Hsiao-hsüeh, *Hsieh Ling-yün shih hsüan*, pp. 54–55; *Wei Chin nan-pei ch'ao wen-hsüeh shih ts'an-k'ao tzu-liao*, pp. 472–74. Previous translations: Frodsham, *Murmuring Stream*, 1: 128; Frodsham and Ch'eng, *Anthology of Chinese Verse*, pp. 130–31.

16   Hsieh probably wrote this poem when he was governor of Yung-chia (in southern Chekiang), 422–23 (Frodsham, *Murmuring Stream*, 1: 34–39). The river would then be the Yung-chia (Ou). *Ku-yü* ("solitary islet") may be an ordinary noun preceded by a modifying adjective, or it may be a place name, as suggested by Huang Chieh and Frodsham, who identify it as a small island with two peaks in the Yung-chia River, four *li* south of Wen-chou.

17   "Spending the Night at My Lodge on the Cliff of Rock Gate," Huang Chieh, *Hsieh K'ang-lo shih chu*, 3.14b–15a.

18   See Wu Ch'i (1615–75), *Liu-ch'ao hsüan shih ting-lun*, cited without contradiction in Huang Chieh, *Hsieh K'ang-lo shih chu*, 2.22a; and in *Wei Chin*, p. 473, n. 5. In Wu's interpretation, the poet, having formerly explored the northern bank and more recently the southern bank, is tired of the South and longs again for the North; while crossing from South to North he discovers the island.

19   Text: *Ch'üan Sui-shih* (in Ting Fu-pao), 1.1619. Previous translations: Waley, *Chinese Poems* (1946), p. 115; Peter Olbricht in Gundert, p. 59.

20   "Canción," from *Galán, valiente y discreto*, in Castro, *Poetas líricos de los siglos XVI y XVII*, 2: 422b.

21   Text and commentaries: Tai Chün-jen, *Sung-shih hsüan*, p. 13; Imazeki and Karashima, pp. 63–65; Ch'eng and Miao, *Sung-shih hsüan chu*, pp. 17–18; Ch'en Po-ku, *Sung-shih hsüan chiang*, p. 32.

22   This matter is well brought out and analyzed by Hoffmann, *Die Lieder des Li Yü*, p. 63 and passim.

23   Text and commentary: Tai Chün-jen, p. 145; Imazeki and Karashima, pp. 180–81.

CHAPTER 2

1   First of twelve or thirteen poems. Text and commentaries: Ch'en Hung-chih, *Li Ch'ang-chi ko-shih chiao-shih*. pp. 80–81; Wang Ch'i, *Li Ch'ang-chi ko-shih*, 1.60; Chiang Shang-hsien, *T'ang Sung ming-chia shih*, pp. 396–97; Saitō, *Tōshisen*, pp. 94–95. Previous translation: Frodsham, *The Poems of Li Ho*, p. 59.

2 "The Twelve Months, Inscribed on a Brocade Sash: The Fifth Month,"
   Ch'üan Liang-wen (in Yen K'o-chün), 19.8b. The borrowing is noted in Wang
   Ch'i's commentary.

3 Second of two poems. Text and commentaries: Su Shih, Tung-p'o hsien-sheng
   shih, 10.22a; Ogawa, So Shoku, 1: 73–74; Kondō, So Tōbo, pp. 112–13; Ch'ien
   Chung-shu, Sung-shih hsüan chu, p. 77; Chiang Shang-hsien, T'ang Sung ming-
   chia shih, pp. 468–69; Imazeki and Karashima, Sōshi sen, pp. 119–20; Ch'eng
   and Miao, Sung-shih hsüan chu, p. 48; Wang Li, Ku-tai Han-yü, pp. 1398–99.
   Previous translation: Pénélope Bourgeois and Max Kaltenmark in Demiéville, Anthologie, p. 347.

4 First of four poems. Text and commentaries: Wang Ch'i, Li T'ai-po ch'üan-chi,
   23.515; Aoki, Ri Haku, pp. 81–82; Takebe, Ri Haku, 1: 23–24; Chiang,
   T'ang Sung ming-chia shih, pp. 158–60; Yü Shou-chen, T'ang-shih san-pai shou,
   no. 19. Previous translations: Bynner and Kiang, Jade Mountain, pp. 59–60;
   Obata, Works of Li Po, no. 54; Günther Eich in Gundert, Lyrik des Ostens, p.
   79; Tsang Bing-ching in Payne, White Pony, p. 208; Liu, The Art of Chinese
   Poetry, p. 25; Tch'en Yen-hia and Jean-Pierre Diény in Demiéville, p. 226;
   Lai Ming, History of Chinese Literature, p. 160; Liu Wu-chi, Introduction to
   Chinese Literature, p. 75.

5 Text and commentary: Yang Wan-li, Ch'eng-chai chi, 36.16a–b; Chou Ju-
   ch'ang, Yang Wan-li hsüan-chi, pp. 218–19.

6 Text and commentaries: Yang Wan-li, 7.5b; Chou Ju-ch'ang, p. 64; Imazeki
   and Karashima, pp. 252–53.

7 Preface to "Tired, I Fall Asleep in 'Snow-Fisher Boat,' " in Chou Ju-ch'ang,
   p. 63.

8 "River Snow," in Yü Shou-chen, no. 241.

9 Hsiao T'ung, Wen hsüan (Shih-chieh), 56.778–80.

10 From "Tzu-yeh Songs of the Four Seasons." Text and commentary: Kuo
    Mao-ch'ien, Yüeh-fu shih chi, 44.6a; Wei Chin nan-pei ch'ao wen-hsüeh shih ts'an-
    k'ao tzu-liao, p. 361. Previous translation: Frodsham and Ch'eng, Anthology,
    p. 101.

11 First two poems from a cycle of nine. Text and commentary: T'ang Kuei-
    chang, Ch'üan Sung-tz'u, p. 3649; Hu Yün-i, Sung-tz'u hsüan, pp. 148–49.

12 Text and commentaries: Hsiao T'ung, Wen hsüan (Ssu-pu ts'ung-k'an), 23.
    20b–21a; (Shih-chieh), 23.316–17; Ch'üan san-kuo shih (in Ting Fu-pao),
    3.181; Shiba and Hanabusa, Monzen, pp. 37–38; Shen Te-ch'ien, Ku-shih
    yüan, pp. 157–58; Uchida, Koshi gen, pp. 298–99; Iritani, Koshisen, pp. 123–
    26; Yü Kuan-ying, Han Wei liu-ch'ao shih hsüan, p. 117; Wei Chin, pp. 132–33.
    Previous translation: Watson, Chinese Lyricism, p. 36. The title is traditional,
    but its syntax and the significance of "seven" are uncertain. Lü Hsiang (early
    eighth century), in his commentary to a poem by Ts'ao Chih with the same
    title, asserts that seven kinds of grief are aroused by seven senses (Hsiao T'ung
    [Ssu-pu ts'ung-k'an], 23.19a). Li Yeh (1192–1279; his name is sometimes
    given as Li Chih) connects the title with "the seven feelings" (cited by Huang
    Chieh, Ts'ao Tzu-chien shih chu, 1.3). Both explanations are unconvincing.
    More plausible is the suggestion made by Huang Chieh (ibid.) and Yü Kuan-

ying (*Han Wei liu-ch'ao shih hsüan*, p. 131, n. 1; *Ts'ao Ts'ao Ts'ao P'ei Ts'ao Chih shih hsüan*, p. 101) that the original *yüeh-fu* song bearing this title was divided into seven stanzas (*chieh*). Another theory holds that the title designates a cycle of seven poems. (See Suzuki, *Gyokudai shin'ei shū*, 1: 203; Shiba and Hanabusa, p. 36.) It is true that Wang Ts'an, Ts'ao Chih, and others each wrote more than one poem titled "Seven: Grief." But the three by Wang Ts'an which are extant today were obviously written at different times and places. This fact militates against the last-mentioned theory.

Poems consisting of seven parts were common in Han times (see Poem 106).

13   Ta-chiang ("Great River") normally refers to the Yangtze, but since the Yangtze is more than 100 miles south of Hsiang-yang, the administrative center of Chin and Liu Piao's headquarters where Wang Ts'an was presumably staying at the time, Iritani Sensuke suggests that the "Great River" must here be the Han, on which Hsiang-yang is located (*Koshisen*, p. 124). Shiba and Hanabusa assume that the poem speaks of Wang Ts'an's proceeding *toward* Ching, but this is hard to reconcile with line 2. Besides, a trip from Ch'ang-an to Ching would most likely go downstream, not upstream (l. 3), no matter which river was used. All these difficulties vanish when we take the river voyage as a fantasy. For a detailed account of Wang Ts'an's travels, see Miao Yüeh, "Wang Ts'an hsing nien k'ao," in his *Tu shih ts'un-kao*, pp. 116–26.

14   Text and commentary: Kuo Mao-ch'ien, *Yüeh-fu shih chi*, 86.3a (printed as two songs of two lines each); *Wei-Chin*, p. 373 (printed as one song). The first two lines only are cited in Li Tao-yüan, *Shui-ching chu*, 34.3b (section "Chiang-shui chu").

15   Text and commentaries: Wang Ch'i, *Li T'ai-po*, 23.523; Takebe, *Ri Haku*, 1: 31; Aoki, *Ri Haku*, p. 202; Kao Pu-ying, *T'ang Sung shih chü-yao*, 8.8a; Kanno, *Tōshi sen shōsetsu*, p. 173; Saitō, *Tōshi sen*, 2: 169–70; Takagi, *Tōshi sen*, 2: 124–25; Chiang Shang-hsien, *T'ang Sung ming-chia shih*, p. 205. Previous translations: Obata, no. 29; Günther Eich in Gundert, p. 72; Liu Wu-chi, p. 77; Yeh Sing-hwa, *Selection of Chinese Poetry*, p. 62.

16   "In Praise of Impoverished Gentlemen," first of seven poems, in Ikkai, *Tō Emmei*, p. 164; trans. Hightower, *The Poetry of T'ao Ch'ien*, pp. 203–04. The similarity between T'ao's and Li's poems is noted by Kanno, p. 713. Other implications of the imagery in T'ao's poem need not concern us here.

17   "Congratulating the Groom," in T'ang Kuei-chang, *Ch'üan Sung-tz'u*, p. 1915. The couplet is cited in conjunction with Li Po's poem by Yeh Chia-ying, "Wen T'ing-yün tz'u kai-shuo," pp. 63–64, reprinted in her *Chia-ling t'an tz'u*, p. 28.

18   Text and commentaries: Wang An-shih, 30.5a; Imazeki and Karashima, pp. 95–96; Shimizu, *Ō Anseki*, pp. 86–87. Previous translation: Jan Ulenbrook in Gundert, p. 131.

19   "Entering the Jo-yeh Stream Valley," *Ch'üan Liang-shih* (in Ting Fu-pao), 10.1178–79. Wang An-shih is said to have told his friend Huang T'ing-chien that he believed his own version to be superior to Wang Chi's. (See Shimizu, p. 86.)

CHAPTER 3

1 Text and commentaries: Ting Yen, *Ts'ao-chi ch'üan-p'ing*, 5.70; Huang Chieh, *Ts'ao Tzu-chien shih chu*, 2.99–100; Yü Kuan-ying, *Ts'ao Ts'ao Ts'ao P'ei Ts'ao Chih shih hsüan*, p. 27; Ku Chih, *T'sao Tzu-chien shih chien*, 3.9b–10a; Kuo Mao-ch'ien, *Yüeh-fu shih chi*, 40.2b; Itō, *Sō Shoku*, pp. 182–83. Previous translation: Kent, *Worlds of Dust and Jade*, p. 76. Earlier versions of this poem and Poem 31 were included in my article "Fifteen Poems by Ts'ao Chih" in *Journal of the American Oriental Society* 84 (1964), pp. 2 and 8.

2 Huang Chieh, *Ts'ao Tzu-chien shih chu*, 2.100; Chu Chia-cheng (1602–84) and Ch'en Tso-ming (seventeenth century), both quoted by Huang Chieh, ibid.; Lu K'an-ju and Feng Yüan-chün, *Chung-kuo shih shih*, p. 314; Itō, p. 183; Yü Kuan-ying, *Ts'ao Ts'ao Ts'ao P'ei Ts'ao Chih shih hsüan*, pp. 84–85.

3 Yü Kuan-ying, "Lun Chien-an Ts'ao shih fu-tzu ti shih," p. 153; Cheng Meng-t'ung and Huang Chih-hui, "Shih Lun Ts'ao Chih ho t'a-ti shih-ko," p. 103.

4 I have dealt with these matters more fully in "Fifteen Poems by Ts'ao Chih."

5 Text and commentaries: Hsiao Chi-tsung, *Meng Hao-jan shih shuo*, p. 206; Yu Hsin-li, *Meng Hao-jan chi chien-chu*, p. 281.

6 Cf. Frankel, "The 'I' in Chinese Lyric Poetry."

7 Text and commentaries: Yang Wan-li, *Ch'eng-chai chi*, 5.4a; Chou Ju-ch'ang, *Yang Wan-li hsüan-chi*, pp. 51–53; Tai Chün-jen, *Sung-shih hsüan*, pp. 158–59; Ogawa, *Sōshi sen*, pp. 228–30.

8 This interpretation of Yang's poem is based on Chou Ju-ch'ang's commentary.

9 Text and commentary: T'ang, *Ch'üan Sung-tz'u*, p. 935; Lo Ch'i, *Chung-kuo li-tai tz'u hsüan*, p. 202; Hu Yün-i, *Sung-tz'u hsüan*, p. 205. Previous translation: Kotewall and Smith, *Penguin Book of Chinese Verse*, p. 47.

10 *Ch'üan san-kuo shih* (in Ting Fu-pao), 3.183–84.

11 Texts in Kuo, *Yüeh-fu shih chi*, 69.1b–3b.

12 Text and commentaries: Hsiao Chi-tsung, *Meng Hao-jan shih shuo*, pp. 142–43; Yu, *Meng Hao-jan chi chien-chu*, pp. 246–47; Kao, *T'ang Sung shih chü-yao*, 4.16b. Previous translation: Rust, *Meng Hao-jan*, p. 4.

13 From "On My Return to the South Garden in Midsummer, I Send This to My Old Companions in the Capital," in Hsiao Chi-tsung, p. 45.

14 From "Going from Lo-yang to Yüeh, " in Hsiao Chi-tsung, p. 112.

15 From "At the Capital, Seeing Off the Eldest Son of the Hsin Clan on His Way to O," in Hsiao Chi-tsung, p. 139.

16 From "Six or Seven Miles West of Cloud Gate Temple, Hearing That Hermit Fu's Cell Is Most Secluded, I Go There with the Eighth Son of the Hsüeh Clan," in Hsiao Chi-tsung, p. 2. This Hsüeh is probably identical with the Hsüeh of our poem.

CHAPTER 4

1 See Arberry, *The Seven Odes*.

2 Text and commentary: Ch'ien Chung-lien, *Han Ch'ang-li shih hsi-nien chi-shih*,

7.315–16; Chu Hsi, *Chu Wen-kung chiao Ch'ang-li hsien-sheng chi*, 4.14a. Previous translation: von Zach, *Han Yü's Poetische Werke*, book IV, poem 23.

3　See Ch'ien Chung-lien, *Han Ch'ang-li shih*, p. 315, and Hanabusa, *Kan Yu kashi sakuin*, p. 68.

4　Text and commentaries: T'ang, *Ch'üan Sung-tz'u*, p. 222; T'ang Kuei-chang, *Sung-tz'u san-pai shou chien-chu*, pp. 40–41; Hsü K'o, *Li-tai tz'u hsüan chi-p'ing*, p. 41; Cheng Ch'ien, *Tz'u hsüan*, pp. 28–29; Lung Yü-sheng, *T'ang Sung ming-chia tz'u hsüan*, p. 94; Chiang, *T'ang Sung ming-chia tz'u*, pp. 121–23; Hu, *Sung-tz'u hsüan*, pp. 48–49. Previous translation: Ayling and Mackintosh, *Collection of Chinese Lyrics*, no. 34.

5　From the first of a series of eight poems titled "Kung chung hsing-lo tz'u," in Wang Ch'i, *Li Ta'i-po*, 5.146.

6　First of two poems. Text and commentaries: Hsiao T'ung, *Wen hsüan* (Ssu-pu ts'ung-k'an), 20.40a–b; (Shih-chieh), 20.277–78; Ting Yen, *Ts'ao-chi*, 4.36; Huang Chieh, *Ts'ao Tzu-chien*, 1.8–9; Ku Chih. *Ts'ao Tzu-chien*, 1.1b–2b; Yü Kuan-ying, *Ts'ao Ts'ao*, pp. 37–38; Itō, *Sō Shoku*, pp. 29–31. Previous translations: von Zach, *Die Chinesische Anthologie*, book XX, poem 18; Waley, *Chinese Poems* (1946), pp. 79–80; Kent, *Worlds of Dust and Jade*, p. 38; Watson, *Chinese Lyricism*, pp. 39–40; Sackheim, *Silent Zero*, p. 102.

7　Text: Kao, *T'ang Sung shih chü-yao*, 8.41b.

8　Text and commentary: Ch'ien Chung-lien, *Han Ch'ang-li*, 7.338–40. Previous translation: von Zach, *Han Yü*, V.3–4.

9　The connection between "Master of Jade River" and "Jade Emperor" is pointed out by von Zach. Han Yü places his friend in this lofty position for the purposes of this poem only. In another poem, written probably at about the same time, he describes Lu T'ung's dwelling and circumstances in less glorious terms:

> The Master of Jade River lives in the city of Lo-yang,
> In a broken-down house with just a few rooms.
> He has a single manservant with a long beard but no headcloth
> And a single maidservant with bare feet, old and toothless.
> Diligently he supports more than ten persons,
> His mother at the top, his wife and children below.

("Sent to Lu T'ung," in Ch'ien Chung-lien, *Han Ch'ang-li*, 7.340.) Both descriptions are probably exaggerated.

CHAPTER 5

1　*Hsien-Ch'in wen-hsüeh shih ts'an-k'ao tzu-liao*, p. 68, n. 4.

2　"I call it a 'carrier-sound', because its original function was obviously to carry the singing voice through parts of the melody for which there were no corresponding words" (Hawkes, *Ch'u Tz'ŭ*, p. 5).

3　In Karlgren's reconstruction the rhyming syllables all end in ŏg or ôg, see his "Grammata serica recensa."

4　Cf. the dew imagery in Herrick's "Corinna's going a-Maying," discussed by Brooks, *The Well Wrought Urn*, p. 73.

5　Text: *Ch'üan Sung-shih* (in Ting Fu-pao), 5.722; Kuo, *Yüeh-fu shih chi*, 69.2a.

6 Two poems from a series of six. Text: *Ch'üan Ch'en-shih* (in Ting Fu-pao), 1.1346; Kuo, 69.2b.

7 Second of two poems. Text and commentaries: Feng Chi-wu, *Fan-ch'uan shih chi-chu*, 4.311–12; Yü Shou-chen, *T'ang-shih san-pai shou*, no. 291; Chiang, *T'ang-Sung ming-chia shih*, p. 414. Previous translations: Bynner and Kiang, *Jade Mountain*, p. 177; Payne, *White Pony*, p. 319; Günther Debon in Gundert, *Lyrik des Ostens*, p. 121; Kotewall and Smith, *Penguin Book of Chinese Verse*, p. 24; Graham, *Poems of the Late T'ang*, p. 134; Watson, *Chinese Lyricism*, p. 121.

8 Eleventh of twelve poems. Text: Wang Ch'i, *Li T'ai-po*, 25.570. Previous translations: C. H. Kwock and Vincent McHugh in Birch, *Anthology of Chinese Literature*, p. 226; Scott, *Love and Protest*, p. 71.

CHAPTER 6

1 Text and commentaries: Fong, *Tz'u shih ta-ch'üan*, 1.27–28; Hsü K'o, *Li-tai tz'u-hsüan chi-p'ing*, pp. 4–6; Chiang, *T'ang Sung ming-chia tz'u*, pp. 17–22 (Poems 42 and 43).

2 See Yü P'ing-po, *Tu tz'u ou te*, p. 3; and Yeh Chia-ying, "Wen T'ing-yün tz'u kai-shuo," pp. 71–72, reprinted in her *Chia-ling t'an tz'u*, p. 41.

3 Text and commentaries: Yü Shou-chen, *T'ang-shih san-pai shou*, no. 243; Chiang, *T'ang Sung ming-chia shih*, pp. 401–02; Kao, *T'ang Sung shih chü-yao*, 8.14b–15a. Previous translation: Bynner and Kiang, *Jade Mountain*, p. 11.

4 The song's nature and origin are not clear from the conflicting accounts that have been preserved. The sources are collected and discussed by Wen Ju-hsien, *Tz'u-p'ai hui shih*, pp. 201–04; and Gimm, *Das Yüeh-fu tsa-lu*, pp. 343–45. According to some sources, Ho Man-tzu was originally the name of the singer and dancer who created the piece.

5 Gimm suggests it may have been an ecstatic cult dance from Central Asia. This plausible theory goes well with the first line of our poem, though that line does not unquestionably identify the singer as a foreigner, since *ku kuo* "old country," "homeland" could refer either to a foreign country or to a region of China.

CHAPTER 7

1 Text and commentaries: Kuo, *Yüeh-fu shih chi*, 38.9a–b; *Ch'üan Han-shih* (in Ting Fu-pao), 4.72–73; Shen Te-ch'ien, *Ku-shih yüan*, pp. 67–68; *Liang Han wen-hsüeh shih ts'an-k'ao tzu-liao*, pp. 524–27; Huang, *Han Wei yüeh-fu feng chien*, 4.38–40; Yü Kuan-ying, *Yüeh-fu shih hsüan*, pp. 35–37; idem, *Han Wei liu-ch'ao shih hsüan*, pp. 38–40; P'an, *Yüeh-fu shih ts'ui chien*, pp. 34–37; Wang Li, *Ku-tai Han-yü*, pp. 1310–12; Iritani, *Koshisen*, pp. 72–80. Previous translations: Waley, *Chinese Poems* (1946), pp. 49–50; Yves Hervouet and Max Kaltenmark in Demiéville, *Anthologie*, pp. 107–08; Sackheim, *Silent Zero*, pp. 48–49.

2 Chiu-chiang ("Nine Rivers") is in modern Anhwei Province; Ch'i and Lu are in Shantung. The three place names put the scene of the poem in what is now Honan Province, as noted by Yü, *Yüeh-fu shih hsüan*, p. 36.

3 Different assumptions are revealed by Ch'en Tso-ming, who comments on

the poem as follows: "When one savors the poem in its totality, it seems that the episode of the melon cart is a real event which the poem actually commemorates, and the preceding episodes of traveling as a peddler and fetching water are only supplementary. Otherwise, why would the poem relate and lament the small incident of the cart so minutely?" (Quoted with approval in *Liang Han*, p. 525, n. 1.)

4   The poem seems to imply that he is not allowed to rest on his return. This point is made in the *Liang Han* commentary, p. 526, n. 11.

5   Such an interpretation is suggested by Li Tzu-te, quoted in Huang, *Han Wei yüeh-fu feng chien*, 4.40.

6   "Barbara Allen," in Hodgart, *Faber Book of Ballads*, p. 235, after Campbell and Sharp, eds., *English Folksongs from the Southern Appalachians*. This is a seventeenth-century English ballad (Child, no. 84) which became popular in the U.S.

7   In the orally transmitted Spanish ballads (*romances*), the narrator's past tense often intrudes into a speech that deals with events occurring at the time of the ballad's action. The Hungarian scholar Joseph Szertics has pointed out that in such cases the narrator blends his own voice with that of the interlocutors (*Tiempo y verbo en el Romancero Viejo*, pp. 82, 195). Stephen Gilman has termed this feature "double directionality," see his "On 'Romancero' as a Poetic Language."

8   Text and commentaries: Wu Chao-i, *Chien-chu yü-t'ai hsin-yung*, 1.15a–b; Suzuki, *Gyokudai shin'ei shū*, 1: 100–04; Kuo, *Yüeh-fu shih chi*, 73.1b–2a; Shen Te-ch'ien, *Ku-shih yüan*, p. 47; Uchida, *Koshi gen*, pp. 121–23; *Ch'üan Han-shih* (in Ting Fu-pao), 2.46; *Liang Han wen-hsüeh shih ts'an-k'ao tzu-liao*, pp. 540–41; Yü, *Yüeh-fu shih hsüan*, p. 152; Yü, *Han Wei liu-ch'ao shih hsüan*, pp. 27–28; Hsü Ch'eng-yü, *Yüeh-fu ku-shih*, pp. 68–69. Previous translations: Demiéville, *Anthologie*, p. 110; Sackheim, *Silent Zero*, p. 62. As for the title of the poem, Tung is a surname and Chiao-jao ("Graceful") is a girl's personal name. "Tung Chiao-jao" was perhaps the title of an earlier *yüeh-fu* song, as suggested by Yü Kuan-ying (*Han Wei liu-ch'ao shih hsüan*, p. 28). In T'ang poetry it was the type name of a beautiful girl, especially a professional singing-girl. (See *Liang Han*, p. 540, n. 1.)

9   I follow the generally accepted view about the distribution and attribution of the spoken portions, as set forth in *Liang Han*: lines 11–12 and 17–20 are spoken by the flowering trees and lines 13–16 by the mulberry-picking girl. However, according to Suzuki Torao and Uchida Sennosuke it is a dialogue between a passerby and the mulberry girl. But line 12, in the original wording, seems to me to indicate that the trees are speaking themselves, not being spoken about.

10 Text and commentaries: Kuo, *Yüeh-fu shih chi*, 25.10a–11a; *Wei Chin nan-pei ch'ao wen-hsüeh shih ts'an-k'ao tzu-liao*, pp. 379–82; Yü, *Yüeh-fu shih hsüan*, pp. 119–22; Yü, *Han Wei liu-ch'ao shih hsüan*, pp. 334–38; P'an, *Yüeh-fu shih ts'ui chien*, pp. 101–05; Hsü Ch'eng-yü, *Yüeh-fu ku-shih*, pp. 151–55; Liang Jung-jo, *Chu-yin ku-chin wen hsüan chu*, pp. 25–27. Previous translations: Waley, *Chinese Poems* (1946), pp. 113–15; Wong T'ong-wen and Jean-Pierre Diény

in Demiéville, *Anthologie*, pp. 189–91; Frodsham and Ch'eng, *Anthology*, pp. 104–06; Sackheim, *Silent Zero*, pp. 50–52.

11 This ambiguity is noted by Wong and Diény.

12 Previous translators seem to have misunderstood it by taking it literally.

13 The *hu-wen* aspect of this couplet has been recognized by some commentators, such as Yü Kuan-ying, Hsü Ch'eng-yü, the *Wei Chin* editors, and P'an Ch'ung-kuei. Others, however, have taken the two lines literally, e.g., Liang Jung-jo, Waley, Wong and Diény, and Frodsham and Ch'eng. Lines 33–34 have never before been taken as *hu-wen*, as far as I am aware.

CHAPTER 8

1 Text and commentaries: Hsiao T'ung, *Wen hsüan* (Ssu-pu ts'ung-k'an), 16.35a–41a; (Shih-chieh), 16.221–23; *Ch'üan Liang-wen* (in Yen), 33.6a–7a; Hsü Lien, *Liu-ch'ao wen-chieh chien-chu*, 1.16–23; Chang Jen-ch'ing, *Li-tai p'ien-wen hsüan*, 1: 95–108; *Wei Chin nan-pei ch'ao wen-hsüeh shih ts'an-k'ao tzu-liao*, pp. 630–39; Wang Li, *Ku-tai Han-yü*, pp. 1214–23. Previous translations: Margouliès, *Le "fou" dans le Wen-siuan*, pp. 75–81; Margouliès, *Anthologie raisonnée de la littérature chinoise*, pp. 307–09 (see Erwin von Zach, "Zu G. Margouliès' Übersetzung des Pieh-fu," *T'oung Pao*, n.s. 25 [1928]: 359–60); Watson, *Chinese Rhyme-Prose*, pp. 96–101.

2 "Tseng hsien-na-shih ch'i-chü T'ien she-jen," in Hung, *Tu-shih yin-te*, 18.282.

3 Text and commentary: Ts'ui Pao, *Ku-chin chu*, 2.3a; Kuo, *Yüeh-fu shih chi*, 27.3b–4a; Yü, *Yüeh-fu shih hsüan*, p. 10. Previous translations: Waley, *Chinese Poems* (1946), pp. 55–56; Watson, *Early Chinese Literature*, p. 290; Yves Hervouet and Max Kaltenmark in Demiéville, *Anthologie*, p. 97; Frodsham and Ch'eng, *Anthology of Chinese Verse*, p. 2; Hightower, *The Poetry of T'ao Ch'ien*, p. 250.

4 Hsiao T'ung, *Wen hsüan* (Shih-chieh), 29.403–04.

5 "Ch'iu-liang shih chi cheng-tzu shih-erh hsiung," in Ch'en Hung-chih, *Li Ch'ang-chi ko-shih*, 3.262–63.

6 *Metamorphoses* 13.621–22.

7 Quevedo, *Obras en verso*, pp. 14–15.

8 "Madrigal" from *La Guirlande de Julie*, in Livet, *Précieux et précieuses*, p. 396.

9 "Fu-p'ing p'ien," in Huang Chieh, *Ts'ao Tzu-chien*, 2.94–95, 1. 22.

10 "Sung Wang ch'i wei Sung-tzu te Yang-t'ai yün," in Hsiao Chi-tsung, *Meng Hao-jan shih shuo*, pp. 61–62.

11 "Meng Li Po" (second of two poems), in Hung, *Tu-shih yin-te*, 5.79–80.

12 Hsiao T'ung, *Wen hsüan* (Shih-chieh), 13.179–81.

13 Text and commentaries: T'ang, *Ch'üan Sung-tz'u*, p. 280; Ogawa, *So Shoku*, 2: 109–13; Chiang, *T'ang Sung ming-chia tz'u*, pp. 160–63; T'ang, *Sung-tz'u san-pai shou chien-chu*, pp. 50–52; Hu, *T'ang Sung tz'u i-pai shou*, pp. 41–42; Hu, *Sung-tz'u hsüan*, pp. 63–65; Lo Ch'i, *Chung-kuo li-tai tz'u hsüan*, pp. 132–33; Ch'iu and Li, *Tz'u hsüan*, pp. 35–39; Kondō, *So Tōbo*, pp. 144–47; Wang Li, *Ku-tai Han-yü*, pp. 1473–74. Previous translations: Yu Min-chuan in Payne, *White Pony*, pp. 348–49; Kotewall and Smith, *Penguin Book of Chinese Verse*, pp. 41–42; Lai Ming, *History of Chinese Literature*, pp. 223–24; Liu Wu-chi,

Introduction to Chinese Literature, p. 111; Ayling and Mackintosh, *Collection of Chinese Lyrics*, no. 45; Chen Shih-chuan, *T'ang Sung tz'u hsüan i*, pp. 82–84.

14 "Yen ko hsing," in Huang Chieh, *Wei Wu-ti Wei Wen-ti shih chu*, pp. 50–51.

15 Text and commentaries: She Hsüeh-man, *Li hou-chu tz'u hsin-shang*, p. 78; T'ang, *Nan-T'ang erh chu tz'u hui-chien*, pp. 11b–12a; Murakami, *Ri Iku*, pp. 82–83. Previous translations: Hoffmann, *Die Lieder des Li Yü*, pp. 150–52; Hoffmann and Günther Debon in Gundert, *Lyrik des Ostens*, p. 126; Hsiung Ting in Payne, p. 328; Ayling and Mackintosh, no. 18; Chen Shih-chuan, p. 40; Yeh Sing-hwa, *Selection of Chinese Poetry*, p. 85.

16 Text and commentaries: She Hsüeh-man, pp. 81–82; T'ang, *Nan-T'ang*, pp. 4a–6b; Murakami, pp. 84–85. Previous translations: Hoffmann, pp. 138–42; Hsiung Ting in Payne, pp. 330–31; Feifel, *Geschichte der chinesischen Literatur*, p. 238; Lai Ming, p. 212; Liu Wu-chi, pp. 104–05; Ayling and Mackintosh, no. 25; Chen Shih-chuan, p. 38; Yeh Sing-hwa, p. 88; Cyril Birch in Birch, *Anthology*, p. 352.

17 "Raising Barriers," l. 20; trans. Hawkes, *Ch'u Tz'ŭ*, p. 148.

18 "The God of the Yellow River," l. 16; trans. Hawkes, *Ch'u Tz'ŭ*, p. 42.

19 "Sung-yüan ch'ü," in Hung Shun-lung, *Hsieh Hsüan-ch'eng chi chiao chu*, 2.165–67.

20 Wu Yüan-heng (758–815), "Sung Liu lang-chung," in *Ch'üan T'ang-shih*, case 7, vol. 5, 1.5b.

21 Niu Ch'iao (*chin-shih* 878), "Kan en to," in Fong, *Tz'u shih ta-ch'üan*, 2.3, ll. 1–2.

22 Wang Po (649?–76?), "Ch'iu-jih pieh Wang chang-shih," in Wang Po, *Wang Tzu-an chi*, 3.6b, ll. 3–4.

23 Kuo, *Yüeh-fu shih chi*, 38.1a–2a.

24 "T'ung Hsin Pu-chien ying-ch'ou Ssu-hsüan shang-jen Lin-ch'üan" (last of four poems), in Ch'en Hsi-chin, *Lo Lin-hai chi chien-chu*, 2.73–74, ll. 7–8.

25 Huo Sung-lin, *Po Chü-i shih hsüan i*, p. 270.

26 Text and commentaries: Chao, *Wang yu-ch'eng chi chien-chu*, 13.11a; Tsuru, *Ō I*, pp. 27–28; Yü Shou-chen, *T'ang-shih san-pai shou*, no. 222. Previous translations: Bynner and Kiang, *Jade Mountain*, p. 189; Payne, *White Pony*, p. 181; Chang and Walmsley, *Poems by Wang Wei*, no. 21.

27 Trans. Hawkes, *Ch'u Tz'ŭ*, pp. 119–20.

28 See Sun, "The Grass Motif in Chinese Poetry."

29 Text and commentaries: She Hsüeh-man, pp. 74–75; T'ang, *Nan-T'ang*, p. 9b; Murakami, pp. 60–62. Previous translations: Hoffmann, pp. 76–77; Hsiung Ting in Payne, p. 329; Ayling and Mackintosh, no. 22; Yeh Sing-hwa, p. 84.

30 The effect of placing this image at the very end of Poem 53 is pointed out by Hoffmann, pp. 151–52.

31 Text and commentaries: T'ang, *Ch'üan Sung-tz'u*, p. 617; Chiang, *T'ang Sung ming-chia tz'u*, pp. 253–56; T'ang, *Sung-tz'u san-pai shou chien-chu*, pp. 93–94.

32 "Chin-shan ssu," in Wang An-shih, *Lin-ch'üan hsien-sheng wen-chi*, 36.4b–5a, l. 16. The derivation is noted by Chiang Shang-hsien, p. 253.

33 For an impressionistic essay on "Willows and Parting" in Sung *tz'u*, see Chou Kuo-ts'an, *Sung-tz'u shang-hsi*, pp. 41–46.

34 *San-fu huang-t'u*, 6.3b.

35 Text: Kuo, *Yüeh-fu shih chi*, 25.7b.

36 Text: Kuo, 22.5b–6a; *Ch'üan Liang-shih* (in Ting Fu-pao), 3.943. The poet reigned 549–55 as Emperor Yüan of the Liang dynasty.

37 Text: Liu Yü-hsi, *Liu Meng-te wen-chi*, 9.10a–b; Kuo, 81.5a.

38 Seventh and eighth of eight poems. Text: Ku Chao-ts'ang and Chou Ju-ch'ang, *Po Chü-i shih hsüan*, pp. 314–15; Kuo, 81.4a–b.

39 Text and commentaries: T'ang, *Ch'üan Sung-tz'u*, p. 123; Chiang, *T'ang Sung ming-chia tz'u*, pp. 111–12; T'ang, *Sung-tz'u san-pai shou chien-chu*, pp. 21–22; Ch'iu and Li, *Tz'u hsüan*, pp. 21–23; Lo Ch'i, *Chung-kuo li-tai tz'u hsüan*, pp. 96–97. Previous translation: Chen Shih-chuan, *T'ang Sung tz'u hsüan i*, p. 60.

40 This interpretation is given by Ch'iu and Li.

41 Text and commentaries: T'ang, *Ch'üan Sung-tz'u*, p. 277; Ogawa, *So Shoku*, 2:145–48; Chiang, *T'ang Sung ming-chia tz'u*, pp. 174–76; T'ang, *Sung-tz'u san-pai shou chien-chu*, pp. 52–54; Hu, *Sung-tz'u hsüan*, pp. 84–86; Lo Ch'i, pp. 164–65; Kondō, *So Tōbo*, pp. 246–49; Wang Li, *Ku-tai Han-yü*, pp. 1477–78. Previous translations: Ayling and Mackintosh, *Collection of Chinese Lyrics*, no. 47; Chen Shih-chuan, pp. 94–96.

42 Quoted by Chiang Shang-hsien.

43 Last couplet of "Honoring the Good," the fifth of the "Nine Regrets" by Wang Pao, trans. Hawkes, *Ch'u Tz'ŭ*, p. 146.

44 Huang Chieh, *Ts'ao Tzu-chien*, 2.94–95.

45 Text: T'ang, *Ch'üan Sung-tz'u*, p. 458; Jao, *Huai-hai chü-shih ch'ang-tuan chü*, 1.16–17; Jen-han chü-shih, *Huai-hai chü-shih ch'ang-tuan chü chiao chu*, 1.11–12. Previous translation: Chen Shih-chuan, p. 110. An earlier version of my translation was published in "Classical Chinese," in *Versification: Major Language Types*, edited by W. K. Wimsatt (New York University Press, 1972, © by New York University), p. 33. It is used here by permission of New York University Press.

46 Text and commentary: T'ang, *Ch'üan Sung-tz'u*, p. 888; Chiang, *T'ang Sung ming-chia tz'u*, pp. 298–99.

CHAPTER 9

1 *Li chi*, sec. 41, "The Behavior of the Confucian." For this reference I am indebted to Anne M. Birrell.

2 I have dealt with this matter from a different viewpoint, using some of the same materials, in "The Contemplation of the Past in T'ang Poetry," in *Perspectives on the T'ang*, ed. Wright and Twitchett.

3 Text in *Ch'üan Han-shih* (in Ting Fu-pao), 2.34–35.

4 Third, seventh, and eighth of the series. Text and commentaries: Hsiao T'ung, *Wen hsüan* (Ssu-pu ts'ung-k'an), 21.4a–b, 6b–8b; (Shih-chieh), 21.282–83, 283–84; *Ch'üan Chin-shih* (in Ting Fu-pao), 4.385, 386; Shiba and Hanabusa, *Monzen*, pp. 153, 156–57; *Wei Chin nan-pei ch'ao wen-hsüeh*

shih ts'an-k'ao tzu-liao, pp. 291–92, 296–98; Yü Kuan-ying, *Han Wei liu-ch'ao shih hsüan*, pp. 174–75, 178–81; Wang Li, *Ku-tai Han-yü*, pp. 1324–25 (Poem 67 only). Previous translations: von Zach, *Die Chinesische Anthologie*, XXI. 5, 9, 10; Watson, *Chinese Lyricism*, p. 126 (Poem 69, ll. 1–4 only).

5   Translations: von Zach, *Die Chinesische Anthologie*, XXI. 4; Frodsham and Ch'eng, *Anthology of Chinese Verse*, pp. 95–96.

6   Text and commentaries: Hsü P'eng, *Ch'en Tzu-ang chi*, p. 17; Kanno, *Tōshi sen shōsetsu*, pp. 390–92; Takagi, *Tōshi sen*, 1: 250–53; Saitō, *Tōshi sen*, 1: 266–68; Chiang Hsia-an, *T'ang-shih hsüan p'ing-shih*, pp. 240–42; Wang Yao-ch'ü, *Ku T'ang-shih ho-chieh*, 2.88–89.

7   Text and commentaries: Hsü P'eng, p. 17; Kanno, pp. 392–95; Takagi, 1: 253–57; Saitō, 1: 268–69; Chiang Hsia-an, pp. 242–43.

8   *Chin shu*, 34.6b.

9   *Mu t'ien-tzu chuan*, 3.15b.

10   Text and commentaries: Hsiao Chi-tsung, *Meng Hao-jan shih shuo*, pp. 65–66; Yu, *Meng Hao-jan chi chien-chu*, pp. 147–48; Chiang, *T'ang Sung ming-chia shih*, pp. 66–67; Yü Shou-chen, *T'ang-shih san-pai shou*, no. 120. Previous translations: Bynner and Kiang, *Jade Mountain*, p. 109; Rust, *Meng Hao-jan*, p. 2. This poem, as well as Poems 73 and 75–79, were translated and discussed in my essay "The Contemplation of the Past in T'ang Poetry," in *Perspectives on the T'ang*, ed. Wright and Twitchett, pp. 345–48 and 358–63.

11   *Chin shu*, 34.5a.

12   *Han-shih wai-chuan*, 7.15b. Previous translation: Hightower, *Han shih wai chuan*, p. 248.

13   For a full translation and discussion of the "Nine Arguments," see Hawkes, *Ch'u Tz'ŭ*, pp. 92–100.

14   Hsiao T'ung, *Wen hsüan* (Ssu-pu ts'ung-k'an), 13.4b–10a. Previous translation: von Zach, *Die Chinesische Anthologie*, XIII. 2.

15   Sec. 26, "External Things."

16   Liao K'uang-t'u, "Chiu-jih p'ei Tung nei-chao teng kao," in Chin Jen-jui, *T'ang-shih i-ch'ien shou*, p. 480.

17   Text and commentaries: *Ō Shōrei shishū*, 4.56–57; Kanno, pp. 624–25; Saitō, 2: 108–109; Wang Yao-ch'ü, 2.37.

18   Text: *Ch'üan T'ang-shih*, case 3, vol. 6, fol. 4a–b.

19   Text and commentaries: Hung, *Tu-shih yin-te*, 30.471–73; Ch'iu Chao-ao, *Tu-shih hsiang-chu*, 17.29b–36a; Yang Lun, *Tu-shih ching-ch'üan*, 13.26b–29a; Ch'ien Ch'ien-i, *Tu kung-pu chi*, 15.7a–9a; Kao, *T'ang Sung shih chü-yao*, 5.29a–31b; Kurakawa, *To Ho*, 1:164–73; Wang Li, *Ku-tai Han-yü*, pp. 1382–86; Feng Chih, *Tu Fu shih hsüan*, pp. 222–25; Hsiao Ti-fei, *Tu Fu yen-chiu*, 2: 179–82 (Poems 76–78 only). Previous translations: von Zach, *Tu Fu's Gedichte*, book XV, poems 55–59; Hung, *Tu Fu: China's Greatest Poet*, p. 236 (Poems 76 and 78 only); Bynner and Kiang, *Jade Mountain*, p. 157 (Poems 78 and 80 only); Hsieh Wen T'ung in Payne, *White Pony*, p. 227 (Poem 78 only); Hawkes, *Primer*, nos. 27–28 (Poems 78 and 80 only); Yeh Sing-hwa, *Selection of Chinese Poetry*, pp. 54–55 (Poem 76 only).

20   "Chao-chün's Grief," in Kuo, *Yüeh-fu shih chi*, 59.1a–b.

21   See Hsiao Ti-fei, 2:182.

22   Kuo, 59.1b–2b, 29.1b–7b.

23   Hawkes, *Primer*, p. 175.

24   Hung, *Tu Fu: China's Greatest Poet*, pp. 228, 229.

25   Ni, *Yü Tzu-shan chi chu*, 2.3a.

26   The derivation of Yü Hsin's couplet is indicated in Ni Fan's commentary. Tu Fu's source is noted by Kao Pu-ying.

27   Wang Li takes "river(s) and pass(es)" to stand for the Southland, which seems unlikely to me.

28   Hsiao T'ung, *Wen hsüan* (Shih-chieh), 19.249.

29   This series is noted by Hsiao Ti-fei.

30   Kao, *T'ang Sung shih chü-yao*, 5.29b.

31   Yü Hsin, "K'u-shu fu," in Ni, 1.16b. The provenience of the phrase is noted by Ch'iu Chao-ao.

32   This is Yang Lun's and Kao Pu-ying's interpretation. Ch'iu Chao-ao takes it differently: just as Sung Yü was Ch'ü Yüan's disciple, so Tu Fu models himself after Sung Yü.

33   Chiang Yen, "Hen fu," in Hsiao T'ung, *Wen-hsüan* (Shih-chieh), 16.220; Ts'ui Kuo-fu (flourished first half of eighth century), "Wang Chao-chün," in Kuo, *Yüeh-fu shih chi*, 29.3b. The former antecedent is noted by Tu Fu's commentators but the latter is not.

34   "Chao-chün tz'u ying-chao," in Ni, 5.1b. Noted by Ch'iu Chao-ao, 17.32b.

35   See Hung, *Tu Fu: China's Greatest Poet*, pp. 222, 228–29.

36   Text and commentaries: T'ang, *Ch'üan Sung-tz'u*, p. 204; Shimizu, *Ō Anseki*, pp. 64–68; Chiang, *T'ang Sung ming-chia tz'u*, pp. 155–57; Lung Yü-sheng, *T'ang Sung ming-chia tz'u hsüan*, p. 90; Hsü K'o, *Li-tai tz'u-hsüan chi-p'ing*, pp. 38–39; T'ang, *Sung-tz'u san-pai shou chien-chu*, pp. 37–38; Hu, *T'ang Sung tz'u i-pai shou*, pp. 34–37; Hu, *Sung-tz'u hsüan*, pp. 53–55; Ch'iu and Li, *Tz'u hsüan*, pp. 28–31; Lo Ch'i, *Chung-kuo li-tai tz'u hsüan*, pp. 105–06. Previous translations: Odile and Max Kaltenmark in Demiéville, *Anthologie*, p. 384; Chen Shih-chuan, *T'ang Sung tz'u hsüan i*, pp. 76–78.

37   "T'ai-ch'eng ch'ü" (first of two poems), in Feng Chi-wu, *Fan-ch'uan shih chi chu*, p. 260. This source of Wang's poem is cited by T'ang Kuei-chang and Lo Ch'i.

38   *Ch'üan Ch'en-shih* (in Ting Fu-pao), 1.1346.

39   *Sui shu*, 22.21a ("Treatise on the Five Elements"), cited by Hu, *Sung-tz'u hsüan*, pp. 54–55.

40   "P'o Ch'in-huai," in Feng Chi-wu, pp. 273–74. This source is cited by T'ang Kuei-chang and Lo Ch'i.

41   This aspect of Wang's poem is noted by Ch'iu and Li.

42   See Ch'iu and Li, p. 29.

CHAPTER 10

1   Text and commentaries: Hsiao Chi-tsung, *Meng Hao-jan shih shuo*, pp. 76–77; Yu, *Meng Hao-jan chi chien-chu*, pp. 68–69; Kao, *T'ang Sung shih chü-yao*, 4.18b–19a.

2 Text and commentaries: Lu Chao-lin, *Yu-yu tzu chi*, 2.2a–4b; Kanno, *Tōshi sen shōsetsu*, pp. 67–87; Takagi, *Tōshi sen*, 1:35–51; Saitō, *Tōshi sen*, 1:56–69; Chiang Hsia-an, *T'ang-shih hsüan p'ing-shih*, pp. 29–42; Hsü Wen-yü, *T'ang-shih chi-chieh*, 1:14–19. The poem is discussed by Wen I-to in "Kung-t'i shih ti tzu-shu" (in his *T'ang-shih tsa-lun*), pp. 14–16.

3 This connection is noted by Kanno.

4 "Hsiao Shih ch'ü," *Ch'üan Ch'en-shih* (in Ting Fu-pao), 3.1409.

5 *Han shu*, 83.16a.

6 *Shih chi*, 120.8b.

7 Kuo, *Yüeh-fu shih chi*, 47.10a.

8 Collected in Kuo, 47.10b–12a.

9 Text: Kuo, 47.10a; *Ch'üan Sung-shih* (in Ting Fu-pao), 5.745.

10 Ni, *Yü Tzu-shan chi chu*, 5.6b–7a and 7b–8a. The commentators of Lu's poem have overlooked these two antecedents of line 33.

11 Text: Kuo, 48.1a; *Ch'üan Liang-shih* (in Ting Fu-pao), 1.896.

12 Kuo, 47.9a–10a.

13 *Shih chi*, 109.10b; *Han shu*, 54.23b.

14 *Liang Han wen-hsüeh shih ts'an-k'ao tzu-liao*, p. 70.

15 These sources are noted by Kanno and other commentators of Lu's poem.

16 Trans. Hawkes, *Ch'u Tz'ŭ*, p. 119. The allusion is noted by Kanno.

17 This is because the phrase "South Mountain" occurs repeatedly in no. 172 of *The Classic of Songs*, a poem invoking the blessings of a long and happy life.

18 Hung, *Tu-shih yin-te*, 1.9–10; translation and discussion in Hawkes, *Primer*, no. 2.

19 Ku and Chou, *Po Chü-i shih hsüan*, pp. 14–27; trans. Bynner and Kiang, *Jade Mountain*, pp. 120–25; Demiéville, *Anthologie*, pp. 297–302.

CHAPTER 11

1 Ts'ao Chih, "T'ai-shan Liang-fu hsing," in Huang Chieh, *Ts'ao Tzu-chien*, 2.82, l. 5.

2 Ch'ü Yüan (fourth to third century B.C.), "Li sao," l. 10; Poem 106, l. 189.

3 Li Po, "Sung T'ung ch'an-shih huan Nan-ling Yin-ching-ssu," in Wang Ch'i, *Li T'ai-po*, 18.405–06, l. 2.

4 T'ao Ch'ien, "Yin chiu," no. 5, in Ku Chih, *T'ao Ching-chieh*, 3.9a, l. 2.

5 Tu Fu, "Tan-ch'ing yin," in Hung, *Tu-shih yin-te*, 8.121, l. 7.

6 "Ta tzu-yeh ko," in Kuo, *Yüeh-fu shih chi*, 45.2b, l. 1.

7 Ts'ao Chih, "T'ai-shan Liang-fu hsing," in Huang Chieh, *Ts'ao Tzu-chien*, 2.82, l. 6.

8 Meng Hao-jan, "Yung-chia pieh Chang Tzu-jung," in Hsiao Chi-tsung, *Meng Hao-jan shih shuo*, p. 137, l. 5.

9 Ch'ü Yüan, "Li sao," l. 9.

10 Ts'ao Chih, "T'ai-shan Liang-fu hsing," in Huang Chieh, *Ts'ao Tzu-chien*, 2.82, l. 2.

11 Meng Hao-jan, "Tzu Lo chih Yüeh," in Hsiao Chi-tsung, p. 112, l. 4.

12 *Shih ching*, no. 189, in Karlgren's translation (*The Book of Odes*, pp. 130–31). Quoted with Professor Karlgren's permission.

13   Li Yü, "Ch'ang hsiang ssu," in She Hsüeh-man, *Li hou-chu*, p. 50.

14   Hsüeh Ang-fu (flourished early fourteenth century), "Shan-p'o yang," in Lo K'ang-lieh, *Yüan-ch'ü san-pai shou chien*, p. 105.

15   See J. L. La Drière, "Prosody," in Preminger, *Encyclopedia of Poetry and Poetics*, p. 677.

16   These and nine other instances of such pairs in parallel couplets are given in Wang Li, *Han-yü shih-lü hsüeh*, pp. 167–68.

17   Text and commentary: Liu Tsung-yüan, *Liu Ho-tung chi*, 42.704; Kao, *T'ang Sung shih chü-yao*, 5.36b–37a.

18   Text and commentaries: Feng Chi-wu, *Fan-ch'uan shih*, pp. 202–03; Ichino, *To Boku*, pp. 240–41; Kao, 5.40b–41a.

19   Luis de Góngora (1561–1627), "Romance" beginning "En un pastoral albergue," in Millé, *Obras completas de Don Luis de Góngora y Argote*, p. 122.

20   Thomas Gray (1716–71), "Elegy Written in a Country Churchyard," in Eastman, *Norton Anthology of Poetry*, pp. 488–90.

21   Heinrich Heine (1797–1856), untitled poem in Echtermeyer and von Wiese, *Deutsche Gedichte*, p. 447.

22   Victor Hugo (1802–85), "Booz endormi," from *Légende des siècles*, in Seghers, *Livre d'Or*, p. 193.

23   *Shih ching*, no. 2, ll. 10–11, translation adapted from Karlgren, *Book of Odes*, p. 3.

24   *Shih ching*, no. 26, l. 25; no. 29, ll. 1, 7, 13, 19.

25   Hsieh T'iao, "Yung chu," in Lee, *Hsieh Hsüan-ch'eng*, p. 153, ll. 3–4.

26   Yü Hsin, "Ho K'an fa-shih," in Ni, *Yü Tzu-shan*, 4.33b, ll. 1–2.

27   Lu Chi (261–303), "Yin ma ch'ang-ch'eng k'u hsing," in Hsiao T'ung, *Wen hsüan* (Shih-chieh), 28.386, l. 9.

28   Yü Hsi (late fifth to early sixth century), "Yung Huo chiang-chün pei fa," in Hsiao T'ung (Shih-chieh), 21.291, l. 23.

29   Tu Fu, "Meng Li Po" (second of two poems), in Hung, *Tu-shih yin-te*, 5.79–80, l. 15.

30   Meng Chiao (751–814), "Hsia ai" (third of ten poems), in Hua, *Meng Tung-yeh*, 10.185, ll. 1–2.

31   "Nineteen Old Poems," no. 5, in Hsiao T'ung (Shih-chieh), 29.402, l. 11.

32   Tu Fu, "Ch'un wang," in Hung, *Tu-shih yin-te*, 19.295–96, l. 1.

33   Juan Chi (210–63), "Yung huai," no. 39, in Ku Chih, *Juan Ssu-tsung*, fol. 30a-b, l. 8.

34   Yen Yen-chih (384–456), "Ho Hsieh chien Ling-yün," in Hsiao T'ung (Shih-chieh), 26.357, l. 23.

35   Text and commentary: *Wang Chien shih chi*, p. 20; Hsü Ch'eng-yü, *Chang Wang yüeh-fu*, pp. 104–05.

36   Text and commentary: *Wang Chien shih chi*, p. 20; Hsü Ch'eng-yü, *Chang Wang yüeh-fu*, pp. 105–06.

37   Pao Chao (born between 405 and 416, died 466), "Tai pai chu ch'ü" (first of two poems), in Ch'ien Chung-lien, *Pao ts'an-chün*, 4.100–01, l. 8.

38   Yang Wan-li, "Tu Chang Wen-ch'ien shih," in Chou Ju-ch'ang, *Yang Wan-li*, pp. 233–34, l. 3.

39   Chia Chih (718–72), "Sung Li shih-lang fu Ch'ang-chou," in Kanno, *Tōshi sen shōsetsu*, pp. 877–78, l. 1.

40   Po Chü-i, "Hsi-hu wan kuei hui wang Ku-shan-ssu tseng chu k'o," in Ku and Chou, *Po Chü-i*, pp. 287–88, l. 1.

41   Fan Ch'eng-ta (1126–93), "Ssu shih t'ien-yüan tsa hsing," in Imazeki and Karashima, *Sōshi sen*, p. 217, l. 2.

42   Yang Wan-li, "Ho Chao Ting-fu fu-p'an t'ou-tseng ho hsüeh chih chü," in Yang Wan-li, *Ch'eng-chai chi*, 11.10a, l. 2.

43   Ts'en Shen (715–70), "Pai hsüeh ko sung Wu p'an-kuan kuei ching," in Chiang, *T'ang Sung ming-chia shih*, p. 141, l. 12.

44   Chü-chien (1168–1246), "Liu hsü," in Imazeki and Karashima, p. 346, l. 1.

45   Pao Chao, "Ni hsing-lu man," no. 3, in Ch'ien Chung-lien, *Pao ts'an-chün*, 4.104, ll. 1–2.

46   Lo Pin-wang, "Shang li-pu shih-lang ti-ching p'ien," in Ch'en Hsi-chin, *Lo Lin-hai*, 1.1–16, ll. 43–44.

47   T'an Yung-chih (tenth century), "Chi Tso hsien-pei," in Chin, *T'ang-shih i-ch'ien shou*, pp. 489–90, l. 1.

48   Text and commentary: Wang Ch'i, *Li T'ai-po*, 25.566.

49   Pao Chao, "Tai pai chu ch'ü" (first of two poems), in Ch'ien Chung-lien, *Pao ts'an-chün*, 4.100–01, l. 3.

50   Li Po, "Hsüan-chou Hsieh-T'iao-lou chien-pieh chiao-shu Shu-yün," in Wang Ch'i, *Li T'ai-po*, 18.418, l. 5.

51   Pao Chao, "Tai pai chu ch'ü" (second of two poems), in Ch'ien Chung-lien, *Pao ts'an-chün*, 4.101, l. 3.

52   Po Chü-i, "Ch'ang-hen ko," in Ku and Chou, *Po Chü-i*, pp. 14–27, l. 59.

53   Wei Ying-wu (736–830?), "Hsiu-hsia jih fang Wang shih-yü pu yü," in Wei Ying-wu, *Wei Chiang-chou chi*, 5.15a, l. 1.

54   Li Yü, "Lang t'ao sha," in She Hsüeh-man, *Li hou-chu*, pp. 83–84, l. 8.

55   Pao Chao, "Mei-hua lo," in Ch'ien Chung-lien, *Pao ts'an-chün*, 4.114–15, l. 8.

56   Po Chü-i, "Ch'ang-hen ko," in Ku and Chou, pp. 14–27, l. 26.

57   Li Shang-yin (813?–58), "Wu ch'ou kuo yu ch'ou ch'ü Pei-Ch'i ko," in Chang Ts'ai-t'ien, *Yü-ch'i sheng*, pp. 412–13, l. 1.

58   Su Shih, "Tung-lan li-hua," in Kao, *T'ang Sung shih chü-yao*, 8. 45a-b, l. 1.

59   Ts'ao P'ei (187–226), "Yen ko hsing" (third of three poems), in Huang Chieh, *Wei Wu-ti*, pp. 50–51, l. 1.

60   Wang Chih-huan (695–765?), "Ch'u sai," in Chiang, *T'ang Sung ming-chia shih*, pp. 45–46, l. 2.

61   Ho Chih-chang (659–744), "Hui hsiang ou shu," in Chiang, *T'ang Sung ming-chia shih*, pp. 26–27, l. 1.

62   Liu Yü-hsi (772–843), "Chu-chih tz'u," in Chiang, *T'ang Sung ming-chia shih*, pp. 360–61, l. 3.

63   Pao Chao, "Tai pai chu ch'ü" (second of two poems), in Ch'ien Chung-lien, *Pao ts'an-chün*, 4.101, l. 2.

64   Tu Mu, "Chi Yang-chou Han Ch'o p'an-kuan," in Feng Chi-wu, *Fan-ch'uan shih*, 4.282–83, l. 1.

65   Han Yü, "Pa yüeh shih-wu yeh tseng Chang kung-ts'ao," in Chiang, *T'ang*

Sung ming-chia shih, pp. 342–45, l. 15.

66 Lu Yu (1125–1210), "Hua shih p'ien yu chu-chia yüan," in Imazeki and Karashima, *Sōshi sen*, pp. 190–91, l. 1.

67 Pao Chao, "Ni hsing-lu nan," no. 13, in Ch'ien Chung-lien, *Pao ts'an-chün*, 4.111–12, l. 6.

68 Kao Shih (707–65), "Pieh Tung ta," in Kanno, *Tōshi sen shōsetsu*, pp. 913–14, l. 1.

69 Po Chü-i, "Ch'ang-hen ko," in Ku and Chou, *Po Chü-i*, pp. 14–27, l. 48.

70 P'an Lang (tenth to eleventh century), "Su Ling-yin-ssu," in Imazeki and Karashima, pp. 48–49, l. 1.

71 Wang Wei, "Ch'un-jih yü P'ei Ti kuo Hsin-ch'ang-li fang Lü i-jen pu yü," in Chao, *Wang yu-ch'eng*, 10.19a-b, ll. 5–6.

72 Su Shih, "Ho Tzu-yu Min-ch'ih huai chiu," in Ch'ien Chung-shu, *Sung-shih hsüan chu*, p. 73, l. 5.

73 Li Po, "Tsao fa Po-ti-ch'eng," in Wang Ch'i, *Li T'ai-po*, 22.496, l. 2.

74 Ts'en Shen, "Wei yüan-wai chia hua-shu ko," in Kanno, pp. 160–61, ll. 1–2.

75 Liu Ch'ang-ch'ing (710–80), "Teng Yü-kan ku-ch'eng," in Chiang, *T'ang Sung ming-chia shih*, pp. 218–20, l. 8.

76 Huang-fu Jan (723–67), "Ch'un ssu," in Chiang, *T'ang Sung ming-chia shih*, pp. 307–08, l. 1.

77 Yang Wan-li, "Yu ho feng yü" (second of two poems), in Chou Ju-ch'ang, *Yang Wan-li hsüan-chi*, pp. 39–40, ll. 5–6.

78 Eastman, *Norton Anthology of Poetry*, pp. 461–69.

79 Hugo, *Œuvres choisies*, 2 : 74–96.

80 Eastman, pp. 866–67.

81 Tso Ssu, "Yung shih," no. 6, in Hsiao T'ung, *Wen hsüan* (Shih-chieh), 21.283, ll. 9–12.

82 Meng Chiao, "Ch'iu huai," no. 8, in Hua, *Meng Tung-yeh*, 4.59–60, ll. 7–10. See another instance in Poem 92 below. Further examples are given in Wang Li, *Han-yü shih-lü hsüeh*, pp. 479–80; and in Wu Hsüan-t'ao, *Ku-tien shih-ko ju-men*, pp. 49–50.

83 Text and commentaries: T'ang, *Ch'üan Sung-tz'u*, p. 1920; Teng, *Chia-hsüan tz'u*, pp. 137–38; Hu, *Sung-tz'u hsüan*, pp. 278–79. Previous translations: Hsiung Ting in Payne, *White Pony*, p. 358; A. T'ang and Max Kaltenmark in Demiéville, *Anthologie*, p. 406; Kotewall and Smith, *Penguin Book of Chinese Verse*, p. 49; Liu Wu-chi, *Introduction to Chinese Literature*, p. 122; Ayling and Mackintosh, *Collection of Chinese Lyrics*, no. 58; Scott, *Love and Protest*, pp. 20, 115; Chen Shih-chuan, *T'ang Sung tz'u hsüan i*, pp. 190–92.

84 See Wang Li, *Han-yü shih-lü hsüeh*, pp. 177–79; Wu Hsüan-t'ao, p. 48.

85 Pao Chao, "Tai Tung-wu yin," in Ch'ien Chung-lien, *Pao ts'an-chün*, 3.71–73, ll. 17–18.

86 Text and commentaries: Lee, *Hsieh Hsüan-ch'eng*, 1.27–28; Hung Shun-lung, *Hsieh Hsüan-ch'eng*, 2.196–97. Previous translations: Lai Ming, *History of Chinese Literature*, p. 141; Frodsham and Ch'eng, *Anthology of Chinese Verse*, p. 159.

87 Yü Hsin, "Ni yung huai," no. 11, in Ni, *Yü Tzu-shan*, 3.20b–21a, ll. 11–12.

88 Wang Li misses the juxtaposing function of *huo* . . . *cha* when he glosses *cha* as "suddenly" (*Ku-tai Han-yü*, p. 1215, n. 4).

CHAPTER 12

1 *Shih ching*, no. 124, ll. 13–20, translation and notes by Karlgren, *Book of Odes*, p. 80. Quoted with Professor Karlgren's permission.

2 "Chan ch'eng-nan," in Kuo, *Yüeh-fu shih chi*, 16.5a, ll. 1–2.

3 Tu Fu, "K'o chih," in Hung, *Tu-shih yin-te*, 21.355, ll. 3–4.

4 Tu Fu, "K'uang-fu," ibid., 21.343–44, ll. 3–4.

5 Yang Wan-li (1127–1206), "Ch'un-wan wang Yung-ho," in his *Ch'eng-chai chi*, 2.20a, ll. 3–4.

6 Góngora, *Soledades*, "Soledad Segunda," ll. 24–25.

7 Ibid., l. 41.

8 Horace, *Ad Pisones*. l. 29, cited by Wimsatt, *Hateful Contraries*, p. 161, n.

9 Pedro Calderón (1600–81), *Argenis y Poliarco*, act 2, in his *Comedias*, 1 : 386a.

10 Góngora, *Soledades*, "Soledad Segunda," ll. 214–15.

11 *The Nine Songs*, "Hsiang chün," ll. 21–22, as translated by Hawkes, *Ch'u Tz'ŭ*, p. 38.

12 Góngora, *Soledades*, "Soledad Segunda," ll. 419–20.

13 Vega, *Rimas humanas y divinas*, p. 56, verso.

14 I have discussed this matter in "Poetry and Painting."

15 Vega, *La siega* (auto sacramental), in his *Obras*, 2 : 311a.

16 Maurice Scève (born early sixteenth century, died ca. 1563), "Délie, objet de la plus haute vertu," cxliv, in Seghers, *Livre d'Or*, pp. 80–81, ll. 3–4.

17 Amadis Jamyn (1538–92), "Stances de l'impossible," in Seghers, pp. 100–01. This device is called adynaton in Greek rhetoric.

18 Hofmannswaldau, *Helden-Briefe*, pp. 4–5 ("Eginhard an Emma").

19 Cruz, *Obras escogidas*, p. 56.

20 Text: *Han-shan*, fol. 21a–b.

21 Text: *Han-shan*, fol. 8b. Previous translation: Watson, *Cold Mountain*, no. 23.

22 Text and commentary: *Han-shan*, fol. 17b; Iriya, *Kansan*, p. 87. Previous translations: Waley, *Chinese Poems* (1961), p. 111; Watson, *Cold Mountain*, no. 68.

23 "Yu-chou hsin-sui tso," in Kanno, *Tōshi sen shōsetsu*, p. 530.

24 "Che yang-liu ko-tz'u," no. 5, in Kuo, *Yüeh-fu shih chi*, 25.7a.

25 From *Cherubinischer Wandersmann*, in Wehrli, *Deutsche Barocklyrik*, p. 45.

26 Lines 123–28 of the same poem is another instance of triple parallelism that happens to be in prose.

27 Ssu-ma Hsiang-ju (ca. 179–117 B.C.), "Shang-lin fu," in Hsiao T'ung, *Wen hsüan* (Shih-chieh), 8.112.

28 Text and commentary: Sui Shu-sen, *Ch'üan Yüan san-ch'ü*, p. 651; Lo K'ang-lieh, *Yüan-ch'ü san-pai shou chien*, p. 97.

29 Text and commentary: Sui Shu-sen, p. 824; Lo K'ang-lieh, pp. 130–31.

30 Text and commentary: Sui Shu-sen, p. 806; Lo K'ang-lieh, p. 148. Lu-ch'ing is the courtesy name of the man of letters Ko Sheng-chung (1059–1131). I

do not know whether the title of this poem refers to him or to another man of the same name. The poem itself seems to point to a place that has not been inhabited for some time.

31 Text and commentary: Sui Shu-sen, pp. 756–57; Chiang, *Tz'u ch'ü hsin-shang*, pp. 212–13.

32 Text and commentary: Sui Shu-sen, p. 1032; Lo K'ang-lieh, pp. 157–58.

33 Text and commentary: Sui Shu-sen, p. 197; Lo K'ang-lieh, p. 32. Previous translations: Wilhelm, "Stockades of the Soul," p. 219; Li Tche-houa and Yves Hervouet in Demiéville, *Anthologie*, p. 446.

34 Text and commentaries: Sui Shu-sen, p. 242; Lo K'ang-lieh, pp. 43–44; Chiang, *Tz'u ch'ü hsin-shang*, pp. 207–08; Wang Li, *Ku-tai Han-yü*, p. 1511. Previous translations: Wilhelm, "Stockades," p. 220; Li Tche-houa and Yves Hervouet in Demiéville, p. 444; James Liu, *Art of Chinese Poetry*, pp. 32–33; Lai Ming, *History of Chinese Literature*, pp. 227–28; Yang and Metzger, *Fifty Songs from the Yüan*, no. 11.

35 Proposed by Ku Chieh-kang and Yü P'ing-po in *Ku-shih pien*, vol. 3, see *Hsien-Ch'in wen-hsüeh shih ts'an-k'ao tzu-liao*, p. 44, n. 1.

36 Cited in *Hsien-Ch'in*, p. 44, n. l.

37 Text and commentaries: Hsiao T'ung, *Wen hsüan* (Ssu-pu ts'ung-k'an), 29. 15b–18a; (Shih-chieh), 29.406–07; Shiba and Hanabusa, *Monzen*, pp. 30–32; Wu Chao-i, *Chien-chu yü-t'ai hsin-yung*, 9.5a–6b; *Ch'üan Han-shih* (in Ting Fu-pao), 2.37–38; *Liang Han wen-hsüeh shih ts'an-k'ao tzu-liao*, pp. 596–98; Yü, *Han Wei liu-ch'ao shih hsüan*, pp. 8–10. Previous translations: von Zach, *Die Chinesische Anthologie*, XXIX. 27–30; Demiéville, pp. 86–87.

38 Wu Chao-i, 9.11a–12b and 13b–14a.

CHAPTER 13

1 Hsü Shih-ying, "Mei Sheng 'Ch'i fa' yü ch'i mu-ni-che."

2 Text and commentaries: Hsiao T'ung, *Wen hsüan* (Ssu-pu ts'ung-k'an), 34.1a–17b; (Shih-chieh), 34.474–80; Yü Kuang-hua, *P'ing-chu Chao-ming wen-hsüan*, 8.17a–21a; *Liang Han wen-hsüeh shih ts'an-k'ao tzu-liao*, pp. 6–27. Previous translations: von Zach, *Die Chinesische Anthologie*, XXXIV. 1; Scott, *Love and Protest*, pp. 36–48. Partial translations: Waley, *Temple*, pp. 35–38 (mostly the frame); Moule, "The Bore on the Ch'ien-t'ang River in China," pp. 162–65 (Sixth Stimulus); Hervouet, *Un poète de cour sous les Han*, p. 160, n. 1. (ll. 96–111); Watson, *Chinese Rhyme-Prose*, pp. 17–18 (ll. 96–129). Wu Hsiao-ju, "Mei Sheng 'Ch'i fa' Li Shan chu ting-pu" is helpful for the understanding of several difficult passages. After completing my draft, I was privileged to look through a draft translation of the "Seven Stimuli" by David R. Knechtges and Jerry Swanson, subsequently published in their article, "Seven Stimuli for the Prince: The *Ch'i-fa* of Mei Ch'eng," *Monumenta Serica* 29 (1970–71): 99–116.

3 I have not found the sources for ll. 48–50 and 53–54. The three other quotations are from *Lü shih ch'un-ch'iu*, 1.6a (sec. 2, "Pen sheng").

4 I accept Ho I-men's emendation, substituting *fa* "come forth" for *fei* "abolish," see Yü Kuang-hua, 8.17b.

5   A dance tune, mentioned in "Chao hun," ll. 104 and 109 (trans. Hawkes, *Ch'u Tz'ŭ*, p. 108).

6   The music of these two Northern Chinese states was considered provocative and immoral in ancient China; see Diény, *Aux Origines de la poésie classique*, pp. 21–40.

7   Quotations from *Huang-ti nei-ching su-wen*, 51.3b (sec. 56, "P'i-pu lun-p'ien").

8   *Han Shu*, 64B.13b. For this reference I am indebted to David R. Knechtges.

9   Hsiao T'ung, *Wen hsüan* (Ssu-pu ts'ung-k'an), 34.20a.

10 *Li-tai fu-hui, wai-chi*, 18.6b. The preface, lacking in other editions of the *fu*, may not be by Wang himself, but for our present purpose this is immaterial.

11 For a later elaboration of *ch'in* theory, again in the form of a *fu*, see the "Ch'in fu" by Chi K'ang (223–62; his name is sometimes read Hsi K'ang), text and translation in van Gulik, *Hsi K'ang and His Poetical Essay on the Lute*.

12 Some of the following discussion is based on Böttger, *Die ursprünglichen Jagd-methoden der Chinesen* and especially on Schafer, "Hunting Parks and Animal Enclosures in Ancient China."

13 Such an interpretation is suggested by Burton Watson, *Early Chinese Literature*, p. 268.

14 The alternation of prose and poetry, typical of the *fu* genre in Han times, is actually a shifting back and forth between more prosaic and more poetic passages, with fluid borders between the two styles. See appendix 1.

15 For an illuminating discussion of this problem, see Wimsatt, *Hateful Contraries*, pp. 44–45 and passim.

Bibliography

Aoki Masaru 青木正兒, ed. and trans. *Ri Haku* 李白. Kanshi taikei 漢詩大系, no. 8. Tokyo: Shūeisha 集英社, 1965.

Arberry, A. J. *The Seven Odes: The First Chapter in Arabic Literature.* London: Allen and Unwin, 1957.

Ayling, Alan, and Duncan Mackintosh, trans. *A Collection of Chinese Lyrics.* New York and London: Chelsea House, [1969?].

Birch, Cyril, ed. *Anthology of Chinese Literature from Early Times to the Fourteenth Century.* New York: Grove Press, 1965.

Bodde, Derk. *China's First Unifier, a Study of the Ch'in Dynasty as Seen in the Life of Li Ssŭ.* Leiden: Brill, 1938.

Böttger, Walter. *Die ursprünglichen Jagdmethoden der Chinesen.* Berlin: Akademie-Verlag, 1960.

Brooks, Cleanth. *The Well Wrought Urn.* New York: Harcourt, Brace, 1947.

————, and Robert Penn Warren. *Understanding Poetry.* 3rd ed. New York: Holt, Rinehart and Winston, 1960.

Bynner, Witter, and Kiang Kang-hu, trans. *The Jade Mountain.* New York: Knopf, 1929.

Calderón de la Barca, Pedro. *Comedias.* Edited by Juan Jorge Keil. 4 vols. Leipzig: Fleischer, 1827–30.

Castro, Adolfo de, ed. *Poetas líricos de los siglos XVI y XVII.* Biblioteca de Autores Españoles, vols. 32 and 42. Madrid: Rivadeneyra, 1854–57.

Chan-kuo ts'e 戰國策. Ssu-pu ts'ung-k'an.

Chang Jen-ch'ing 張仁青, ed. *Li-tai p'ien-wen hsüan* 歷代駢文選. 2 vols. Taipei: National Teachers' College and Chung-hua 中華, 1963–65.

Chang P'u 張溥, ed. *Liang Chien-wen ti chi* 梁簡文帝集, in *Han Wei liu-ch'ao pai-san ming-chia chi* 漢魏六朝百三名家集 (Chang P'u's original wood-block ed. of Ch'ung-wen era [1628–44]).

Chang Ts'ai-t'ien 張采田. *Yü-ch'i sheng nien-p'u hui-chien* 玉谿生年譜會箋. Shanghai: Chung-hua 中華, 1963.

Chang Yin-nan and Lewis C. Walmsley, eds. and trans. *Poems by Wang Wei.* Rutland, Vt. and Tokyo: Tuttle, 1958.

Chao Tien-ch'eng 趙殿成, ed. *Wang yu-ch'eng chi chien-chu* 王右丞集箋註. Original wood-block ed., preface by editor's elder brother Chao Tien-tsui 趙殿最 dated 1738.

Chen Shih-chuan 程石泉, ed. and trans. *T'ang Sung tz'u hsüan i* 唐宋詞選譯 (*Chinese Lyrics from the Eighth to the Twelfth Centuries*). Taipei: Commercial Press, 1969.

Ch'en Hsi-chin 陳熙晉, ed. *Lo Lin-hai chi chien-chu* 駱臨海集箋注. Shanghai: Chung-hua 中華, 1961.

Ch'en Hung-chih 陳弘治, ed. *Li Ch'ang-chi ko-shih chiao-shih* 李長吉歌詩校釋. Taipei: Chia-hsin Cement Co., 1969.

Ch'en Po-ku 陳伯谷. *Sung-shih hsüan chiang* 宋詩選講. Hong Kong: Shanghai Book Co., 1963.

Ch'en shu 陳書. Po-na ed.

Cheng Ch'ien 鄭騫, ed. *Tz'u hsüan* 詞選. Taipei: Chung-hua wen-hua 中華文化, 1954.

Cheng Meng-t'ung 鄭孟彤 and Huang Chih-hui 黃志輝. "Shih lun Ts'ao Chih ho t'a-ti shih-ko 試論曹植和他的詩歌." *Wen-hsüeh i-ch'an tseng-k'an* 文學遺產增刊, no. 5 (Peking, 1957): 95–109.

Ch'eng Ch'ien-fan 程千帆 and Miao K'un 繆琨, eds. *Sung-shih hsüan chu* 宋詩選註. Hong Kong: Hsin yüeh 新月, 1961.

Chiang Hsia-an 江俠菴, ed. *T'ang-shih hsüan p'ing-shih* 唐詩選評釋. 2 vols. Hong Kong: Commercial Press, 1958.

Chiang Shang-hsien 姜尚賢, ed. *T'ang Sung ming-chia shih hsin hsüan* 唐宋名家詩新選. Tainan, 1964.

———, ed. *T'ang Sung ming-chia tz'u hsin hsüan* 唐宋名家詞新選. Tainan, 1963.

———. *Tz'u ch'ü hsin-shang* 詞曲欣賞. Tainan, 1964.

Ch'ien Ch'ien-i 錢謙益, ed. *Tu kung-pu chi* 杜工部集. Wood-block ed., preface by Chi Chen-i 季振宜 dated 1667.

Ch'ien Chung-lien 錢仲聯, ed. *Han Ch'ang-li shih hsi-nien chi-shih* 韓昌黎詩繫年集釋. 2 vols. Shanghai: Ku-tien wen-hsüeh 古典文學, 1957.

———, ed. *Pao ts'an-chün chi-chu* 鮑參軍集注. Shanghai: Ku-tien wen-hsüeh 古典文學, 1958.

Ch'ien Chung-shu 錢鍾書, ed. *Sung-shih hsüan chu* 宋詩選註. Peking: Jen-min wen-hsüeh 人民文學, 1958.

Child, Francis James, ed. *The English and Scottish Popular Ballads.* 5 vols. New York: Dover, 1965. (First published in Boston: Houghton Mifflin, 1884–98.)

Chin Jen-jui 金人瑞, ed. *T'ang-shih i-ch'ien shou* 唐詩一千首. 2 vols. Hong Kong: Tung-nan 東南, 1957.

Chin shu 晉書. Po-na ed.

Ch'iu Chao-ao 仇兆鰲, ed. *Tu-shih hsiang-chu* 杜詩詳註. Shanghai: Sao-yeh shan-fang 掃葉山房, 1915.

Ch'iu Feng 秋峯 and Li Jung-te 李榮德, eds. *Tz'u hsüan* 詞選. Singapore: Shanghai Book Co., 1966.

Chou Ju-ch'ang 周汝昌, ed. *Yang Wan-li hsüan-chi* 楊萬里選集. Shanghai: Chung-hua 中華, 1962.

Chou Kuo-ts'an 周國燦. *Sung-tz'u shang-hsi* 宋詞賞析. Hong Kong: San-yü t'u-shu wen-chü kung-ssu 三育圖書文具公司, 1965.

Chu Hsi 朱熹, ed. *Chu Wen-kung chiao Ch'ang-li hsien-sheng chi* 朱文公校昌黎先生集. Ssu-pu ts'ung-k'an.

Ch'u-hsüeh chi 初學記. Peking: Chung-hua 中華, 1962.

Ch'üan T'ang-shih 全唐詩. Original wood-block ed., Peking, 1707.

Cruz, Sor Juana Ines de la. *Obras escogidas*. Edited by Manuel Toussaint. Mexico City: Editorial "Cultura," 1928.

Demiéville, Paul, ed. *Anthologie de la poésie chinoise classique*. Paris: Gallimard, 1962.

Diény, Jean-Pierre. *Aux Origines de la poésie classique en Chine*. Leiden: Brill, 1968.

Downer, G. B., and A. C. Graham. "Tone Patterns in Chinese Poetry." *Bulletin of the School of Oriental and African Studies* 26 (University of London, 1963): 145–48.

Eastman, Arthur M., ed. *The Norton Anthology of Poetry*. New York: Norton, 1970.

Echtermeyer, Theodor, and Benno von Wiese, eds. *Deutsche Gedichte von den Anfängen bis zur Gegenwart*. Düsseldorf: Bagel, 1960.

Feifel, P. Eugen. *Geschichte der chinesischen Literatur*. 2d ed. Darmstadt: Wissenschaftliche Buchgesellschaft, 1959.

Feng Chi-wu 馮集梧, ed. *Fan-ch'uan shih chi chu* 樊川詩集注. Shanghai: Chung-hua 中華, 1962.

Feng Chih 馮至, ed. *Tu Fu shih hsüan* 杜甫詩選. Hong Kong: Ta-kuang 大光, 1961.

Fong Nai Bun 方乃斌, ed. *Tz'u shih ta-ch'üan* 詞史大全, vol. 1. Hong Kong: K'uei-lu 葵廬, 1963.

Franke, Herbert. "Die Geschichte des Prinzen Tan von Yen." *Zeitschrift der Deutschen Morgenländischen Gesellschaft* 107 (1956): 412–58.

Frankel, Hans H. "The Contemplation of the Past in T'ang Poetry." In *Perspectives on the T'ang*, edited by Arthur F. Wright and Denis Twitchett, pp. 345–65. New Haven: Yale University Press, 1973.

―――. "The Date and Authorship of the *Lung-ch'eng lu*." *Silver Jubilee Volume of the Zinbun-Kagaku-Kenkyusyo, Kyoto University* (1954): 129–49.

―――. "Fifteen Poems by Ts'ao Chih: An Attempt at a New Approach." *Journal of the American Oriental Society* 84 (1964): 1–14.

―――. "The Formulaic Language of the Chinese Ballad 'Southeast Fly the Peacocks.'" *Bulletin of the Institute of History and Philology*, Academia Sinica (Taipei), vol. 39, part 2 (1969): 219–44.

―――. "The 'I' in Chinese Lyric Poetry." *Oriens* 10 (1957): 128–30.

―――. "The Plum Tree in Chinese Poetry." *Asiatische Studien* 6 (1952): 88–115.

————. "Poetry and Painting: Chinese and Western Views of Their Convertibility." *Comparative Literature* 9 (1957): 289–307.

Frodsham, John D. *The Murmuring Stream: The Life and Works of the Chinese Nature Poet Hsieh Ling-yün (385–433), Duke of K'ang-Lo*. 2 vols. Kuala Lumpur: University of Malaya Press, 1967.

————, trans. *The Poems of Li Ho (791–817)*. Oxford: Clarendon Press, 1970.

————, and Ch'eng Hsi, eds. and trans. *An Anthology of Chinese Verse: Han Wei Chin and the Northern and Southern Dynasties*. Oxford: Clarendon Press, 1967.

Gilman, Stephen. "On 'Romancero' as a Poetic Language." In *Homenaje a Casalduero*, pp. 151–60. Madrid: Gredos, 1972.

Gimm, Martin. *Das Yüeh-fu tsa-lu des Tuan An-chieh: Studien zur Geschichte von Musik, Schauspiel und Tanz in der T'ang-Dynastie*. Wiesbaden: Harrassowitz, 1966.

Góngora, Luis de. *Las Soledades*. Edited by Dámaso Alonso. Madrid: Árbol, 1935.

Graham, Angus C., trans. *The Book of Lieh-tzŭ: A New Translation*. London: John Murray, 1960.

————. *Poems of the Late T'ang*. Harmondsworth, Middlesex: Penguin Books, 1965.

Gundert, Wilhelm, ed. *Lyrik des Ostens: China*. Munich: Deutscher Taschenbuch Verlag, 1962.

Han-shan tzu shih-chi 寒山子詩集. Ssu-pu ts'ung-k'an.

Han-shih wai-chuan 韓詩外傳. Ssu-pu ts'ung-k'an.

Han shu 漢書. Po-na ed.

Hanabusa Hideki 花房英樹, comp. *Kan Yu kashi sakuin* 韓愈歌詩索引 (*A Concordance to the Poems of Han Yü*). Kyoto: Kyoto Prefectural University, 1964.

Hawkes, David, trans. *Ch'u Tz'ŭ: The Songs of the South, An Ancient Chinese Anthology*. Oxford: Clarendon Press, 1959.

————. *A Little Primer of Tu Fu*. Oxford: Clarendon Press, 1967.

Hervouet, Yves. *Un poète de cour sous les Han: Sseu-ma Siang-jou*. Paris: Presses Universitaires de France, 1964.

Hightower, James Robert. *Han shih wai chuan*. Cambridge: Harvard University Press, 1952.

————. *The Poetry of T'ao Ch'ien*. Oxford: Clarendon Press, 1970.

Hodgart, Matthew, ed. *The Faber Book of Ballads*. London: Faber and Faber, 1965.

Hoffmann, Alfred. *Die Lieder des Li Yü*. Cologne: Greven, 1950.

Hofmannswaldau, Christian Hofmann von. *Helden-Briefe*. Leipzig and Breslau, 1699.

Hou-Han shu 後漢書. Po-na ed.

Hsi-ching tsa-chi 西京雜記. Ssu-pu ts'ung-k'an.

Hsiao Chi-tsung 蕭繼宗, ed. *Meng Hao-jan shih shuo* 孟浩然詩說. Tai-chung: Tunghai University, 1961.

Hsiao Ti-fei 蕭滌非. *Tu Fu yen-chiu* 杜甫研究. 2 vols. Tsinan: Shan-tung jen-min 山東人民, 1956.

Hsiao T'ung 蕭統, ed. *Liu-ch'en chu wen hsüan* 六臣註文選. Ssu-pu ts'ung-k'an.

―――, ed. *Wen hsüan* 文選. Taipei: Shih-chieh 世界, 1962.

Hsieh Chen 謝榛. *Ssu-ming shih-hua* 四溟詩話. In *Hsü li-tai shih-hua* 續歷代詩話, edited by Ting Fu-pao 丁福保. (Taipei: I-wen 藝文, n.d.)

Hsien-Ch'in wen-hsüeh shih ts'an-k'ao tzu-liao 先秦文學史參考資料. Pre-pared by Department of Chinese Literature, Peking University. Hong Kong: Chiao-yü 教育, 1961. (First published in Shanghai, 1957.)

Hsü Ch'eng-yü 徐澄宇, ed. *Chang Wang yüeh-fu* 張王樂府. Shanghai: Ku-tien wen-hsüeh 古典文學, 1957.

―――, ed. *Yüeh-fu ku-shih* 樂府古詩. Hong Kong: Chin-tai t'u-shu kung-ssu 今代圖書公司, n.d. (His preface dated Shanghai, 1955.)

Hsü K'o 徐珂, ed. *Li-tai tz'u-hsüan chi-p'ing* 歷代詞選集評. Hong Kong: Commercial Press, 1959.

Hsü Lien 許槤, ed. *Liu-ch'ao wen-chieh chien-chu* 六朝文絜箋注. Shanghai: Chung-hua 中華, 1962.

Hsü P'eng 徐鵬, ed. *Ch'en Tzu-ang chi* 陳子昂集. Shanghai: Chung-hua 中華, 1960.

Hsü Shih-ying 許世瑛. "Mei Sheng 'Ch'i fa' yü ch'i mu-ni-che 枚乘「七發」與其摹擬者." *Ta-lu tsa-chih* 大陸雜誌 6 (1953): 251–57.

Hsü Wen-yü 許文雨, ed. *T'ang-shih chi-chieh* 唐詩集解. 3 vols. Taipei: Cheng-chung 正中, 1954.

Hu Yün-i 胡雲翼, ed. *Sung-tz'u hsüan* 宋詞選. Shanghai: Chung-hua 中華, 1965. (First published in 1962.)

―――, ed. *T'ang Sung tz'u i-pai shou* 唐宋詞一百首. Shanghai: Chung-hua 中華, 1961.

Hua Ch'en-chih 華忱之, ed. *Meng Tung-yeh shih-chi* 孟東野詩集. Peking: Jen-min wen-hsüeh 人民文學, 1959.

Hua-yang-kuo chih 華陽國志. Ssu-pu ts'ung-k'an.

Huang Chieh 黃節, ed. *Han Wei yüeh-fu feng chien* 漢魏樂府風箋. Hong Kong: Commercial Press, 1961. (Preface dated 1923.)

―――, ed. *Hsieh K'ang-lo shih chu* 謝康樂詩註. Taipei: I-wen 藝文, n.d. (Preface dated 1924.)

―――, ed. *Ts'ao Tzu-chien shih chu* 曹子建詩注. Taipei: Shih-chieh 世界, 1962. (Preface dated 1928.)

———, ed. *Wei Wu-ti Wei Wen-ti shih chu* 魏武帝魏文帝詩註. Hong Kong: Commercial Press, 1961.

Huang-ti nei-ching su-wen 黃帝內經素問. Ssu-pu ts'ung-k'an.

Hugo, Victor. *Œuvres choisies*. Edited by P. Moreau and J. Boudout. 2 vols. Paris: Hatier, 1950.

Hung Shun-lung 洪順隆, ed. *Hsieh Hsüan-ch'eng chi chiao chu* 謝宣城集校注. Taipei: Chung-hua 中華, 1969.

Hung, William. *Tu Fu: China's Greatest Poet*. Cambridge: Harvard University Press, 1952.

Hung Yeh 洪業 and others, comp. and ed. *Tu-shih yin-te* 杜詩引得 (*A Concordance to the Poems of Tu Fu*). Peiping: Yenching University, 1940.

Huo Sung-lin 霍松林, ed. *Po Chü-i shih hsüan i* 白居易詩選譯. Hong Kong: Chien-wen 建文, n.d.

I-wen lei-chü 藝文類聚. Ssu-pu chi-yao 四部集要. Taipei, 1960.

Ichino Sawatorao 市野澤寅雄, ed. and trans. *To Boku* 杜牧. Kanshi taikei 漢詩大系, no. 14. Tokyo: Shūeisha 集英社, 1965.

Ikkai Tomoyoshi 一海知義, ed. and trans. *Tō Emmei* 陶淵明. Chūgoku shijin senshū 中國詩人選集, no. 4. Tokyo: Iwanami 岩波, 1958.

Imazeki Tempō 今關天彭 and Karashima Takeshi 辛島驍, eds. and trans. *Sōshi sen* 宋詩選. Kanshi taikei 漢詩大系, no. 16. Tokyo: Shūeisha 集英社, 1966.

Iritani Sensuke 入谷仙介, ed. and trans. *Koshisen* 古詩選. Shintei Chūgoku kotensen 新訂中國古典選, no. 13. Tokyo: Asahi Shimbunsha 朝日新聞社, 1966.

Iriya Yoshitaka 入矢義高, ed. and trans. *Kansan* 寒山. Chūgoku shijin senshū 中國詩人選集, no. 5. Tokyo: Iwanami 岩波, 1958.

Itō Masafumi 伊藤正文, ed. and trans. *Sō Shoku* 曹植. Chūgoku shijin senshū 中國詩人選集, no. 3. Tokyo: Iwanami 岩波, 1958.

Jao Tsung-i 饒宗頤, ed. *Huai-hai chü-shih ch'ang-tuan chü* 淮海居士長短句. Hong Kong: Lung-men 龍門, 1965.

Jen-han chü-shih 忍寒居士, ed. *Huai-hai chü-shih ch'ang-tuan chü chiao chu* 淮海居士長短句校注. In *Su-men ssu hsüeh-shih tz'u chiao chu* 蘇門四學士詞校注. Taipei: Shih-chieh 世界, 1967.

Kanno Dōmei 簡野道明, ed. and trans. *Tōshi sen shōsetsu* 唐詩選詳說. Tokyo: Meiji 明治, 1966. (First published in 1929.)

Kao Pu-ying 高步瀛, ed. *T'ang Sung shih chü-yao* 唐宋詩舉要. 2 vols. Taipei: I-wen 藝文, 1960.

Karlgren, Bernhard, trans. *The Book of Odes*. Stockholm: Museum of Far Eastern Antiquities, 1950.

———. "Grammata Serica recensa." *Bulletin of the Museum of Far Eastern Antiquities* (Stockholm), no. 29 (1957): 1–332.

Kent, George W., ed. and trans. *Worlds of Dust and Jade: 47 Poems and Ballads of the Third Century Chinese Poet Ts'ao Chih*. New York: Philosophical Library, 1969.

Ko Hung 葛洪. *Shen-hsien chuan* 神仙傳. In *Tseng-ting Han Wei ts'ung-shu* 增訂漢魏叢書 (wood-block edition of 1791).

Kondō Mitsuo 近藤光男, ed. and trans. *So Tōba* 蘇東坡. Kanshi taikei 漢詩大系, no. 17. Tokyo: Shūeisha 集英社, 1964.

Kotewall, Robert, and Norman L. Smith, comp. and trans. *The Penguin Book of Chinese Verse*. Edited by A. R. Davis. Harmondsworth, Middlesex: Penguin Books, 1962.

Ku Chao-ts'ang 顧肇倉 and Chou Ju-ch'ang 周汝昌, eds. *Po Chü-i shih hsüan* 白居易詩選. Peking: Tso-chia 作家, 1962.

Ku Chih 古直, ed. *Juan Ssu-tsung shih chien* 阮嗣宗詩箋. Taipei: Kuang-wen 廣文, 1966.

———, ed. *T'ao Ching-chieh shih chien* 陶靖節詩箋. Taipei: Kuang-wen 廣文, 1964.

———, ed. *Ts'ao Tzu-chien shih chien* 曹子建詩箋. Taipei: Kuang-wen 廣文, 1966.

Kuo Mao-ch'ien 郭茂倩, ed. *Yüeh-fu shih chi* 樂府詩集. 4 vols. Peking and Shanghai: Wen-hsüeh ku-chi 文學古籍, 1955. (Photolith reprint in 3 vols., Taipei: Shih-chieh 世界, 1961.)

Kurakawa Yōichi 黑川洋一, ed. and trans. *To Ho* 杜甫. 2 vols. Chūgoku shijin senshū 中國詩人選集, nos. 9–10. Tokyo: Iwanami 岩波, 1957–58.

Lai Ming. *A History of Chinese Literature*. New York: Capricorn Books, 1966.

Lee Chik-fong 李直方, ed. *Hsieh Hsüan-ch'eng shih chu* 謝宣城詩注. Hong Kong: Universal Book Co., 1968.

Li-tai fu-hui 歷代賦彙. Compiled on order of K'ang-hsi Emperor. Palace wood-block ed., 1706.

Li Tao-yüan 酈道元. *Shui-ching chu* 水經注. Ssu-pu ts'ung-k'an.

Liang Han wen-hsüeh shih ts'an-k'ao tzu-liao 兩漢文學史參考資料. Prepared by Department of Chinese Literature, Peking University. Shanghai: Kao-teng Chiao-yü 高等教育, 1960.

Liang Jung-jo 梁容若 and others, eds. *Chu-yin ku-chin wen hsüan chu* 注音古今文選註. 2 vols. Taipei: Kuo-yü jih-pao she 國語日報社, 1956.

Lieh-tzu 列子. *Ch'ung-hsü chih-te chen ching* 沖虛至德眞經. Ssu-pu ts'ung-k'an.

Liu, James Jo-yü. *The Art of Chinese Poetry*. Chicago: University of Chicago Press, 1962.

Liu Tsung-yüan 柳宗元. *Liu Ho-tung chi* 柳河東集. 2 vols. Shanghai: Chung-hua 中華, 1960.

Liu Wu-chi. *An Introduction to Chinese Literature*. Bloomington: Indiana University Press, 1966.

Liu Yü-hsi 劉禹錫. *Liu Meng-te wen-chi* 劉夢得文集. Ssu-pu ts'ung-k'an.

Livet, Charles-Louis. *Précieux et précieuses*. 3d ed. Paris: Welter, 1895.

Lo Ch'i 羅淇, ed. *Chung-kuo li-tai tz'u hsüan* 中國歷代詞選. 4th ed. Hong Kong: Shanghai Book Co., 1970.

Lo K'ang-lieh 羅忼烈, ed. *Yüan-ch'ü san-pai shou chien* 元曲三百首箋. Hong Kong: Lung-men 龍門, 1967.

Lu Chao-lin 盧照隣. *Yu-yu tzu chi* 幽憂子集. Ssu-pu ts'ung-k'an.

Lu K'an-ju 陸侃如 and Feng Yüan-chün 馮沅君. *Chung-kuo shih shih* 中國詩史. 3 vols. Peking: Tso-chia 作家, 1957.

Lü shih ch'un-ch'iu 呂氏春秋. Ssu-pu ts'ung-k'an.

Lung Kuang-yao 龍光耀. *Tz'u i lun-shih* 詞藝論釋. Taichung: Ming-kuang 明光, 1969.

Lung Yü-sheng 龍瑜生, ed. *T'ang Sung ming-chia tz'u hsüan* 唐宋名家詞選. Shanghai: Ku-tien wen-hsüeh 古典文學. 1956.

Margouliès, Georges, ed. and trans. *Anthologie raisonnée de la littérature chinoise*. Paris: Payot, 1948.

—— *Le "fou" dans le Wen-siuan*. Paris: Geuthner, 1926.

Meier, John, ed. *Balladen*. 2 vols. Leipzig: Reclam, 1935–36.

Miao Yüeh 繆鉞. *Tu shih ts'un-kao* 讀史存稿. Peking: San-lien 三聯, 1963.

Millé y Giménez, Juan, and Isabel Millé y Giménez, eds. *Obras completas de Don Luis de Góngora y Argote*. Madrid: Aguilar, [1932].

Moule, Arthur Christopher. "The Bore on the Ch'ien-t'ang River in China." *T'oung Pao*, n. s., 22 (1923): 135–88.

Mu t'ien-tzu chuan 穆天子傳. Ssu-pu ts'ung-k'an.

Murakami Tetsumi 村上哲見, ed. and trans. *Ri Iku* 李煜. Chūgoku shijin senshū 中國詩人選集. no. 16. Tokyo: Iwanami 岩波, 1959.

Nan shih 南史. Po-na ed.

Ni Fan 倪璠, ed. *Yü Tzu-shan chi chu* 庾子山集注. Taipei: Chung-hua 中華, 1966.

Ō Shōrei shishū 王昌齡詩集. Kyoto: Hōyū shoten 朋友書店, 1970.

Obata Shigeyoshi, trans. *The Works of Li Po the Chinese Poet Done into English Verse*. New York: Dutton, 1922.

Ogawa Tamaki 小川環樹, ed. and trans. *So Shoku* 蘇軾. 2 vols. Chūgoku shijin senshū 中國詩人選集, ser. 2, Nos. 5–6. Tokyo: Iwanami 岩波, 1962.

——, ed. *Sōshi sen* 宋詩選. Chikuma sōsho 筑摩叢書, no. 74. Tokyo: Chikuma shobō 筑摩書房, 1967.

P'an Ch'ung-kuei 潘重規, ed. *Yüeh-fu shih ts'ui chien* 樂府詩粹箋. Hong Kong: Jen-sheng 人生, 1963.

Payne, Robert, ed. *The White Pony*. New York: John Day, 1947.

Po-wu chih 博物志. Attributed to Chang Hua 張華 (232–300). Ku-chin i-shih 古今逸史.

Pound, Ezra, trans. *The Confucian Odes: The Classic Anthology Defined by Confucius*. New York: New Directions, 1959. (First published by Harvard University Press, 1954.)

Preminger, Alex, ed. *Encyclopedia of Poetry and Poetics*. Princeton: Princeton University Press, 1965.

Quevedo Villegas, Francisco de. *Obras completas: Obras en verso*. Edited by Luis Astrana Marín. Madrid: Aguilar, 1932.

Rust, Ambros. *Meng Hao-jan (691–740): Sein Leben und religiöses Denken nach seinen Gedichten*. Ingenbohl, Switzerland: Theodosius, 1960.

Sackheim, Eric. *. . . the silent Zero, in search of Sound . . .* Tokyo: Mushinsha and New York: Grossman, 1968.

Saitō Shō 齋藤晌, ed. and trans. *Tōshi sen* 唐詩選. 2 vols. Kanshi taikei 漢詩大系, nos. 6–7. Tokyo: Shūeisha 集英社, 1964–65.

San-fu huang-t'u 三輔黃圖. Ssu-pu ts'ung-k'an, ser. 3.

Schafer, Edward H. "Hunting Parks and Animal Enclosures in Ancient China." *Journal of the Economic and Social History of the Orient* 11 (1968): 316–43.

———. *The Vermilion Bird: T'ang Images of the South*. Berkeley and Los Angeles: University of California Press, 1967.

Scott, John, ed. and trans. *Love and Protest: Chinese Poems from the Sixth Century B. C. to the Seventeenth Century A.D.* New York: Harper and Row, 1972.

Seghers, Pierre, ed. *Le Livre d'Or de la Poésie française*. Verviers, Belgium: Gerard, n.d.

She Hsüeh-man 佘雪曼, ed. *Li hou-chu tz'u hsin-shang* 李後主詞欣賞. Hong Kong, 1955.

Shen Te-ch'ien 沈德潛, ed. *Ku-shih yüan* 古詩源. Hong Kong: Shanghai Book Co., 1962.

Shiba Rokurō 斯波六郎 and Hanabusa Hideki 花房英樹, eds. and trans. *Monzen* 文選. Sekai bungaku taikei 世界文學大系, 70. Tokyo: Chikuma Shobō 筑摩書房, 1963.

Shih chi 史記. Po-na ed.

Shimizu Shigeru 清水茂, ed. and trans. *Ō Anseki* 王安石. Chūgoku shijin senshū 中國詩人選集, ser. 2, no. 4. Tokyo: Iwanami 岩波, 1962.

Shuo-wen chieh-tzu 說文解字. Ssu-pu ts'ung-k'an.

Su Shih 蘇軾. *Chi-chu fen-lei Tung-p'o hsien-sheng shih* 集註分類東坡先生詩. Ssu-pu ts'ung-k'an.

Sui shu 隋書. Po-na ed.

Sui Shu-sen 隋樹森, ed. *Ch'üan Yüan san-ch'ü* 全元散曲. 2 vols. Peking: Chung-hua 中華, 1964.

Sun, Phillip S. Y. "The Grass Motif in Chinese Poetry." *Tamkang Review* 1.1 (April 1970): 29–41.

Sung shu 宋書. Po-na ed.

Suzuki Torao 鈴木虎雄, ed. and trans. *Gyokudai shin'ei shū* 玉臺新詠集. 3 vols. Iwanami bunko 岩波文庫. Tokyo: Iwanami, 1953–56.

Szertics, Joseph. *Tiempo y verbo en el Romancero Viejo*. Madrid: Gredos, 1967.

Tai Chün-jen 戴君仁, ed. *Sung-shih hsüan* 宋詩選. Hsien-tai kuo-min chi-pen chih-shih ts'ung-shu 現代國民基本知識叢書, ser. 2. Taipei: Chung-hua wen-hua 中華文化, 1954.

T'ai-p'ing huan-yü chi 太平寰宇記. Taipei: Wen-hai 文海, 1963.

T'ai-p'ing yü-lan 太平御覽. Ssu-pu ts'ung-k'an, ser. 3.

Takada Shinji 高田眞治, ed. and trans. *Shikyō* 詩經. 2 vols. Kanshi taikei 漢詩大系, nos. 1–2. Tokyo: Shūeisha 集英社, 1966.

Takagi Masakazu 高木正一, ed. and trans. *Tōshi sen* 唐詩選. 2 vols. Chūgoku koten sen 中國古典選, nos. 14–15. Tokyo: Asahi shimbun sha 朝日新聞社, 1965–66.

Takebe Toshio 武部利男, ed. and trans. *Ri Haku* 李白. 2 vols. Chūgoku shijin senshū 中國詩人選集, nos. 7–8. Tokyo: Iwanami 岩波, 1957–58.

T'ang Kuei-chang 唐圭璋, ed. *Ch'üan Sung-tz'u* 全宋詞. 5 vols. Shanghai: Chung-hua 中華, 1965.

———, ed. *Nan-T'ang erh chu tz'u hui-chien* 南唐二主詞彙箋. Taipei: Cheng-chung 正中, 1966.

———, ed. *Sung-tz'u san-pai shou chien-chu* 宋詞三百首箋注. Hong Kong: Chung-hua 中華, 1961.

Teng Kuang-ming 鄧廣銘, ed. *Chia-hsüan tz'u pien-nien chien-chu* 稼軒詞編年箋注. Shanghai: Chung-hua 中華, 1962.

Ting Fu-pao 丁福保, ed. *Ch'üan Han san-kuo Chin nan-pei ch'ao shih* 全漢三國晉南北朝詩. 2 vols. Shanghai: Chung-hua 中華, 1959.

Ting Yen 丁晏, ed. *Ts'ao-chi ch'üan-p'ing* 曹集銓評. Taipei: Shih-chieh 世界, 1962.

Ts'ui Pao 崔豹. *Ku-chin chu* 古今註. Ssu-pu ts'ung-k'an, ser. 3.

Tsuru Haruo 都留春雄, ed. and trans. *Ō I* 王維. Chūgoku shijin senshū 中國詩人選集, no. 6. Tokyo: Iwanami 岩波, 1958.

Uchida Sennosuke 內田泉之助, ed. and trans. *Koshi gen* 古詩源, part 1. Kanshi taikei 漢詩大系, no. 4. Tokyo: Shūeisha 集英社, 1964.

van Gulik, Robert Hans. *Hsi K'ang and His Poetical Essay on the Lute*. Rev. ed. Tokyo: Sophia University and Tuttle Co., 1969.

Vega Carpio, Lope Félix de. *Obras*. Edition of Real academia española. 15 vols. Madrid: Rivadeneyra, 1890–1913.

———. *Rimas humanas y divinas*. Fascimile reprint of Madrid 1634 ed. Madrid: Cámara oficial del Libro, 1935.

von Zach, Erwin, trans. *Die Chinesische Anthologie: Übersetzungen aus dem "Wen hsüan."* 2 vols. Cambridge: Harvard University Press, 1958.

————, trans. *Han Yü's Poetische Werke*. Cambridge: Harvard University Press, 1952.

————, trans. *Tu Fu's Gedichte*. 2 vols. Cambridge: Harvard University Press, 1952.

Waley, Arthur, trans. *The Book of Songs*. Boston and New York: Houghton Mifflin, 1937.

————, trans. *Chinese Poems*. London: Allen and Unwin: 1946; London: Unwin Books, 1961.

————, trans. *The Temple and Other Poems*. London: Unwin, 1923.

Wang An-shih 王安石. *Lin-ch'uan hsien-sheng wen-chi* 臨川先生文集. Ssu-pu ts'ung-k'an.

Wang Ch'i 王琦, ed. *Li Ch'ang-chi ko-shih Wang Ch'i hui-chieh* 李長吉歌詩王琦彙解. In *San chia p'ing-chu Li Ch'ang-chi ko-shih* 三家評註李長吉歌詩. Shanghai: Chung-hua 中華, 1959.

————, ed. *Li T'ai-po ch'üan-chi* 李太白全集. 2 vols. Hong Kong: Kuang-chih 廣智, n.d.

Wang Chien shih chi 王建詩集. Shanghai: Chung-hua 中華, 1959.

Wang Ch'ung 王充. *Lun heng* 論衡. Ssu-pu ts'ung-k'an.

Wang Li 王力. *Han-yü shih-lü hsüeh* 漢語詩律學. Shanghai: Shang-hai chiao-yü 上海教育, 1962.

————. *Ku-tai Han-yü* 古代漢語. 3 vols. Peking: Chung-hua 中華, 1962–64.

Wang Po 王勃. *Wang Tzu-an chi* 王子安集. Ssu-pu ts'ung-k'an.

Wang Yao-ch'ü 王堯衢, ed. *Ku T'ang-shih ho-chieh* 古唐詩合解. Taipei: Wen-hua t'u-shu 文化圖書, 1968.

Watson, Burton. *Chinese Lyricism*. New York: Columbia University Press, 1971.

————, ed. and trans. *Chinese Rhyme-Prose*. New York: Columbia University Press, 1971.

————, ed. and trans. *Cold Mountain: 100 Poems by the T'ang Poet Han-shan*. New York: Grove, 1962.

————, *Early Chinese Literature*. New York: Columbia University Press, 1962.

Wehrli, Max, ed. *Deutsche Barocklyrik*. 3d ed. Basel and Stuttgart: Benno Schwabe, 1962.

Wei Chin nan-pei ch'ao wen-hsüeh shih ts'an-k'ao tzu-liao 魏晉南北朝文學史參考資料. Prepared by Department of Chinese Literature, Peking University. 2 vols. Peking: Chung-hua 中華, 1962.

Wei Ying-wu 韋應物. *Wei Chiang-chou chi* 韋江州集. Ssu-pu ts'ung-k'an.

Wen I-to 聞一多. *T'ang-shih tsa-lun* 唐詩雜論. Peking: Ku-chi 古籍, 1956.

Wen Ju-hsien 聞汝賢. *Tz'u-p'ai hui shih* 詞牌彙釋. Taipei, 1963.

Wilhelm, Hellmut. "Shih Ch'ung and His Chin-ku-yüan." *Monumenta Serica* 18 (1959): 314–27.

———. "The Stockades of the Soul: Some Chinese Post-Classical Songs." In *Geist und Werk* (Festschrift Daniel Brody), pp. 217–24. Zürich: Rhein-Verlag, 1958.

Wimsatt, William K. *Hateful Contraries: Studies in Literature and Criticism.* Kentucky Paperbacks. Lexington: University of Kentucky Press, 1966.

Wu Chao-i 吳兆宜, ed. *Chien-chu yü-t'ai hsin-yung* 箋注玉臺新詠. Taipei: Kuang-wen 廣文, 1967.

Wu Hsiao-ju 吳小如. "Mei Sheng 'Ch'i fa' Li Shan chu ting-pu 枚乘「七發」李善注訂補." *Wen shih* 文史, no. 2 (April 1963): 129–37.

Wu Hsüan-t'ao 吳玄濤. *Ku-tien shih-ko ju-men* 古典詩歌入門. Hong Kong: Wan-li 萬里, 1963.

Wu Yüeh ch'un-ch'iu 吳越春秋. Ssu-pu ts'ung-k'an.

Yang Lun 楊倫, ed. *Tu-shih ching-ch'üan* 杜詩鏡銓. Wang san-i chai 望三益齋 wood-block ed., 1872.

Yang, Richard F. S., and Charles R. Metzger, eds. and trans. *Fifty Songs from the Yüan.* London: Allen and Unwin, 1967.

Yang Wan-li 楊萬里. *Ch'eng-chai chi* 誠齋集. Ssu-pu ts'ung-k'an.

Yeh Chia-ying 葉嘉瑩. *Chia-ling t'an tz'u* 迦陵談詞. Taipei: Ch'un-wen-hsüeh 純文學, 1970.

———. "Wen T'ing-yün tz'u kai-shuo 溫庭筠詞概說." *Tan-chiang hsüeh-pao* 淡江學報, no. 1 (1958): 55–80.

Yeh Hsiao-hsüeh 葉笑雪, ed. *Hsieh Ling-yün shih hsüan* 謝靈運詩選. Hong Kong: Hsin-yüeh 新月, 1962.

Yeh Sing-hwa 葉新華, ed. and trans. *Chung-kuo shih tz'u hsüan i* 中國詩詞選譯 (*Selection of Chinese Poetry*). Taipei: Wen-ying 文英, 1970.

Yen K'o-chün 嚴可均, ed. *Ch'üan shang-ku san-tai Ch'in Han san-kuo liu-ch'ao wen* 全上古三代秦漢三國六朝文. 4 vols. Peking: Chung-hua 中華, 1958.

Yoshikawa Kōjirō 吉川幸次郎, ed. and trans. *Shikyō kokufū* 詩經國風. 2 vols. Chūgoku shijin senshū 中國詩人選集, nos. 1–2. Tokyo: Iwanami 岩波, 1958.

Yu Hsin-li 游信利, ed. *Meng Hao-jan chi chien-chu* 孟浩然集箋注. Taipei: Chia-hsin Cement Co., 1968.

Yü Kuan-ying 余冠英, ed. *Han Wei liu-ch'ao shih hsüan* 漢魏六朝詩選. Peking: Jen-min wen-hsüeh 人民文學, 1961.

———. "Lun Chien-an Ts'ao shih fu-tzu ti shih 論建安曹氏父子的詩." *Wen-hsüeh i-ch'an tseng-k'an* 文學遺產增刊, no. 1 (Peking, 1955): 139–58.

———, ed. *Ts'ao Ts'ao Ts'ao P'ei Ts'ao Chih shih hsüan* 曹操曹丕曹植詩選. Hong Kong: Ta-kuang 大光, 1966.

———, ed. *Yüeh-fu shih hsüan* 樂府詩選. Hong Kong: Shih-chieh ch'u-pan she 世界出版社, n.d. (Preface to 1st ed. dated 1950; postface to revised ed. dated 1954.)

Yü Kuang-hua 于光華, ed. *P'ing-chu Chao-ming wen-hsüan* 評註昭明文選. Taipei: Wan-kuo t'u-shu kung-ssu 萬國圖書公司, 1956.

Yü P'ing-po 俞平伯. *Tu tz'u ou te* 讀詞偶得. Hong Kong: Wan-li 萬里, 1959.

Yü Shou-chen 喻守眞, ed. *T'ang-shih san-pai shou hsiang hsi* 唐詩三百首詳析. Hong Kong: Chung-hua 中華, 1957.

Yüan K'o 袁珂. *Chung-kuo ku-tai shen-hua* 中國古代神話. Shanghai: Shang-wu 商務, 1957.

Index and Glossary